None so Fit to Break the Chains

Historical Materialism Book Series

The Historical Materialism Book Series is a major publishing initiative of the radical left. The capitalist crisis of the twenty-first century has been met by a resurgence of interest in critical Marxist theory. At the same time, the publishing institutions committed to Marxism have contracted markedly since the high point of the 1970s. The Historical Materialism Book Series is dedicated to addressing this situation by making available important works of Marxist theory. The aim of the series is to publish important theoretical contributions as the basis for vigorous intellectual debate and exchange on the left.

The peer-reviewed series publishes original monographs, translated texts, and reprints of classics across the bounds of academic disciplinary agendas and across the divisions of the left. The series is particularly concerned to encourage the internationalization of Marxist debate and aims to translate significant studies from beyond the English-speaking world.

For a full list of titles in the Historical Materialism Book Series
available in paperback from Haymarket Books, visit:
https://www.haymarketbooks.org/series_collections/1-historical-materialism

None so Fit to Break the Chains

Marx's Ethics of Self-Emancipation

Dan Swain

Haymarket Books
Chicago, IL

First published in 2019 by Brill Academic Publishers, The Netherlands
© 2019 Koninklijke Brill NV, Leiden, The Netherlands

Published in paperback in 2020 by
Haymarket Books
P.O. Box 180165
Chicago, IL 60618
773-583-7884
www.haymarketbooks.org

ISBN: 978-1-64259-335-8

Distributed to the trade in the US through Consortium Book Sales and
Distribution (www.cbsd.com) and internationally through Ingram
Publisher Services International (www.ingramcontent.com).

This book was published with the generous support of Lannan
Foundation and Wallace Action Fund.

Special discounts are available for bulk purchases by organizations and
institutions. Please call 773-583-7884 or email info@haymarketbooks.org
for more information.

Cover design by Jamie Kerry and Ragina Johnson.

Printed in the United States.

10 9 8 7 6 5 4 3 2 1

Library of Congress Cataloging-in-Publication data is available.

Contents

Acknowledgements

Many friends, comrades and colleagues have helped me complete this book. It began life as a PhD thesis at the University of Essex, and owes an enormous debt to its supervisor Fabian Freyenhagen. Its examiners, Peter Dews and Sean Sayers, also deserve thanks, as well as others in the School of Philosophy and Art History at Essex, Jörg Schaub, Timo Juetten, Wayne Martin, Dan Watts, Fiona Hughes and participants in the Critical Theory Colloquium. I also benefitted from participation in a series of seminars in critical political philosophy at the University of Cambridge, and particular thanks are owed to Raymond Guess, Paul Raekstad and (especially) Lorna Finlayson. The book is the outcome of the project 'Towards a New Ontology of Social Cohesion', grant number GA19–20031S of the Czech Science Agency (GAČR), realised at the Institute of Philosophy of the Czech Academy of Sciences, and I am grateful to colleagues there and the wider academic community in Prague for providing the intellectual and practical environment in which to complete it. Neil Davidson, Colin Barker and Andrew Feenberg have all offered critical comments on various ideas in this book. In the course of writing, many people, including several of the above, helped me better understand the meaning of the word comrade, but in particular Mark Bergfeld and Rob Owen stand out. Finally, I would like to thank my partner, Julita Skotarska, and my parents, Nigel Swain and Eve Rosenhaft, to whom this book is dedicated.

Note on References

References to works by Marx and Engels are to the following English-language editions and collections, unless otherwise stated:

Capital Vol. 1	*Capital Vol. 1*, 1990, Ben Fowkes trans., London: Penguin.
Capital Vol. 3	*Capital Vol. 3*, 1991, David Fernbach trans., London: Penguin.
Communist Manifesto	*The Communist Manifesto*, 1985, London: Penguin.
Early Writings	*Early Writings*, 1974, Gregor Benton and Rodney Livingston trans., London: Penguin.
First International and After	*The First International and After: Political Writings Volume 3*, 1974, David Fernbach ed., London: Penguin.
German Ideology	*The German Ideology*, 1998, New York: Prometheus Books.
Grundrisse	*Grundrisse*, 1993, Martin Nicolaus trans., London: Penguin.
MECW	*Marx and Engels Collected Works Vol. 1–50*, 1975–2004, London: Lawrence and Wishart.
Surveys from Exile	*Surveys from Exile: Political Writings Volume 2*, 2010, David Fernbach ed., London: Verso.
The Revolutions of 1848	*The Revolutions of 1848: Political Writings Volume 1*, 2010, David Fernbach ed., London: Verso.

On a small number of occasions I have made use of the original German, indicating the page and volume of the *Marx-Engels Werke*.

Introduction

> None so fitted to break the chains as they who wear them, none so well
> equipped to decide what is a fetter.
>
> JAMES CONNOLLY, 1915

∙ ∙
∙

1 'Our Notion from the Very Beginning'

In his preface to the 1888 English edition of the *Communist Manifesto*, Engels asserts that 'our notion, from the very beginning, was that "the emancipation of the working class must be the act of the working class itself"'. This book begins with the notion that this commitment ought to be considered of central importance to any attempts to interpret Marx's ethics. It influences his conception of what is wrong with capitalism, his notions of freedom and domination. It influences his conception of both the form and content of any alternative to capitalism, and how much it is possible to say about it. Moreover, it influences his sense of himself as an activist and politically engaged critical theorist, and of the role of other activists and theorists.

The point of this book, then, is to foreground the principle of self-emancipation, and to use it as a guiding thread to interpret a number of different aspects of Marx's ethical thought. This principle is often overlooked in explicit treatments of Marx's ethics.[1] It is important to be clear what I mean in saying this. There is no shortage of interpretations and analyses of the relationship between Marxism and ethics. Marx's apparent disavowal of at least some kinds of moral judgements, combined with trenchant and uncompromising denunciation of capitalist social relations, inevitably draws people towards interrogating whether Marx has an ethics, and what he means by it (and the origins of this book are no exception). Thus there has been a great deal written considering metaethical and methodological questions of the status of morality in

---

1 Throughout the book, I treat the terms 'moral' and 'ethical' (and 'ethics' and 'morality') as synonymous. However, I lead with the term 'ethics', since it generally has a broader connotation than morality (which is, often, understood as being about justice and justice only) and it is part of my point to suggest the values and guidance I ascribe to Marx are broad.

Marx.[2] There has also been a great deal dedicated to the interpretive question of 'what (for Marx) is wrong with capitalism?', and the corollary of what a good society might involve.[3] Finally, there are treatments that consider the ethics of revolution and social change, what is permissible and impermissible.[4]

Among these there are plenty of interpretations that stress the importance of freedom and emancipation, that emphasise how Marx sees capitalism as thwarting the development of distinctively human powers, and that insist that a truly human society would permit them.[5] If this were all this book was arguing, there would be little new to say. However, very few of these discussions consider explicitly the additional question of *self*-emancipation. Marx did not just believe that the good society was one in which people were emancipated, and thus capable of realising their human powers freely. He also believed that this society itself must be the product of self-directed emancipatory activity. Discussion of this point, and a consideration of how it shaped Marx's project, is strikingly absent.[6]

This absence is all the more peculiar since in activist circles, many of which identify themselves as socialist or Marxist, this principle is widely discussed, often to the point of dogma. Nor is it absent from a broader literature about Marx. In particular, it is given a central place in several explicit treatments of Marx's theory of revolution, most obviously Hal Draper's, who also helped to popularise the idea with his famous pamphlet *The Two Souls of Socialism*.[7] Draper's commitment to socialism from below was widely shared by various traditions of 'unorthodox' Marxism in the second half of the twentieth century.

Yet these two sets of discussions rarely seem to meet. As someone whose Marxism developed as part of one such tradition, I found myself frequently baffled at the failure to engage with and take seriously the idea of self-emancipation in academic discussions of Marx's ethics. It seemed clear that several of the puzzles and problems discussed about Marx had their answer in this commitment, most obviously (as I will discuss in Chapter 4) his hostility towards the

---

2 For example, Kain 1988; Ash 1964; Kautsky 1918; Nielsen 1989; Kamenka 1962; Blackledge 2012.
3 For example, Callinicos 2006; Geras 1985; Wood 2004; Cohen 2001.
4 For example, Lukes 1987; Lebowitz 2003; Merleau-Ponty 1969.
5 Brenkert 1983; Elster 1985; Wood 2004; Blackledge 2012; Lukes 1987.
6 Two notable exceptions are Blackledge 2012 and Lebowitz 2003, who both develop interpretations that emphasise the standpoint of the proletariat's emancipation for understanding Marx's criticism (Lebowitz less explicitly in the language of ethics). Nonetheless, their emphases and focuses are quite different from mine, and I raise some disagreements in Chapter 2. See also Geras 2017, Chapter 6, for an explicit discussion of self-emancipation in similar terms to how I discuss it in Chapter 2 of this book.
7 Draper 1977. See also Löwy 2005, Kouvelakis 2003.

utopian socialists and his reticence about providing a detailed vision of communism. Moreover, it shaped his sense of the role of both theorists and activists within working-class movements. It helps us understand better Marx's impatience and hostility to certain other individuals, and how he conceived himself as different. For example, much of what is often put down to a belief in historical inevitability or teleology can be understood instead as reflecting a deep sensitivity to what encourages and thwarts self-emancipation (see especially Chapters 3 and 4).

It is necessary to say a few things about the character of this interpretation. I make no claim that this is the only way to read Marx, or that the principle of self-emancipation is some sort of magic key to ordering all of Marx's works. There are probably many areas of Marx's work that foregrounding self-emancipation will not help us to understand. What I do, however, suggest, is that if we want to understand the questions of what Marx thought was wrong with capitalism, and what we should do about it, this principle, which for Engels was 'their idea all along', is of central importance. At various stages I introduce the work of other thinkers to help build on or clarify what I take Marx to be saying (notably in Chapters 2, 4 and 8). In such cases, I make no claim that this is what Marx 'actually thought'. Rather, these comparisons are either intended to develop gaps in Marx's argument, or demonstrate that his position is defensible, even if in terms he does not use.[8]

But no interpretation is entirely neutral or innocent, and this is even truer of interpretations of Marx by Marxists. I write this as someone who has held various roles (paid and unpaid, elected and unelected) in socialist organisations, and has been forced to think through the practical questions that this fact involves in a direct way (sometimes more than I ever wanted to). While I think self-emancipation is central to understanding Marx, it is also of urgent

---

8   Two other points are worth making about my interpretive framework. On several occasions (e.g. Chapters 2 and 7) I trace the development of Marx's ideas on a certain topic and emphasise various changes. On other occasions (e.g. Chapter 1 Section 2), I emphasise continuity and reject the idea that Marx's ideas fundamentally change. Neither of these is based on a grand interpretive theory which locates a break or shift at a particular time. Rather, his ideas on different topics change at different times, as is perfectly natural. Secondly, it is important to say something briefly about Engels, and the relationship between him and Marx. Engels and Marx were lifelong collaborators, and worked very closely together. Engels and Marx were, of course, different individuals, with different styles, emphases and pre-occupations. Nonetheless, in the main, I do not think it is right to suggest that there are substantial differences in their thought, such as would justify strongly separating Marx's thought from that of Engels, or considering the later Engels to be an unreliable commentator on Marx's own thought. Where there are differences I refer to them directly, but, unless otherwise specified, I consider Engels endorsing a position as evidence that Marx also held it.

political importance in the present day. As movements of resistance to capitalism grow and develop, many of the dilemmas posed by a commitment to self-emancipation, in particular, questions of political power, and the dynamics between mobilising and empowering people, become more acute. Organisations and movements, whether new ones, or old ones with new leaders, are faced with concrete questions about state power, organisational forms, and the content of political programmes. I do not think that this book will offer easy answers for what to do in such situations, but I hope it can draw out a framework in which to think about the questions, which might help shed some light on them.

I also hope that some of the reflections in this work will also be of relevance to broader political traditions than just Marxism. The interpretation of Marx I present here is concerned with a particularly radicalised commitment to self-determination. To the extent that this is a value held far more widely than merely by Marx and Marxists, these reflections ought to be of broader interest. If it is correct that a commitment to self-determination has some of the consequences I suggest Marx believed it does, then this has relevance for many other traditions of political philosophy. Notably, in Chapter 4 I argue that a substantial part of Marx's criticism of the utopian socialists also applies to a dominant trend of liberal political philosophy (Chapter 4, Section 3). To the extent that this criticism emerges from a concern with freedom as self-determination that most liberals claim to share, it is not an easy one for them to evade. Moreover, I hope that some of the questions of how to link critical theoretical practice with a commitment to self-emancipation might be of interest and relevance to critical projects from other traditions.

Finally, it is worth noting that the opposite approach to self-emancipation, the notion that particular individuals play decisive, leading roles without the active participation of most people, remains the dominant conception of how we do politics. For several weeks in 2015 the *Guardian* website carried a banner headline that read 'Dear Bill Gates, will you lead us in the fight against climate change'. This reflects how politics is seen by most media, most politicians, and most people. Politics as usual is not a politics of self-emancipation. I hope that this book can contribute towards making the case that collective self-emancipation is neither a fantasy nor a meaningless slogan, but a commitment that can guide political and ethical practice in the here and now.

2 Ethics and Politics

It is useful, at the outset, to make some comments about ethics and politics. At this point, readers might be asking 'what's all this got to do with ethics?' Rather, it might be argued, Marx's commitment to self-emancipation was a political one, a claim about how to achieve political transformation, and thus about where to direct political energies. It was not, however, a concern about individual ethics.

If this is a claim that what is at stake is neither a universal categorical imperative nor a system of rights and correlative duties, I can only agree.[9] If it is, however, to claim that this approach has nothing to do with ethics *in general*, I can only respond that Marx was consistently concerned with the question 'what is to be done', and, moreover, what should *I* do. If you believed, like he did, that society was marked by a series of fundamental wrongs, and that those wrongs needed to be overthrown, what are you going to do about it? By adding the principle of self-emancipation, Marx complicates this question even further. It turns out that you cannot simply lead people from society as it is to a better one. You cannot merely dedicate intellectual energy to designing a better alternative and then propagate and argue for it. Rather, you must participate in and seek to advance a movement that emancipates itself. Doing this poses a series of questions that are precisely about how you should act towards that movement, or rather, the people within it. These are questions of *behaviour*. They are strategic, but not solely strategic; they are political, but not solely political. Rather, I think, it makes sense to call them ethical.

In considering the relationship between ethics and politics, there are, loosely, two extremes I want to avoid. An example of the first extreme might be something like Peter Singer's discussion of global justice, in which all political questions appear reducible to the fundamental imperative to help those in need.[10] On this sort of model, the correct political course will be divined simply by thinking through the correct ethical positions, and combining them appropriately. There is nothing distinctive and irreducible about politics which cannot be rephrased as a question about individual ethics, about how individuals should act towards one another. At the other extreme is the position

---

9   I agree with Lukes 1987 that Marx saw his ethics of emancipation as opposed to an ethics of *Recht*, and with Wood 2004 and others that he was right to. It does not follow from this alone that he was not interested in how we should treat each other, since there are many other ways to cash out moral values, most notably in terms of virtues. See Blackledge 2012 and Brenkert 1983.

10   See Singer 1972.

that the young Lukács – in an essay written before he became a supporter of theirs – ascribes to the Bolsheviks. This is the idea that correct political tactics can (and often do) diverge absolutely from the correct ethical position, 'that good can issue from evil, that it is possible to … lie your way to truth'.[11] On this view, to ask 'what is to be done?' politically and to ask it ethically is to ask very different questions which are likely to disclose very different answers.

Between these two extremes, I suggest that the practice of politics discloses important ethical questions, which are intimately connected to that practice (See Chapter 7). The 'correct' political answer may not always be the correct ethical answer, but good politics should be capable of engaging in these questions. On the other hand, these questions may not be visible until politics is engaged in, and thus politics is not merely the aggregate of the ethical.[12]

These ethical questions can be divided, broadly, into two parts, which form the focus of most of this book. The first is best characterised as the ethics of political action. This is about what courses of action are permissible in pursuit of social change, how we should treat one another and what kinds of values and principles we should employ, within movements for emancipatory change. These questions are discussed explicitly in Chapters 7 and 8, where I consider Marx's own arguments and various ways in which they might be supplemented and developed.

The second set of questions can be characterised as the ethics of critical theory.[13] This is not just about how activists should relate to one another in a social movement, but about the role of committed political and social theorists within those movements. One of the core claims of this book is that these questions should be treated as the same sort of questions as the former set. They are as much ethical questions as they are theoretical questions. Partly, this requires a recognition that political theory is not something that stands above

---

11   Lukács 1995, p. 220.
12   Bernard Williams says of two positions similar to those I discuss that 'They represent a
       Manichaean dualism of soul and body, high-mindedness and the pork barrel, and the
       existence of each helps to explain how anyone could have accepted the other' (Williams
       2005, p. 12).
13   In employing the term critical theory to describe this set of questions and practices I do
       not mean to identify Marx directly with the various generations of the Frankfurt School,
       but rather with a broad tradition of critical theory that understands theorists as necessar-
       ily politically committed, and thus required to reflect on their own critical methodologies
       given their particular social context and goals. Indeed, this broad tradition, in particular
       influenced by discussion with Fabian Freyenhagen, Lorna Finlayson and Raymond Geuss,
       is a significant influence on the ideas in this book.

politics, but is itself substantively political.[14] This in part explains why Marx prosecutes what appear to be methodological and theoretical differences with all the vigour of substantive political differences. Bad theoretical practices can thwart emancipatory possibilities just as bad political practices can (see especially Chapter 4). Questions of what is good theory cannot be easily separated from what is good politics.

In emphasising these questions, I might be accused of a certain myopia, another 'intellectual' preoccupied with what intellectuals should do. Let me say some things to pre-empt this. Firstly, while these questions structure the approach, I do consider a variety of more 'traditional' questions concerning Marx and ethics (especially Chapters 1, 5 and 6). Secondly, however, I want to stress that this is not intended to be limited to the practice of Marxist academics. Rather, it is the question of how anyone committed to building an alternative to capitalism should frame and shape their critical activity. It is about how we *do* criticism, and this is not just the preserve of professional academics with book contracts and publishing agendas. Thirdly, and perhaps most importantly, this was Marx's question. Marx came to an awareness that the society he wanted to see could only be built by the self-activity of vast numbers of other people. He thus faced the question of how his 'intellectual' activities – journalism, propaganda, analysis and philosophy – could serve this movement rather than pre-empt or foreclose it. As Darren Webb puts it:

> The problems were those of generating radical hope without foreclosing the future; of capturing the spirit of revolution whilst remaining faithful to the principles of proletarian self-emancipation and self-determination. So important did Marx consider these problems that resolving them became his own political and theoretical 'project'.[15]

If we still agree with Marx, as I do, that such a movement of emancipation is possible and desirable, this is also the question for Marxists today – and for anyone interested in cooperating with others to change the world for the better.

---

14   Finlayson 2015.
15   Webb 2000, p. 2.

3   Overview of Chapters

In Chapter 1, I offer an interpretation of Marx's conception of freedom, and why capitalism fails to meet it. In particular, I suggest that there are two necessary components to the Marxist account of freedom. Firstly, there is self-objectification in nature through labour (with both nature and labour broadly defined). To this extent, Marx largely follows Hegel. In addition to this, however, is the unavoidable social and political form that this labour takes. For Marx, true self-realisation is possible only if labour is collectively controlled and directed. To this extent, I suggest that Marx shares important affinities with thinkers concerned with self-determination and autonomy.

Chapter 2 addresses self-emancipation directly, tracing the origins of this idea in Marx's thought, and reconstructing an argument, resting in particular on the third thesis on Feuerbach. One important aspect of this discussion is the way in which Marx represents the struggles of the proletariat in the present as simultaneously intimately linked to and importantly distinct from the future goal of communism, which I link in that chapter to contemporary notions of prefigurative politics. Developing this, I also suggest that a comparison between Marx's conception of social emancipation and two different treatments of critical pedagogy – Brecht De Smet's Vygotskian account of the Egyptian Revolution and Jacques Rancière's notion of intellectual emancipation – might help understand both how new social practices might develop, and the particular role those committed to emancipation might play in this development.

Chapters 3 and 4 are then concerned with Marx's role as a critical theorist. Chapter 3 engages directly with the question of historical materialism. It considers the worry (raised by G.A. Cohen and Eugen Kamenka) that Marx's commitment to historical inevitability removes any role for individual decision-making, thus either rendering ethics irrelevant, or at least relegating it to a subordinate role. I first argue that some classical defences of Marx (from Georgi Plekhanov and Karl Kautsky) have failed to understand the full force of this worry, and have therefore been inadequate in responding to them. Whilst they have addressed some of the conceptual and theoretical problems posed by these criticisms, they have been blind to the practical problems which they pose. In particular, they ignore the worry that such an approach to history encourages a prophetic attitude which avoids questions of self-emancipation. In response to this, I offer an interpretation of Marx, influenced by Daniel Bensaïd and Walter Benjamin, in which ethical decision-making is given appropriate importance. This is one which understands the theoretical generalisations that Marx employs in terms of strategic hypotheses, indexed to the goal of self-emancipation. These strategic hypotheses are not a substitute for the independent activity of people, but develop from and help guide it.

Chapter 4 examines and defends Marx's criticism of the utopian socialists. Against those who see this criticism as based on an unwarranted confidence in historical progress, I argue that Marx's rejection of the utopian method is motivated mainly by his concern for self-emancipation. In particular, I suggest that Marx's reticence to offer his own detailed alternative to capitalism is rooted in the concern that this necessarily pre-empts self-emancipation, an argument I develop through comparison with the practice of ideal theory in contemporary political philosophy. I then defend this approach, arguing that there is nothing incoherent or problematic about criticising or resisting capitalism without offering a detailed alternative, but that the details of this alternative must emerge *through* movements of resistance, rather than be specified prior to them.

Chapters 5 and 6 examine two of capitalism's substantive wrongs, according to Marx, in light of the methodology described in Chapter 4. In particular, they suggest ways that these wrongs can be described without reference to a substantive ideal alternative. Chapter 5 discusses exploitation, and in particular makes the case for an interpretation of exploitation that is neither distributive, transactional, nor based on a theory of justice. Rather, I argue that Marx's criticism of exploitation is best understood in terms of systematic relations of domination and vulnerability, which the working class necessarily has an interest in challenging and overcoming. Chapter 6 focuses on alienation, and in particular the question of alienation and human nature. Analogously to the previous chapter, I address the question of whether Marxism requires a substantive conception of human nature which is in tension with an openness to future possibilities.

Chapter 7 turns to Marx's approach to politics, as both an essential sphere of revolutionary activity and the sphere where questions of self-emancipation are most fraught. I consider the various ways in which Marx conceived of the political sphere, and why he considered it essential for movements of emancipation to engage in it. The various ways in which Marx imagined political activity happening all pose difficult ethical questions about relationships within and between social movements and their adversaries. Finally, Chapter 8 discusses some possible answers to these questions. In particular, the ideas of four different thinkers are discussed, two from the revolutions of the beginning of the twentieth century, and two contemporary ones. Each of these offer different ways of answering these ethical questions, and taken together they offer at least some answers. Whilst these answers fall short of the kind of hard and fast rules some might want, I argue that they are far from empty, and taking them seriously can provide an important guide to action. Finally, I return to the question of the relationship between theory and practice, and make some remarks on the enduring legacy of Marxism today.

These chapters add up to an attempt to defend the claim expressed in the quotation from James Connolly at the beginning of this introduction, both as an interpretation of Marx and as a significant claim in its own right. Connolly was in fact writing explicitly about the oppression of women, but I think in Marx the point is (rightly) applied far more generally. There are none so fit to break their chains as those that wear them – emancipation must be self-emancipation. There are none so fit to know what is a fetter – the capacity to both criticise existing society and to found a new one lies with those whom it most oppresses.

Prometheus Plus Spartacus

> Prometheus plus Spartacus equals the starting-point of Marxism.
>
> HAL DRAPER, 'The Principle of Self-Emancipation in Marx', 1971[1]

∴

1 Introduction

To talk about self-emancipation raises the obvious questions 'emancipation from what?' and 'emancipation to what?' What does it mean to talk about emancipation as a goal? To answer this, it is necessary to consider Marx's account of freedom, and in particular how he understood the development of a society which permitted freedom for all. The stated goal, in the *Communist Manifesto*, is 'an association in which the free development of each is the condition for the free development of all'.[2] What is the nature of this free development, and what secures it?

Draper remarks, in an article on Marx and self-emancipation, that 'Prometheus plus Spartacus equals the starting-point of Marxism'. These two figures symbolise the two relationships in which Marx sees freedom as being realised – our relationship with nature and our relationship with others. The two figures also, importantly, represent a reaction against unfreedom, a revolt on the part of the dominated against the conditions of their domination. Prometheus is the titan who rebelled against Zeus, who stole fire from the gods and gave it to man.[3] In Aeschylus' account he is responsible for human civilisation and development. In his own words:

> And verily I discover for them numbers, the surpassing all inventions, the combinations too of letters, and Memory, effective mother-nurse of all arts. I also first bound with yokes beasts submissive to the collars; and

---

1 Draper 1971, p. 97.
2 *Communist Manifesto*, p. 105.
3 For more on the figure of Prometheus in Marx see Prawer 1976, Chapter 1.

in order that with their bodies they might become to mortals substitutes for their severest toils, I brought steeds under cars obedient to the rein, a glory to pompous luxury.[4]

In this version, Prometheus declares that he has saved humanity from Zeus, and as a result he is chained to rocks forever. Prometheus was a particularly significant figure in the Romantic movement, signifying defiance of religious authority, and the primordial creative capacities of mankind. Both Shelley and Goethe wrote poems about him, and Marx himself was influenced strongly by his myth. Aeschylus is recorded, alongside Shakespeare, as Marx's favourite poet, presumably because of *Prometheus Bound*. Prometheus is given pride of place in Marx's 1841 Doctoral Dissertation, in which Marx endorses both his hostility to the gods – 'In simple words I hate the pack of gods' – and his refusal to serve – 'Better to be the servant of this rock/ Than to be faithful to Father Zeus'.[5]

The same (1865) fragment of family life[6] that tells us about Marx's taste in poets tells us that his favourite historical figures were Spartacus and Kepler. Spartacus is, of course, the great protagonist of class struggle in the ancient world. His name is associated with rebellion, and specifically with collective struggle against oppression. It is impossible, now, to hear the name Spartacus without thinking of the slogan, coined for Stanley Kubrick's 1960 film, 'I'm Spartacus'. This is a basic act of collective solidarity, meant to obscure the individual. In a crucial sense, we are all Spartacus, and in that moment there is no (specific individual) Spartacus. Marx, of course, could not have known this particular scene. Nonetheless, Spartacus, a real historical figure, but one far enough away in history that little was known about him, must have represented to Marx class struggle and rebellion against oppression in its purest form.

---

4 Aeschylus 1897.

5 MECW 1, p. 30.

6 MECW 42, p. 47. This is a parlour game in which participants answered a series of questions, and Marx demonstrated probably both the best and worst in his character. Others questions included 'the qualities you like best in Man and in Woman', to which Marx responded 'strength' and 'weakness' respectively and 'your idea of happiness', to which he responds 'to fight'.

2 The Action of Freedom

In a passage in the *Grundrisse*, Marx takes Adam Smith to task for conceiving freedom solely in terms of the absence of burdensome activity. For Smith, citing the Bible, Labour is a curse, and freedom and happiness are found outside it. For Marx, however, labour is an essential part of freedom:

> In the sweat of thy brow shalt thou labour! was Jehovah's curse on Adam. And this is labour for Smith, a curse. 'Tranquillity' appears as the adequate state, as identical with 'freedom' and 'happiness'. It seems quite far from Smith's mind that the individual, 'in his normal state of health, strength, activity, skill, facility', also needs a normal portion of work, and of the suspension [*Aufhebung*] of tranquillity. Certainly, labour obtains its measure [*erscheint das Mass*] from the outside, through the aim to be attained and the obstacles to be overcome in attaining it. But Smith has no inkling whatever that this overcoming of obstacles is in itself a liberating activity [*an sich Betätigung der Freiheit*] – and that, further, the external aims become stripped of the semblance of merely external natural urgencies, and become posited as aims which the individual himself posits – hence as self-realization, objectification of the subject, hence real freedom, whose action is, precisely, labour [*also als Selbstverwirklichung, Vergegenständlichung des Subjekts, daher reale Freiheit, deren Aktion eben die Arbeit*].[7]

Here Labour is represented as the means by which people realise themselves and their freedom in the world. Labour is the *action*, or the *activation* [*Betätigung*] of freedom. Through labour, things that appear as merely external nature, mere obstacles to action, become transformed into internal aims. The labouring subjects objectify themselves in external nature, and in doing so transform nature into an extension of them.

---

7   *Grundrisse*, p. 611. German from *MEW*, vol. 42 p. 512. This passage immediately follows this one from Smith's *Wealth of Nations*: 'Equal quantities of labour must at all times and in all places have the same value for the worker. In his normal state of health, strength and activity, and with the common degree of skill and facility which he may possess, he must always give up the *identical portion* of *his tranquillity*, his *freedom*, and his *happiness*. Whatever may be the quantity or composition of the commodities he obtains in reward of his work, the *price he pays* is always the same. Of course, this price may buy sometimes a lesser, sometimes a greater quantity of these commodities, but only because their value changes, not the value of the labour which buys them. Labour alone, therefore, never changes its own value. It is therefore the *real price* of commodities, money is only their nominal value'.

For Marx, labour is both the way in which human beings are distinguished from the natural world, and the way in which we come to realise ourselves within it. Firstly, human beings are distinguished from animals by their capacity for conscious, purposive activity in the world:

> A spider conducts operations that resemble those of a weaver, and a bee would put many an architect to shame in the construction of its honeycomb cells. But what distinguishes the worst architect from the best of bees is that the architect builds the cell in his mind before he constructs it in wax. At the end of every labour process, a result emerges which had already been conceived by the worker at the beginning, hence already existed ideally. Man not only effects a change of form in the materials of nature; he also realises [*verwirklicht*] his own purpose in those materials.[8]

Moreover, Labour appears as a vital mediating term between human beings and nature:

> Labour is, first of all, a process between man and nature, a process by which man, through his own actions, mediates, regulates and controls the metabolism between himself and nature. He confronts the materials of nature as a force of nature. He sets in motion the natural forces, which belong to his own body, his arms, legs, head and hands, in order to appropriate the materials of nature in a form adapted to his own needs. Through this movement he acts upon external nature and changes it, and in this way he simultaneously changes his own nature. He develops the potentialities slumbering within nature, and subjects the play of its forces to his own sovereign power.[9]

In the *German Ideology* Marx frequently describes labour as 'self-activity', as activity which involves the expression and realisation of the self:

---

8 *Capital Vol. 1*, p. 284. See also *German Ideology*, p. 37: 'Men can be distinguished from animals by consciousness, by religion, or by anything else you like. They themselves begin to distinguish themselves from animals as soon as they begin to produce their means of subsistence, a step which is conditioned by their physical organisation'.

9 *Capital Vol. 1*, p. 283. A more condensed version of this point appears earlier in *Capital*, where labour is 'a condition of human existence which is independent of all forms of society; it is an eternal natural necessity which mediates the metabolism between man and nature, and therefore human life itself'. Ibid, p. 133.

This mode of production must not be considered simply as being the reproduction of the physical existence of the individuals. Rather, it is a definite form of activity of these individuals, a definite form of expressing their life, a definite *mode of life* on their part. As individuals express their life, so they are. What they are, therefore, coincides with their production, both with *what* they produce and with *how* they produce. Hence what individuals are depends on the material conditions of their production.[10]

Through transforming the natural world we also transform ourselves, and become who we are.

To this extent, Marx's account is indebted to Hegel, for whom labour plays a similar role in achieving freedom through changing nature in order to make ourselves feel at home within it.[11] Through transforming nature, objectifying our activity in it, we come to recognise ourselves within it. We see the natural world as an extension of ourselves.[12]

So far so good, but it is important to stress that this is not the end of the story. In the same *Grundrisse* passage, Marx goes on to observe that Smith's mistake was understandable, to the extent that he was fixated on labour in the forms that it had historically existed:

> He is right, of course, that, in its historic forms as slave-labour, serf-labour, and wage-labour, labour always appears as repulsive, always as *external forced labour*; and not-labour, by contrast, as 'freedom, and happiness'. This holds doubly: for this contradictory labour; and, relatedly, for labour which has not yet created the subjective and objective conditions for itself (or also, in contrast to the pastoral etc. state, which it has lost), in which labour becomes attractive work, the individual's self-realisation, which in no way means that it becomes mere fun, mere amusement, as Fourier, with *grisette*-like naïveté, conceives it.[13]

---

10   *German Ideology*, p. 37.

11   See Sayers 2011, Chapter 2, and Fromm 1961.

12   Note in particular this passage from Hegel's lectures on aesthetics, translated and quoted in Sayers 2011, pp. 16–17: 'Man brings himself before himself by *practical* activity, since he has the impulse, in whatever is directly given to him, in what is present to him externally, to produce himself and therein equally to recognise himself. This aim he achieves by altering external things whereon he impresses the seal of his inner being and in which he now finds again his own characteristics. Man does this in order, as a free subject, to strip the external world of its inflexible foreignness and to enjoy in the shape of things only an external realisation of himself'.

13   *Grundrisse*, p. 611.

There are, note, two ways in which labour here can fail to be free. Firstly, through being 'externally forced' and secondly through having 'not yet created the subjective and objective conditions for itself'.

This indicates an important point. To talk about labour in general, solely as the mediation between humans and nature (as Marx does in the passage in *Capital* above), is to talk about an abstraction. There is no labour in general, there is only specific labour under specific social conditions under specific levels of development.[14] Firstly, labour always involves particular, given instruments, particular, given subjects to operate them, and particular, given material to work with. Labour can, thus, sometimes, fail to objectify itself – the tools, or the worker, can simply not be up to the task. More significantly, though, labour always takes place under particular social conditions:

> The production of life, both of one's own in labour and of fresh life in procreation, now appears as a twofold relation: on the one hand as a natural, on the other as a social relation – social in the sense that it denotes the co-operation of several individuals, no matter under what conditions, in what manner, and to what end.[15]

Labour is always social labour, always implying some sort of mode of social co-operation, some set of social relations. Thus, as well as material barriers to realising one's freedom through labour, there can also be social barriers.

What this establishes, in effect, is a second relationship. In addition to the relationship between human beings and nature mediated through labour, there is a relationship between human beings and their own labour, mediated by social forms. These forms are what Mészáros calls 'second-order' mediations, which interpose themselves between subjects and their own labour as a '*historically specific* mediation of the *ontologically fundamental* self-mediation of

---

14   See, for example, the following passages from the *Grundrisse*: 'The human being is in the most literal sense a *Zoon politikon*, not merely a gregarious animal, but an animal which can individuate itself only in the midst of society. Production by an isolated individual outside society – a rare exception which may well occur when a civilized person in whom the social forces are already dynamically present is cast by accident into the wilderness – is as much of an absurdity as is the development of language without individuals living together and talking to each other' (*Grundrisse*, p. 84); 'Hunger is hunger, but the hunger gratified by cooked meat eaten with a knife and fork is a different hunger from that which bolts down raw meat with the aid of hand, nail and tooth. Production thus produces not only the object but also the manner of consumption, not only objectively but also subjectively. Production thus creates the consumer' (*Grundrisse*, p. 92).

15   *German Ideology*, p. 49.

man with nature'.[16] Getting this relationship correct, Marx suggests, is just as important as objectifying oneself through (and in) nature.

This is because, under certain social conditions, labour is not merely objectifying, but also *alienating*.[17] Instead of labour objectifying activity in nature in order to make ourselves feel at home in the world, this activity makes our own labour appear as something alien and dominating. Our own powers become projected against us and outside of us, appearing as an alien, hostile force. This was paradigmatically the case in capitalist society:

> In history up to the present it is an empirical fact that separate individuals have, with the broadening of their activity into world-historical activity, become more and more enslaved under a power alien to them (a pressure which they have conceived of as a dirty trick on the part of the so-called world spirit, etc.), a power which has become more and more enormous and, in the last instance, turns out to be the *world market*.[18]

Under capitalism, a class had been created for whom 'labour, the only connection which still links them with the productive forces and with their own existence, has lost all semblance of self-activity and only sustains their life by stunting it'.[19] Their own activity appears to them as an alien power, confronting and dominating them, and the natural world which these powers shape appears as an alien world, dominating them and sapping their life energy.[20] This establishes an important distinction, between labour in general, and labour in its historically existing, alienated form.[21]

---

16   See Mészáros 1970, p. 79.

17   This distinction is arguably where Marx goes beyond Hegel (see Arthur 1986, Mészáros 1970). But whether or not this is the case is not of primary importance here, since I do not claim that Marx's theory of freedom is necessarily distinctive or unique, merely that it is *his*, and that it is important to his ethics and politics.

18   *German Ideology*, p. 59.

19   *German Ideology*, p. 96.

20   '[L]abour is *external* to the worker, i.e. does not belong to his essential being ... he therefore does not confirm himself in his work, but denies himself, feels miserable and not happy, does not develop free mental and physical energy, but mortifies his flesh and ruins his mind' (*Early Writings*, p. 326).

21   Marx is rarely consistent in which of these he reserves the term 'labour' for. For example, C.J. Arthur argues that 'The category "labour" (*Arbeit*) had settled its meaning by the time Marx wrote *Capital*, as one of his fundamental ahistorical categories ... [Whereas] in such texts as the *1844 Manuscripts* and the *German Ideology* Marx restricts the term to *productive activity carried on under the rule of private property*' (Arthur 1986, p. 13).

Thus not any kind of labour can be the action of freedom; rather (and at the risk of tautology), unalienated, *free* labour is the action of freedom. And so the *Grundrisse* passage proceeds:

> Really free working [*Wirklich freies Arbeiten*], e.g. composing, is at the same time precisely the most damned seriousness, the most intense exertion. The work of material production [*Die Arbeit der materiellen Produktion*] can achieve this character only (1) when its social character is posited [*ihr gesellschaftlicher Charakter gesetzt ist*], (2) when it is of a scientific and at the same time general character, not merely human exertion as a specifically harnessed natural force, but exertion as subject [*als Subjekt*] which appears in the production process not in a merely natural, spontaneous form, but as an activity regulating all the forces of nature.[22]

Here Marx gives two criteria for turning material production into 'really free' labour (which he strikingly compares with composing): Firstly its social character being posited, and secondly that it is exertion 'as subject', acting as a regulating and controlling force in the process, rather than as exertion harnessed from outside.

A sense of what is meant by these conditions is given by this passage from the *German Ideology*:

> Communism differs from all previous movements in that it overturns the basis of all earlier relations of production and intercourse, and for the first time consciously treats all naturally evolved premises as the creations of hitherto existing men, strips them of their natural character and subjugates them to the power of the united individuals.[23]

Thus what is distinctive about communism is that it recognises and acknowledges the social character of production, and that it then brings it under the collective control of everyone:

> Only at this stage [the appropriation of the total productive forces by the united individuals] does self-activity coincide with material life, which corresponds to the development of individuals into complete individuals and the casting off of all natural limitations. The transformation of labour

---

22   *Grundrisse*, p. 611.
23   *German Ideology*, pp. 89–90.

into self-activity corresponds to the transformation of the previously limited intercourse into the intercourse of individuals as such.[24]

Labour would truly become self-activity when those who labour are capable
of bringing the production process under their collective control. Under these
conditions, labour would no longer be alienating, no longer appear as something external and dominating, but as freely undertaken activity. Thus, immediately after Marx has talked about the growth of the world market as a power
standing over and above those who labour, he adds that 'it is just as empir-
ically established that, by the overthrow of the existing state of society by
the communist revolution ... and the abolition of private property which is
identical with it, this power ... will be dissolved; and that then the liberation
of each single individual will be accomplished in the measure in which history
becomes wholly transformed into world history'.[25]

Thus we have two jointly necessary conditions for genuine freedom in
Marx's sense: Firstly, there must be self-realisation in the form of the human-
isation of nature through labour, and secondly there must be conscious self-
direction of this labour. In fact, the second of these conditions the first – it is
only true self-realisation *if* it is also consciously self-directed. Otherwise it is
mere objectification. Thus, while it is useful to think about these as two different relationships (between humans and nature, and between humans and
their own activity), it is important to stress that they are intimately connected.

3   Labour and Objectification

In his early writings, in particular in the *Economic and Philosophical Manuscripts* of 1844, Marx offers a visionary conception of the unity of humanity and
nature. Human beings are to be understood as natural beings, and themselves
a moment in the development of nature itself. The full development of human
beings involves the humanising of nature and the recognition of human beings
as natural:

> [*J*]*ust as* society itself produces *man as man*, so is society produced by
> him. Activity and consumption, both in their content and in their *mode*

---

24   *German Ideology*, p. 97.
25   *German Ideology*, p. 59.

of existence, are *social: social* activity and *social* consumption. The *human* essence of nature exists only for *social* man; for only here does nature exist for him as a *bond* with man – as his existence for the other and the other's existence for him – and as the vital element of human reality. Only then does nature exist as the *foundation* of his own *human* existence. Only here has his *natural* existence become his *human* existence, and nature become man for him. *Society* is therefore the perfected unity in essence of man with nature – the true resurrection of nature – the realised naturalism of man and the realised humanism of nature.[26]

Indeed, this relationship between human beings and nature is of fundamental ontological significance. 'For socialist man', Marx remarks, 'the *whole of what is called world history* is nothing more than the creation of man through human labour, and the development of nature for man'. Marx believes it is through this process that people prove the reality of their own genesis, and render irrelevant any conception of an original or first cause.[27] Thus the Manuscripts contain what appears to be a refutation of the need for any proof of God, since even asking the question is to presuppose man's non-existence. Rather, 'Since the *essentiality* of man and nature, man as the existence of nature for man and nature for the existence of man for man, has become practically and sensuously perceptible, the question of an *alien* being, a being above nature and man – a question which implies an admission of the unreality of nature and of man – has become impossible in practice'.[28]

Thus history is the progressive humanising of nature and recognition of the human as natural. The end of this history is true communism (which in this text Marx distinguishes from crude communism):

> This communism, as fully developed naturalism, equals humanism, and as fully developed humanism equals naturalism; it is the *genuine* resolution of the conflict between man and nature, and between man and man, the true resolution of the conflict between existence and being, between objectification and self-affirmation, between freedom and necessity, between individual and species. It is the solution of the riddle of history and knows itself to be the solution.[29]

---

26   *Early Writings*, pp. 349–50.
27   See Feenberg 2014, Chapter 1.
28   *Early Writings*, p. 357.
29   *Early Writings*, p. 348.

Under this version of communism, the human relationship to nature will be transformed, along with the means by which we relate to nature – our senses. When we have a truly human attitude to nature, the way in which we experience the world changes fundamentally: 'The supersession of private property is therefore the complete *emancipation* of all human senses and attributes; but it is this emancipation precisely because these senses and attributes have become *human*, subjectively as well as objectively. The eye has become a human eye, just as its *object* has become a social, *human* object, made by man for man'.[30] Moreover, our relationships with each other change too, 'activity in direct association with others etc. has become an organ of my *life expression* and a mode of appropriation of human life'.[31] Finally, this also has a consequence for our conception of science and knowledge. With nature humanised, and humanity naturalised, the separation of human and natural sciences no longer makes sense. Indeed, to the extent that nature is accessed through man, then 'Man is the immediate object of natural science', while nature becomes, in fact, 'the immediate object of the science of man ... Natural science will in time subsume the science of man just as the science of man will subsume natural science: there will be *one* science'.[32]

The account in the 1844 manuscripts is a rich and complex one, as much about the completion of the tradition of European Philosophy as it is about human anthropology or society. As such, much of its grand language and expectations do not survive Marx's abandonment of explicit philosophy in the years that followed. Marx's discussions of nature become more influenced by the development of natural sciences, which tend to be granted a greater autonomy in understanding nature than the earlier account suggests. One notable shift in Marx's treatment of nature is towards the language of metabolism.[33] From the notion of communism achieving a fundamental unity between human beings and nature, we now have the idea that labour regulates the metabolism between man and nature. This metabolism implies a subtly different approach. While previously Marx appeared to have a notion of unity with nature being achieved through identity or synthesis – the humanising of nature and naturalising of the human such that they become one and the same – the idea of metabolism seems to suggest a unity in *difference* between human beings and nature. Nature does not collapse entirely into the human world, but retains a degree of independence. Moreover labour no longer achieves

---

30   *Early Writings*, 352.
31   *Early Writings*, 352.
32   *Early Writings*, 355.
33   Schmidt 2014, pp. 76–93.

this identity, but it regulates and mediates a relationship, characterised by metabolic inputs and outputs. In both of these conceptions labour mediates between human beings and nature, but in one this mediation is overcome, in the other it remains as a necessary term.

The idea of metabolism is significant for answering the charge that Marx is 'Promethean' in the negative sense in which this word is sometimes used, i.e. that he sees human freedom as solely a matter of conquest and control over nature. Even in the earlier writings, it is clear that by the humanising of nature Marx does not conceive it as something to be merely used up and dominated – rather, it transforms us as much as we transform it. However, the emphasis on metabolism brings to the fore the importance of maintaining balance between what 'goes in and comes out' of nature. It also gives a framework in which to consider environmental degradation and change in social terms, as the metabolism is badly regulated or broken down. Marx and Engels themselves employed these ideas to discuss soil erosion, and such ideas have been fruitfully developed to discuss contemporary climate change. This is not a consequence of too much mastery over nature, but a consequence of a failure to master nature. It is a funny (though ironically appropriately capitalist) sort of 'mastery' which creates the conditions for systematic crises which undermine the very basis of any activity.

It is tempting to see talk of managing metabolism and talk of objectification and self-realisation through labour as suggesting radically different worldviews between the young and the old Marx. However, there remain several important continuities, in part indicated by the passage from the *Grundrisse* discussed in the previous section.

Firstly, labour remains a fundamental mediation between human beings and nature, and potentially a realm of freedom. It is worth addressing directly a set of interpretations to the contrary, which tend to rely on the following passage from Volume III of *Capital*:

> The realm of freedom really begins only [*das Reich der Freiheit beginnt in der Tat erst da*] where labour determined by necessity and external expediency ends; it lies by its very nature beyond the sphere of material production [*materiellen Produktion*] proper. Just as the savage must wrestle with nature to satisfy his needs, to maintain and reproduce his life, so must civilised man, and he must do it in all forms of society and under all possible modes of production. This realm of natural necessity expands with his development, because his needs do too; but the productive forces to satisfy these expand at the same time. Freedom, in this sphere [*die Freiheit in diesem Gebiet*], can consist only in this, that social-

ised man, the associated producers, govern the metabolism with nature in a rational way, bringing it under their collective control instead of being dominated by it as a blind power; accomplishing it with the least expenditure of energy and in conditions most worthy and appropriate for their human nature. But this always remains a realm of necessity [*ein Reich der Notwendigkeit*]. The true realm of freedom, the development of human powers as an end in itself, begins beyond it, though can only flourish with this realm of necessity as its basis. The reduction of the working day is the basic prerequisite [*die Grundbedingung*].[34]

This passage has been interpreted as signalling a retreat from the position that labour can potentially be free, towards a more 'gloomy' position that labour ought to be merely minimised in order to make room for other, more truly free activities.[35] Rather than make labour free, this seems to suggest, we ought to simply cut it back as much as possible, reduce it to what is purely necessary. This would suggest that the idea that labour might take on the character of composing is fanciful. Indeed, perhaps composing is precisely an example of what happens in the realm of freedom, in which the development of human powers is an end in itself.

Several points can be made in response to this reading. Firstly, the schema described in this quotation is not substantially different from that described in the *Grundrisse* quotation above. Marx is still asserting that freedom *can* exist in material production, and though the language is somewhat different, the themes of rational regulation and collective control persist. Whilst the realm of freedom and the realm of necessity seem to be more clearly distinguished, freedom is possible within both. Secondly, Marx does suggest an interdependence between these two realms: the realm of freedom arises on the realm of necessity, but *only if that realm itself is free*. The realm of necessity, for Marx, is not necessarily a realm of unfreedom, rather it is the realm of necessary labour, i.e. that labour which is necessary to meet the (broad, and expanding) needs of society.[36] This labour may be free or unfree – but if it is unfree no other freedom is possible.

---

34   *Capital Vol. 3*, p. 959. German from *MEW* 25, p. 828.
35   The word 'gloomy' comes from Cohen 1988, p. 207, but similar claims can be found in Berki 1983 and Arendt 1998. While not based on this passage, Van Parijs offers a 'Marxist' definition of work which expressly excludes 'spontaneous activities and activities which are performed for their own sake': Van Parijs 1993, p. 91. Elster 1985, pp. 92–102 does not see any contradiction between this passage and the *Grundrisse* passage, but offers some more general criticisms of Marx's views.
36   Sayers 2011, pp. 66–71. See also Avineri 1968, p. 246.

Nonetheless, Marx's suggestion that real freedom lies beyond the realm of necessity might be taken to suggest that non-labouring activities are somehow a higher form of free activity. As Sayers notes, Marx's pre-occupation with the length of the working day is understandable, given the conditions he was describing and the fact that it was a site of intense political contestation. He understandably wanted to emphasise the possibility that a better organisation of necessary labour would create time and space for workers to do other things, to pursue their own interests, and so on.[37] However, any sense that this ought to be seen in terms of 'higher' forms of human activity in direct contrast to labour ought to be tempered for a range of reasons. Firstly, in the quotation itself Marx is concerned with the development of human powers. While this may well contain a range of activities outside of the narrow confines of necessary labour, much of this activity remains analogous to labour, in the sense that it is conscious and purposive. Indeed, the point about composing in the *Grundrisse* example is that it remains serious work, expenditure of energy towards a goal. Similarly, when in *Capital* Marx uses the example of an architect to characterise human labour, he is concerned with the same process.

Secondly, this schema seems to reinforce an antagonistic opposition that Marx at other times seeks to reject – namely that between labour time and free time.[38] This opposition appears not primarily as two periods of time within the life of one individual, but as the properties of two different classes. The free time of those who do not labour 'whether for idleness or for the performance of activities which are not directly productive (as e.g. war, affairs of state) or for the development of human abilities and social potentialities (art, etc., science) which have no directly practical purpose, has as its prerequisite the surplus labour of the mass of workers'.

> To put it more definitely: the surplus labour time worked by the mass of workers over and above the quantity necessary for the reproduction of their own labour capacity, their own existence, over and above the *necessary* labour, this surplus labour time, which presents itself as surplus value, is simultaneously materialised in extra product, surplus product, and this surplus product is the material basis for the existence of all the classes apart from the working classes, of the whole superstructure of society. It *simultaneously provides free time*, gives them disposable time for the development of their other capacities. Thus the production of sur-

---

37   Sayers 2011, p. 70.
38   A similar point is made by O'Rourke 1974, p. 30 and Sayers 2011, pp. 71–2.

plus labour time on one side is at once the production of *free* time on the other. The whole of human development, so far as it extends beyond the development directly necessary for the natural existence of human beings, consists merely in the employment of this free time and presupposes it as its necessary basis. Thus the free time of society is produced through the production of unfree time, the labour time of workers prolonged beyond that required for their own subsistence. Free time on one side corresponds to subjugated time on the other side.[39]

The distinction between the realm of necessity and the realm of freedom employed in the passage from *Capital Vol. III* above seems to rest on but also to transform this antagonism. It shifts both free time and labour time from being class properties to being general social properties, such that all can share in both. In doing so, it means that both are freer. While the distinction remains, it has lost its antagonistic character.

However, elsewhere Marx suggests that this distinction itself might be entirely overcome. For example, in the *Grundrisse* he suggests that 'It goes without saying, by the way, that direct labour time itself cannot remain in the abstract antithesis to free time in which it appears from the perspective of bourgeois economy'.[40] These remarks suggest a more subtle conception of the relationship between free and labour time than that expressed in *Capital Vol. III*. The stress there on reducing the working day rests on a model in which time for free development is still conditioned by labour time as its opposite. In fact, the development of truly free time can arise only when this abstract opposition is eroded. While there is a clear difference of emphasis here, it is worth stressing that Marx identifies shortening the working day as a necessary prerequisite, rather than as an end in itself. This is compatible with the interpretation offered by Sayers, that 'The purpose of limiting the working day is not to minimise or eliminate work in the realm of necessity as such, but rather to overcome the antagonistic relation which has existed historically between work and freedom'.[41]

The second important continuity between the early and later accounts is Marx's insistence that nature is something always already altered by human hands.[42] There is no innocent, unchanged nature which is not in some sense

---

39   *MECW* 30, p. 191.
40   *Grundrisse*, p. 712.
41   Sayers 2011, pp. 71–2.
42   See Schmidt 2014, Habermas 1972, pp. 27–34.

already a product of human activity, a point which Marx presses against Feuerbach in the *German Ideology*:

> [Feuerbach] does not see that the sensuous world around him is not a thing given direct from all eternity, remaining forever the same, but the product of industry and of the state of society; and, indeed, a product in the sense that it is an historical product, the result of the activity of a whole succession of generations, each standing on the shoulders of the preceding one, developing its industry and its intercourse, and modifying its social system according to changed needs ... [N]ature, the nature that preceded human history, is not by any means the nature in which Feuerbach lives, it is nature which today no longer exists anywhere (except perhaps on a few Australian coral islands of recent origin) and which, therefore, does not exist for Feuerbach either.[43]

In other words, nature includes already the world of human objects, our built environment, our tools and workplaces. This suggests any activity which engages in transformation of the human environment can be understood as an engagement with 'nature'. Moreover, when Marx talks about labour he is clearly also concerned with activity required to maintain and reproduce human society. Expanding the scope of 'labour' to incorporate activity which may not involve a direct interchange with nature, but which is nonetheless a part of social reproduction (in a broad sense which incorporates cultural reproduction) is of both analytical and political significance. Grasping the way in which certain kinds of (often women's) work are central to social reproduction because they reproduce labour-power (and thus workers themselves) allows for both a more expansive conception of those who labour – expanding from coal mines and car plants to colleges and care homes – and a broader conception of class struggle – to include disputes over the means and relations of reproduction as well as production.[44]

This also indicates the importance of recognising the social character of even the scientific and technical knowledge required to carry out that labour:

---

43   *German Ideology*, pp. 45–6. In this context, it is also worth noting that in the *Economic and Philosophical Manuscripts*, Marx talks about 'alienation from product' and 'alienation from nature' as if they are the same thing – what is at stake is the engagement with the external world.

44   See Vogel 2013, Bhattacharya, 2017. This expanded notion of labour also offers a reply to the common argument that developments in immaterial labour have made Marx's ideas somehow invalid or obsolete. See Sayers 2011, Chapter 3, and Swain 2012a, Chapter 10.

> Feuerbach speaks in particular of the perception of natural science; he mentions secrets which are disclosed only to the eye of the physicist and the chemist; but where would natural science be without industry and commerce? Even this 'pure' natural science is provided with an aim, as with its material, only through trade and industry, through the sensuous activity of men.[45]

Marx admits a small qualification, here, which can be seen as a retreat from the more radical position in the *Economic and Philosophical Manuscripts*:[46]

> Of course, in all this, the priority of external nature remains unassailed, and all this has no application to the original men produced by *generatio aequivoca*; but this differentiation has meaning only insofar as man is considered separate from nature.[47]

However, this is not much of a concession, since, as the example of commerce-driven science suggests, in most cases, and in particular in relevant cases of practical engagement with the world, we are not concerned with nature separate from man.

Thus while Marx perhaps no longer envisaged one grand science capable of understanding nature and humanity as one, he still recognised that any valuable scientific endeavour must understand itself as social product, and as implicated in human goals. This turns our attention sharply to the social context in which that knowledge is produced, exercised and deployed, and in particular who gets to produce, exercise and deploy it.

4   Democracy

To the extent that Marx is concerned with the appropriate relationship between the subject and their activity, his account of freedom shares affinities with self-determination or autonomy-based accounts of freedom. Whilst Marx is concerned that subjects *realise* themselves in their relationship with nature, an essential prerequisite for that is the capacity to direct and control

---

45   *German Ideology*, p. 46.
46   See Feenberg 2014, p. 48.
47   *German Ideology*, p. 46.

their activity according to their conscious will. Otherwise labour would not be distinct from instinct-driven behaviour of animals (when, as we saw, it is so distinct for Marx); and otherwise it would not be self-realisation, but mere self-objectification (and merely the realisation of the will of others, and as such alienating). To this extent, I agree with those, like Brenkert and Gould, who have stressed Marx's concern with freedom as self-determination.[48] Self-determination forms an important component of Marx's theory of freedom; whilst objectifying one's powers in nature is essential, it is not sufficient, if that objectification results only in alienation. Rather, as Brenkert identifies, 'self-determination ... occurs when a person essentially directs and controls the form his self-objectification takes'.[49]

Moreover, to the extent that I am concerned with the question of 'emancipation to what', of the goal of Marx's political action, the 'self-determination' element seems more important. Firstly, any labour, even alienated labour under class domination, involves objectification (or at least the attempt at objectification, where this attempt might fail for reasons not to do with restrictions on freedom, but for technical reasons). Thus, if we were interested in what it is to be emancipated and for labour to be free, concentrating on objectification alone would not yield much of a result. Secondly, self-determination is a precondition for any labouring activity to be free. Without getting the relationship between the subject and labour correct, it does not matter what actual labouring activity is undertaken. Thus, if we are asking the question of where to direct political efforts and energies, it is first to establishing 'the appropriation of the total productive forces by the united individuals', rather than anything else. Indeed, it is arguable that for Marx getting the relationship to labour correct will render the question of what people then do with that labour somewhat moot – in that sense, his notion of self-determination is formal, not substantive. Once given genuine control over their activity, people will realise themselves almost automatically, developing their talents in whatever direction they see fit.

It is worth stressing that to talk about freedom in terms of self-determination is not to invoke a *negative* conception of freedom. Marx's own theory of freedom does not squeeze easily into the categories of negative and positive. Indeed, some – for example Geuss[50] – have suggested that Marx's view constitutes a genuine alternative to either negative and positive conceptions, focused

---

48 See Gould 1978, p. 107, Brenkert 1983, Chapter 3.
49 Brenkert 1983, p. 92.
50 Geuss 2005, Chapter 4.

as it is on the realisation of the subject's capacities, without substantively constraining what this would amount to. However, in Berlin's terms the link to self-determination (and self-realisation) suggests a positive conception of freedom. When it comes to the crucial social aspect – the 'second-order mediation' – Marx is certainly not just concerned with the mere absence of outside interference. In this respect, Marx is not that unusual. For example, Republican theories of freedom also combine a commitment to self-determination with an understanding that this can only be achieved given particular social and political institutions, which have to go beyond a minimal state securing negative liberty.[51] Whilst Marx would likely reject the specific institutional forms they recommend, he shares with the Republicans a sense that self-determination requires substantial social forms beyond that of basic minimal liberties.[52] Specifically, for Marx, self-determination was only possible through social forms which permit the democratic management of productive activity – that is what he ultimately means with 'the power of the united individuals'. This indicates how Marx's account of freedom is intimately linked to his conception of democracy; for Marx, real freedom required nothing less than the democratic organisation of our social and productive lives – something which, he thought, capitalism was incapable of delivering.

Why is this impossible under capitalism? Straightforwardly, because it is structurally impossible for those who perform the labour to appear within it 'as subject' in the sense required for truly free activity. There are a number of reasons for this that Marx emphasises:

The first is the necessary role that capital plays as organiser in the labour process. Capitalism's central relationship is the worker's sale of individual labour power to the capitalist. The worker is an isolated bearer of labour power, which the capitalist buys. However, capitalists (usually) do not buy one, isolated labour power, but several, which they put to work together. Capital thus appears as organiser of the cooperation of the separate workers: 'The work of directing, superintending and adjusting becomes one of the functions of capital, from the moment that the labour under capital's control becomes cooperative'.[53] Of course, the capitalist may not do this himself – he may recruit a group of 'officers (management) and NCOs (foremen, overseers), who command during the labour process in the name of capital',[54] but 'that a capitalist should com-

---

51   See Pettit 2001.

52   Though note that he does refer to the Paris commune as a 'social republic'. See Basso, 2015, p. 84.

53   *Capital Vol. 1*, p. 449.

54   *Capital Vol. 1*, p. 450.

mand in the field of production is now as indispensable as that a general should command on the field of battle'.[55]

This leads to a general division of labour between those who design the labour process and those who execute it. The technical and scientific knowledge that directs and designs the work process appears as the special property of a small number of experts, set apart from those who perform the work. Thus the 'plan', as it were, is left out of the hands of most people. Under these conditions, workers lack, to a greater or lesser degree, awareness of why they perform certain activities, and thus the capacity to recognise them as the realisation of themselves. As Braverman puts it:

> It thus becomes essential for the capitalist that control over the labour process pass from the hands of the worker into his own. This transition presents itself in history as the *progressive alienation of the process of production* from the worker; to the capitalist it presents itself as the problem of *management*.[56]

Thus, under capitalist conditions, part of the scientific knowledge required to direct production is management techniques, not just knowledge to regulate the relationship with nature, but knowledge to regulate *people themselves.*

Moreover, this division of labour becomes represented as natural, and the 'science' of management becomes as apparently fixed as the science of nature:

> The individuals composing the ruling class possess among other things consciousness, and therefore think. Insofar, therefore, as they rule as a class and determine the extent and compass of an historical epoch, it is self-evident that they do this in its whole range, hence among other things rule also as thinkers, as producers of ideas, and regulate the production and distribution of the ideas of their age: thus their ideas are the ruling ideas of the epoch.[57]

This fixity is reinforced by a division of labour within the ruling class between those who produce ideas ('its active, conceptive ideologists, who make the formation of the illusions of the class about itself their chief source of livelihood') and those who passively receive them while directing their energies

---

55   *Capital Vol. 1*, p. 448.
56   Braverman 1998, p. 40.
57   *German Ideology*, 67.

towards appropriation.[58] This allows the ideas to gain a veneer of independence from the particular class interests they are connected to. Moreover, to the extent that these ideas are connected to the material reality of the division of labour, they are not 'mere' illusions, capable of being seen through or wished away: they are reinforced by the division of labour itself and cannot be removed without at the same time challenging that division (See Chapter 3).

Under these conditions, the idea of the workers themselves appearing in the process of production as a directing agency themselves is unthinkable. Rather, 'the interconnection between their various labours confronts them, in the realm of ideas, as a plan drawn up by the capitalist, and, in practice, as his authority, as the powerful will of a being outside them, who subjects their activity to his purpose'.[59] Under capitalist relations of production, this could simply not be otherwise – only capital possesses the power to be the organiser in production, because of, on one side, its control of the means of production and, on the other, the separation of the working class into individual bearers of labour power (See Chapter 5). In addition, their products, the machinery they work with, and the world they live in all appear increasingly as an alien world, animated by something else. Thus their own activity appears not as something freely undertaken, but as animated by an alien power, and subject to 'natural' forces outside of their control.

The only alternative to this that would permit the producers themselves to appear as organisers in production is a far deeper democratic organisation of the economy. This is a historically specific claim. In earlier economic forms it may have been possible for the producer to appear as organiser in the labour process on a small scale. Artisans, even peasant farmers, can be the directors of their own working activity, albeit on a small and isolated scale, and generally in conditions of political domination and ignorance. However, the complexity of co-operation brought about by modern manufacture and technology has made this small scale impossible. If workers are to appear as organisers, it must be as a collectively constituted body. If they are all to share in this organisation, it must be democratic. In one passage in the *Grundrisse* Marx schematically divides history into three kinds of social forms:

> Relations of personal dependence (entirely spontaneous at the outset) are the first social forms, in which human productive capacity develops only to a slight extent and at isolated points. Personal independence foun-

---

58 *German Ideology*, pp. 67–8.

59 *Capital Vol. 1*, p. 450.

ded on *objective* [*sachlicher*] dependence is the second great form, in which a system of general social metabolism, of universal relations, of all-round needs and universal capacities is formed for the first time. Free individuality, based on the universal development of individuals and on their subordination of their communal social productivity as their social wealth, is the third stage. The second stage creates the conditions for the third.[60]

The third stage is conceived as merely the 'subordination' of – the exertion of control over – the conditions that exist in the second. This claim is no less necessary for being historically specific, however. So long as we want to maintain the huge advanced developments of capitalism – and we do want most of them – we cannot take a step back to small scale handcrafts. Thus the only option available to *us*, says Marx, is economic democracy.

Marx says little about the social structures, relationships and norms that would make possible this democratic control. He has good reasons for wanting to avoid this, which I will examine in Chapter 4. However, there are a few things that can be said:

Firstly, it requires people recognising that the social relations in which they exist are not natural ones, but rather social products that can be subject to collective change. The relationships and interconnections between people can no longer appear as a natural force external to them, but only as a specific form of society, which can then be brought under democratic control. This involves, in a quite literal sense, coming to see the world differently. While this may not quite be the radical transformation of the senses anticipated by the *Economic and Philosophical Manuscripts*, it nonetheless involves a different way of perceiving reality. Capitalism had, in some ways, accelerated this process: it had 'put an end to all feudal, patriarchal, idyllic relations ... pitilessly torn asunder the motley feudal ties that bound man to his natural superiors, and has left remaining no other nexus between man and man than naked self-interest, than callous "cash payment"'.[61] However, there remained one great barrier to this realisation, namely the world market discussed in the quotations in Section 2 above: an abstract system which presents human activity as an alien force. Recognition of that force as human activity, and thus something that can be brought under human control, is the fundamental next step.

---

60   *Grundrisse*, p. 158.
61   *Communist Manifesto*, p. 82.

Secondly, it is necessary to undermine the distinction between mental and manual labour, or, more specifically, between those who design the labour process and those who carry it out – between task-execution and task-definition.[62] To some extent, this can be carried out through democratisation of workplaces, a system which permits workers a direct say in the decisions of the enterprises they work in. This would already be a radical departure from the 'standard' model of capitalism, in which the capitalist commands like a general on the field of battle, and workers enact a plan they have no role in. However, as Iris Marion Young notes:

> Workplace democracy is less than complete, however, if it only involves participation in top-level decisions through a system of representations. It is at least as important that workers should participate in decisions about their own immediate work context and environment – their own speciality, department, work team, work site and so on.[63]

This, too, however, is unlikely to be enough without a radical transformation of jobs themselves. One suggestion for this comes from Michael Albert's *Parecon* project, which recommends 'balanced job complexes'. The idea here is that individuals would not be limited to a particular task, but have bundles of tasks that balanced between pleasant and unpleasant and empowering and disempowering tasks:

> We need to balance job complexes for desirability and empowerment in each and every workplace, as well as guarantee that workers have a combination of tasks that balance across all workplaces. This and only this provides a division of labour that gives all workers an equal chance of participating in and benefitting from workplace decision-making. This and only this establishes a division of labour which does not produce a class division between permanent order-givers and order-takers.[64]

As well as the democratisation of work, however, it must also be possible to extend democracy to society as a whole. This, too, must involve a richer conception of democracy than currently exists. It must be possible for the united individuals to exert democratic control over the entire economy, and to recog-

---

62   See Braverman 1998, Young 1990.
63   Young 1990, p. 224.
64   Albert 2003, p. 104.

nise it as their own product. This requires more than just the democratisation of individual workplaces, but at the very least a set of democratic relationships between workplaces, and the capacity to make democratic decisions on some relevant geographical scale. Again, how precisely this is to work remains at best underspecified.

Finally, these new democratic forms and structures will only function if they are based on new social relations. There is perhaps a hint of this idea in Marx's early notes on James Mill, in which he imagines producing 'as human beings':

> In that event, each of us would have doubly affirmed himself and his neighbour in production. In my production I would have objectified the *specific character* of my *individuality* and for that reason I would both have enjoyed the *expression* of my own individual *life* during my activity ... In your use or enjoyment of my product I would have the *immediate* satisfaction and knowledge that in my labour I had gratified a *human* need ... I would have acted for you as the *mediator* between you and the species, thus I would be acknowledged by you as the complement of your own being, as an essential part of yourself. I would thus know myself to be confirmed both in your thoughts and your love.[65]

This, however, remains troublingly vague. And it is not a surprise that it should be so, because Marx is anticipating a form of life he does not believe has historically existed. He clearly believed that there was some analogy to be drawn with pre-capitalist societies, in which people related to their labour concretely but in a one-sided fashion.[66] However, he also clearly believes it could be possible for people to relate in a far richer fashion than this. Earlier forms of life could form a useful comparison and perhaps even inspiration, but they were not to provide models or examples. The significance of this point I will return to in later chapters. For present purposes I will just note that I do not think that the vagueness of a conception of what relating 'as human beings' invalidates a critique of existing social relations. It is not necessary for Marx to fully specify what freely determined social relations will look like to say that other social relations are not free.

Thus, while perhaps not quite as radically as the 1844 Manuscripts envisage, the people who inhabit communism will be radically different. They will see the world differently, they will acquire new ideas, new social practices, and new

---

65   *Early Writings*, p. 277.
66   *Grundrisse*, p. 158.

social relationships. Only then will their activity truly be self-activity. The gap between there and here is immense, and yet Marx believes we can and must bridge it. However, he also asserts that to bridge the gap must involve already engaging in something like the very same self-activity that this society secures. Communism must itself be the product of revolutionary self-activity. Prometheus and Spartacus must free themselves. Why that is, and how it might work, is the subject of the next chapter.

From Freedom to Self-Emancipation

'Neighbour', he said, 'although we have simplified our lives a great deal
from what they were, and have got rid of many conventionalities and
many sham wants, which used to give our forefathers much trouble, yet
our life is too complex for me to tell you in detail by means of words how
it is arranged; you must find that out by living amongst us. It is true that I
can better tell you what we don't do than what we do do.'

WILLIAM MORRIS, *News From Nowhere*[1]

∴

1 Introduction

Marx's vision of an emancipated society was one in which social productive
activity was self-activity, in which productive activity was controlled collectively and consciously, through democratic forms. However, he went a step further, in insisting that this emancipated society must also itself be the product of
consciously directed self-activity. The revolution which secured the possibility
of freely self-determined action in the future, must itself be a freely determined
act in its own right. Emancipation must be self-emancipation. The question
that confronts this chapter, then, is why? Why must Spartacus emancipate himself? Or, in a different era of slavery, why is a Toussaint L'Ouverture better than
a William Wilberforce? Why, in other words, must the social conditions of freedom be the result of self-emancipation, rather than of a benevolent liberator,
or a neutral arbiter?

Marx offers surprisingly little to ground his commitment to self-emancipation philosophically. It appears almost as a guiding political assumption,
inserted into the founding statement of the First International, and defended
against revision in the Gotha Programme. However, for all that Marx might
see it as self-evident, it is far from the normal way of thinking about political change, either now or in Marx's time. Contemporary conceptions of social

---

1 Morris 2003, pp. 68–9.

change are still marked deeply by 'great man' ideas, in which individuals harness or motivate popular opinion in order to effect real change, combined with a dismissiveness towards ordinary people as a herd or mass. Brecht de Smet observes that the Egyptian uprising of 2011 took many by surprise precisely because of patronising attitudes that saw the masses as uneducated and undeveloped, and therefore unready for democratic change.[2] At the more comical end of the spectrum, for several weeks in 2015 the *Guardian* website carried a banner headline that read 'Dear Bill Gates, will you lead us in the fight against climate change'. This is the approach which Draper calls the *acherontic* or saviour-leader mode of doing politics, citing Virgil: 'If I cannot change the Powers above, I shall set the Lower Regions [*Acheron*] into motion'.[3] Many of Marx's early contemporaries were entirely content with this approach, looking to the enlightened bourgeoisie, or to a small group of insurrectionary conspirators (of the type Marx described as 'alchemists of revolution'),[4] whilst his *bête noir* in later life, Ferdinand Lassalle, was happy to pin his hopes on Bismarck as a benevolent reformer.[5] Thus this commitment to collective self-emancipation was something that set him apart from most of his contemporaries, and remains an unusual position.

Secondly, as I will discuss further below, Marx's commitment to self-emancipation involves a certain paradox. Put succinctly, self-activity in the future must arise on the basis of self-activity in the present, within a society that consistently thwarts the possibility of self-activity. Indeed, it is this very paradox that has led people, both in Marx's own era and since, to conclude that collective self-emancipation is impossible, and thus to pin hopes on various saviours from outside. The concept intended to solve this paradox is revolutionary praxis, conceived as a process of simultaneous world and self-transformation. Yet, as I will discuss further below, even those accounts of Marx that recognise the centrality of this concept have tended to downplay the degree of paradox involved.

In the following section, I consider the various intellectual themes that feed into Marx's ideas through his early philosophical and journalistic career. While this falls well short of an adequate intellectual history, it provides the groundwork for how Marx came to the principle of self-emancipation. Section 3 then considers more directly the conception of revolutionary praxis described in the *Theses on Feuerbach* and how it provides the answer to why self-emancipation is necessary and how it is possible. Section 4 develops on this conception

---

2 De Smet 2015, p. 3.
3 Draper 1977, p. 215.
4 MECW 10, p. 318.
5 See Draper 1977 and 1990; Löwy 2005.

of revolutionary praxis through comparison and analogy with two different understandings of radical pedagogy, in particular as an attempt to conceptualise the role and challenges of those committed to self-emancipation as a political and ethical project. This chapter thus sets up many of the problems that will be addressed in the following chapters, specifically about the role of both activists and critical theorists and their relationship to the movements they seek to participate in, encourage, and guide.

2   Reckonings

The origins of Marx's commitment to self-emancipation can be traced in his early political and intellectual development, particularly in the period 1842–5. In this time, as is well known, Marx undergoes the transition from radical democrat to communist, he 'discovers' and declares allegiance to the proletariat, he settles accounts with Hegel, and makes and breaks friends and alliances at a pretty rapid pace. In the course of this he writes a series of articles and notebooks through which it is possible to trace the evolution of his thought. These writings contain a vast array of ideas and positions, and it is beyond the scope of this book to write a complete intellectual history of Marx's development in this period, nor could I hope to match those that already exist.[6] However, in this section I want to identify a number of recurring, intertwining and mutating themes that push Marx towards the conclusion that self-emancipation is central.

In this period especially, there is an urgency about Marx's writing that indicates a deep concern with the question of what is to be done. While both Marx's ultimate goal (from a vague conception of a democratic society to communism) and his self-identity (liberal journalist, philosopher, communist) changes and develops, he is persistently concerned with what *people like him should do*. Whether this is best attributed to features of Marx's character, or to the way in which he was forced very directly to confront practical questions in his professional life as either an academic or journalist (or both),[7] there is a continuous drive to make intellectual questions practical questions. This, in part, explains the sheer speed with which he cycles through certain positions, perhaps best

---

6   See, e.g. Cornu 1957, Löwy 2005, Draper 1977, Avineri 1968, Kouvelakis 2003.

7   Draper emphasises Marx's 'year and a half of rubbing his nose against the social and political facts of life, which he encountered as the crusading editor of the most extreme leftist democratic newspaper in pre-1848 Germany' (Draper 1977, p. 31), while Löwy suggests Bruno Bauer's removal from his academic position as a significant factor.

illustrated by the 1843 *Critique of Hegel's Philosophy of Right*, which begins with critical engagement with the old master, and breaks off in outright frustration ('God Help us all',[8] is Marx's final comment). To point this out is not to praise the 'activist' Marx over his ivory tower adversaries. Rather, it is to suggest that right from the beginning, what is to be done was a central question for him.

Another feature that appears strikingly early in Marx's political writings is a consistent suspicion and rejection of a kind of politics which seeks to act on behalf of the masses, without their active participation and involvement. This is first evident in his writings on censorship, in which he regularly excoriates those with paternalistic pretensions towards acting in the interest of the people over their own heads. All defences of censorship (an issue of personal significance for the young journalist), embodied an elitist approach he sought to reject:

> In order to combat *freedom of the press*, the thesis of the *permanent immaturity* of the human race has to be defended ... If the immaturity of the human race is the mystical ground for opposing freedom of the press, then the censorship at any rate is a highly reasonable means against the maturity of the human race.[9]

This approach represents an abominably patronising attitude towards the people that politicians and the state were supposed to represent, and could not help having negative consequences:

> The government hears only its own voice, it knows that it hears only its own voice, yet it harbours the illusion that it hears the voice of the people, and it demands that the people, too, should itself harbour this illusion. For its part, therefore, the people sinks partly into political superstition, partly into political disbelief, or, completely turning away from political life, becomes a rabble of private individuals [*Privatpoebel*].[10]

Against this position – that once representatives were chosen the people should largely butt out of politics – Marx asserts an expansive conception of representation:

> Representation must not be conceived as the representation of something that is not the people itself. It must be conceived only as the people's

---

8   *Early Writings*, p. 198.
9   MECW 1, p. 153.
10   MECW 1, p. 168.

self-representation, as a state action which, not being its sole, exceptional state action, is distinguished from other expressions of its state life merely by the universality of its content.[11]

Moreover, it is a 'senseless contradiction that my self-activity should consist of acts unknown to me and done by another'.[12] Rather, 'a representation which is secluded from the consciousness of its constituents is no representation at all'.[13]

This carries over into Marx's first attempt at a reckoning with Hegel, written in Kreuznach in 1843. In working through Hegel's writings, Marx several times sticks on Hegel's belief that a particular class can summarise or represent society as a whole.[14] He criticises Hegel for attempting to locate the source of sovereignty in a monarch, arguing that he can only do this by twisted logic and by capitulating to society as it actually is:

> Hegel converts every attribute of the constitutional monarch in contemporary Europe into the absolute self-determinations of the *will*. He does not say that the will of the monarch is the final decision, but that the final decision of the will is – the monarch. The first statement is empirical. The second twists the empirical fact into a metaphysical axiom.[15]

Rather than locate the source of sovereignty in a monarch, Marx locates it in the mass of people:

> The state is an abstraction. Only the people is a concrete reality. And it is noteworthy that Hegel, who does not scruple to ascribe living qualities to the abstraction, should concede the right of the concrete reality to a living quality [i.e., to the people] such as sovereignty only with reluctance and with so many reservations.[16]

It is notable, here, that sovereignty is described as a 'living quality'. Partly motivating the declaration that sovereignty lies in the masses is the motivation to undo Hegel's inversion of subject and predicate and present living, acting

---

11   MECW 1, p. 306.
12   MECW 1, p. 148.
13   MECW 1, p. 148.
14   See Avineri 1968, Kouvelakis 2003.
15   *Early Writings*, p. 82.
16   *Early Writings*, pp. 85–6.

human beings at the centre of politics. Marx then uses this as part of a full-blown defence of democracy against monarchy. He describes monarchy as a particular pathological instance of democracy as the genus of politics: 'Democracy is the generic constitution. Monarchy is only a variant, and a bad variant at that'.[17] If the monarch has sovereignty, it is only, ultimately, through the constituting power of the masses.

Thus true democracy, without the mediation of the monarch, would be a superior form. Monarchy cannot do without democracy, but democracy can do without the monarchy:

> In monarchy the whole, the people, is subsumed under one of its forms of existence, the political constitution; in democracy the *constitution itself* appears only as *one* determining characteristic, and indeed as its [the people's] self-determination. In monarchy we have the people of the constitution, in democracy the constitution of the people. Democracy is the solution to the *riddle* of every constitution. In it we find the constitution founded its true ground: *real human* beings and the *real* people; not merely implicitly and in essence. The constitution is thus posited as people's own creation. The constitution is in appearance what it is in reality: the free creation of man.[18]

Here Marx's conception of true democracy as the collective self-determination of the people comes through very clearly. The most significant move Marx makes is to assert that democracy is, in an important sense, both more real and more fundamental monarchy:

> Democracy is the truth of monarchy; monarchy is not the truth of democracy. Monarchy is by necessity democracy in contradiction with itself; the monarchic moment is not an inconsistency within democracy. Monarchy cannot be explained in its own terms; democracy can be so explained. In democracy no moment acquires a meaning other than what is proper to it. Each is really only a moment of the *demos* as a whole. In monarchy a part determines the character of the whole. The whole constitution must adapt itself to one fixed point. Democracy is the generic constitution ... Democracy is both form and content. Monarchy is *supposed* to be only a form, but it falsifies the content.[19]

---

17   *Early Writings*, p. 87.
18   *Early Writings*, p. 87.
19   *Early Writings*, p. 88.

What we see beginning to emerge in these passages is a radical critique of a narrow representational politics, of a politics in which individuals or particular groups seek to act on behalf of the people. Such attempts to represent the people are all mere shadows of 'true democracy', whereas: 'In a democracy the constitution, the law, i.e. the political state, is only a self-determination of the people and a determinate content of the people'.[20]

While these passages stay at the level of representation within the state, we later see a more general criticism of 'acherontic' politics appear in the *Holy Family*. By this point Marx has advanced much further in the process of becoming a communist, and his focus has shifted from a question of representation in the state to the political practice of those who would seek to transform it. Draper identifies Marx's critique of Eugene Sue's *Les Mystères de Paris* as being of particular importance in this context. For many of Marx's contemporaries, Sue's book was a magnificent work demonstrating the importance of philanthropy. For Marx, it was a travesty, indicating the patronising approach of the would-be social reformers: 'Thus in *the Holy Family* Marx wrote the first direct polemic against the pervasive conception that it is the prerogative of some band of superior intellectuals to think for the masses, whose duty in turn is to repay this service by acting as their instruments, flock or raw material'.[21]

The second vital thread in Marx's development is the priority of practical activity. The possible sources of this are many and varied. I have already examined in the previous chapter Marx's Hegelian-influenced belief in the importance of acting to transform the world in order to realise oneself, but Fichte, Moses Hess, August Cieszkowski, and Feuerbach can all be suggested as influences on this particular position.[22] Whatever its source, this priority is central to Marx's ideas. In the *Theses on Feuerbach*, he asserts that Feuerbach 'does not grasp the significance of "revolutionary", of "practical-critical", activity'. He fails to see that 'All social life is essentially practical. All mysteries which lead theory to mysticism find their rational solution in human practice and in the comprehension of this practice'.[23] This connection between consciousness and activity is re-asserted in the *German Ideology*, most famously in the assertion that 'Consciousness can never be anything else than conscious being, and the being of men in their actual life process ... It is not consciousness that determines life,

20 *Early Writings*, p. 89.

21 Draper 1977, p. 226.

22 For discussion of Fichte, see Rockmore 1980, for suggestions of the significance of Hess and Cieszkowski, see Cornu 1957, Liebich 1979. For alternative views on Hess, see Kouvelakis 2003, pp. 121–58.

23 *Early Writings*, p. 422.

but life that determines consciousness'.[24] This is a conception of consciousness as profoundly intertwined with practical activity – consciousness is necessarily consciousness of a certain activity, and thus shaped by that activity, not able to float and fly beyond it. Moreover, our most fundamental social practices, those through which we meet our most basic needs and manage our relationship with nature, have a particularly powerful pull. Thus labour (in the sense it is discussed in the previous chapter) has a particular significance, and a growing one throughout these writings. It briefly appears in the 1843 critique of Hegel, where Marx refers to 'the class of immediate labour, of concrete labour, [that] do not so much constitute a class of civil society as provide the ground on which the circles of civil society move and have their being',[25] and by 1845, in the *German Ideology*, has a central determining role in history and consciousness.

Linked to this is a growing disdain and distrust of the pretensions of theory:

> Where speculation ends, where real life starts, there consequently begins real, positive science, the expounding of the practical activity, of the practical process of development of men. Empty phrases about consciousness end, and real knowledge has to take their place. At its best its place can only be taken by a summing-up of the most general results, abstractions which are derived from the observation of the historical development of men. These abstractions themselves, divorced from real history, have no value whatsoever.[26]

Later he asserts that it is only on the basis of the division between material and mental labour that 'consciousness can really flatter itself that it is something other than consciousness of existing practice, that it *really* represents something rather than represents something real'.[27] Whatever role theoretical reflection had for Marx, it came after practice, rather than preceding it. In this respect, albeit perhaps for very different reasons, Marx is re-affirming Hegel, something which he reminds Bauer et al in the *Holy Family*:

> Already in Hegel the Absolute Spirit of history has its material in the Mass and finds its appropriate expression only in philosophy. The philosopher, however, is only the organ through which the maker of history,

---

24   *German Ideology*, p. 42.
25   *Early Writings*, pp. 146–7.
26   *German Ideology*, p. 43.
27   *German Ideology*, p. 50.

the Absolute Spirit, arrives at self-consciousness retrospectively after the movement has ended. The participation of the philosopher in history is reduced to this retrospective consciousness, for the real movement is accomplished by the Absolute Spirit unconsciously. Hence the philosopher appears on the scene *post festum*.[28]

This attitude, substantially shared by Marx, is summed up by Goethe's Mephistopheles when he says 'All theory is grey, my friend. But forever green is the tree of life'.

These features partly seem to drive Marx to another important point in his early development: The centrality of critique. Motivated on the one hand by a distrust of the pretensions of either theory or demagogic politicians, and on the other by a deep concern for practical matters, Marx asserts directly the importance of criticising and analysing what actually exists. The role for radicals is not to present the world with grand plans, but to turn to examining how the newly desired world exists within the old:

> Hence, nothing prevents us from making criticism of politics, participation in politics, and therefore real struggles, the starting point of our criticism, and from identifying our criticism with them. In that case we do not confront the world in a doctrinaire way with a new principle: Here is the truth, kneel down before it! We develop new principles for the world out of the world's own principles. We do not say to the world: Cease your struggles, they are foolish; we will give you the true slogan of struggle. We merely show the world what it is really fighting for, and consciousness is something that it has to acquire, even if it does not want to.[29]

This shift towards critique drives Marx in several directions. It pushes him towards a closer examination of actually existing social processes and developments within society, to look for struggles that might develop 'principles for the new world'. This, combined with the emphasis on practice, can be seen to drive his concern for political economy, and material production in particular. However, Marx goes further than merely emphasising critique. He also insists that this critique must take sides, that it must be partisan and align itself with a movement. Thus critique cannot be mere narcissistic or self-indulgent critique, it must also risk aligning itself with some particular political grouping.

---

28   MECW 4 p. 86.
29   MECW 3, p. 144.

Thus Marx 'joined the radically critical party ... and recognised that division and conflict were both his own essential concerns and the condition for all historical development'.[30]

This shift also brings into focus something that is both obvious and easy to forget: The future society must be built from the imperfect material existing in the present. This puts into far sharper relief the crucial question of how we get from here to there. That the reform of consciousness cannot be a matter of just telling people to live differently is already announced in the letter to Ruge:

> The reform of consciousness consists entirely in making the world aware of its own consciousness, in arousing it from its dream of itself, in explaining its own actions to it.[31]

Here reform of consciousness is conceived as making plain to people something they already unconsciously know. Later, Marx will talk more explicitly about the production of *communist* consciousness:

> Both for the production on a mass scale of this communist consciousness, and for the success of the cause itself, the alteration of men on a mass scale is necessary, an alteration which can only take place in a practical movement, a revolution; this revolution is necessary, therefore, not only because the ruling class cannot be overthrown in any other way, but also because the class overthrowing it can only in a revolution succeed in ridding itself of all the muck of ages and become fitted to found society anew.[32]

Thus if society is to be transformed, it must be on the basis of a process of self-transformation, in which people change themselves as they change the world. Moreover, this transformation appears necessarily conflictual – it is on the basis of challenges to the existing order.

By the time Marx wrote this, he had also 'discovered' the proletariat. There are probably three important moments in this process: Firstly, his moving to Paris from Cologne, and thus experiencing a far more developed socialist and communist movement. Secondly, the Silesian Weavers' revolt, and the growing confidence that such movements were possible in Germany too. Finally, discussion with Engels about the state of the workers' movement in England.

---

30 Kouvelakis 2003, p. 242 See also Kouvelakis 2003, pp. 281–3.
31 MECW 3, p. 144.
32 *German Ideology*, p. 60.

The proletariat appears first as a political category, or rather as a class without a political category, one which does not fit into the system but on which it nonetheless rests. This means that their entry into the political sphere must, by necessity, transform and revolutionise that sphere. As I will return to in Chapter 7, Marx never moves away from stressing the political importance of the proletariat, but this is developed and embellished through economic analysis, showing that this class is uniquely separated not just from the products of its labour, but from that labour itself, and thus its struggles strike at the very heart of the institution of private property. Thus the political success of the proletariat must also necessitate social and economic transformation towards communism.

The various strands I have picked out combine and reach a certain zenith in the third thesis on Feuerbach. Feuerbach, Marx argues, 'forgets that circumstances are changed by men and that it is essential to educate the educator himself' and 'must, therefore, divide society into two parts, one of which is superior to society'.[33] In contrast to this approach, 'the coincidence of the changing of circumstances and of human activity or self-changing can be conceived and rationally understood only as *revolutionary practice*'.[34] This condensed thesis links the hostility to hierarchy and the pretensions of theory to the emphasis on practical self-transformation. It expresses a fear that a mode of politics which plays the role of educator to the unenlightened masses simply cannot lead to anything resembling emancipation – rather, it reproduces the very hierarchies it hopes to abolish. It is, as such, the closest thing to a philosophical argument one finds in Marx in defence of the principle of self-emancipation. However, it is more an aphorism than an argument, and while the above sketch identifies some of the ideas that feed into it, it does not amount to a philosophical defence either.

3   Linking the Present to the Future

There are many possible candidates for the target of the third thesis,[35] but its negative charge is clear enough: What Marx means by the materialist doctrine

---

33   *Early Writings*, p. 422.
34   *Early Writings*, p. 422.
35   Engels would later gloss it as being about Robert Owen (See Chapter 4), while Löwy identifies it as 'the transcendence, the sublation of the antithesis between 18th century materialism (the changing of circumstances) and 19th century Young Hegelianism' (Löwy 2005, p. 105).

is the – widespread and entirely plausible – claim that people are products of their own environment, and thus that they carry with them various prejudices, desires, beliefs, and even needs (Marx's 'muck of ages'), that are distinctive of their epoch. This much is uncontroversial. What is controversial is the conclusion that, since the masses are necessarily corrupted by current conditions, it is necessary for reformers to educate them from outside. Indeed, some versions of this are even driven to argue that the masses are best kept out, lest they corrupt the transition or development. There are two ways this can proceed – either an enlightened educator shows the masses the way, or the enlightened set about changing conditions, in order to create new, better masses.[36]

Against both of these approaches, Marx levels the simple question 'who educates the educators?' If, indeed, people are products of their time and circumstances, how can anyone transcend this in order to become an enlightened educator-emancipator? The answer, flatly, is they cannot, and all approaches that think in this way merely flatter themselves that they can. In this sense, they have to split society into educators and educated, enlightened and in-need-of-enlightenment, emancipators and emancipated. Moreover, Marx asserts, this split is necessarily a hierarchical one to the extent it posits one group as above, outside of, or beyond society. In this, Marx returns to the themes of his earliest writings on press censorship, in which metaphors of education abound. Most strikingly, in 1842 he had already rhetorically asked 'if we all remain children in swaddling clothes, who is to swaddle us? If we lie in a cradle who is to cradle us? If we are all in jail, who is to be the jail warden?' In this passage we already see, as Draper puts it, 'the basic answer to all arguments old and new for "educational" dictatorships. It already implies that democratic freedom is not a diploma of maturity passed out at a graduation ceremony, but is acquired only in a process of struggle by people *who are not yet 'ready' for freedom*, but who grow up to it only by engaging in the struggle themselves, before anyone certifies them mature'.[37]

That, then, is the negative charge of the third thesis, and it is pretty watertight and compelling. However, Marx's positive alternative is not. The argument might have been taken as a *reductio ad absurdum* of the entire idea that people are determined by circumstances. Indeed, a strikingly similar argument might be employed against Marx himself – if people really were products of their

---

36   See Löwy 2005, p. 67.

37   Draper 1971, p. 48. See also Geras, 2017, Chapter 6, for whom the third thesis 'breaks the circle which cuts men off from the possibility of self-transformation and, doing so, liberates them from the need for liberators'.

own circumstances, how could social change happen at all? But Marx does not intend it like this – instead it is a rejection of the idea that social change can come from outside or above. But, in a sense, all Marx has done is deepen the paradox, or tighten the dilemma. If we are all covered with the muck of ages, all products of our existing society, how can we even conceive of social change happening? It is important to stress here that although Marx has rejected the idea that ideas can only be changed 'from outside', and the elitist conclusions that flow from it, he has not rejected the idea that consciousness is only consciousness of being. Hence communist consciousness, not to mention its success, is something that must be *produced* – it is not available in the present, at least not on a mass scale: There is an important sense in which we do not and cannot know what it is like to live under communism until we have lived it. Marx has thus left only one option for explaining how it can be produced: it must be consciousness of a transformed and transforming practice – of revolutionary praxis.

Marx does not give us a great deal to go on when it comes to describing what this revolutionary praxis looks like in concrete. One famous example, though, appears in the *Economic and Philosophical Manuscripts*:

> When communist workmen gather together their immediate aim is instruction, propaganda, etc. But at the same time they acquire a new need – the need for society – and what appears as a means has become an end. The practical development can be most strikingly observed in the gatherings of French socialist workers. Smoking, eating and drinking, etc. are no longer means of creating links between people. Company, association, conversation, which in its turn has society as its goal, is enough for them. The brotherhood of man is not a hollow phrase, it is a reality, and the nobility of man shines forth upon us from their work-worn figures.

The process described here is something like the following: for the French workers, collective co-operation, communication and co-ordination appears first as a means to meet their more fundamental needs. In order to win from the capitalist class better wages, and thus greater capacity to meet their basic needs, they must work together and collectively organise. However, in the course of this, this need for society becomes not merely an external, instrumental need, but is internalised.[38]

---

38   See Lebowitz 2003, pp. 179–84.

What this demonstrates is how actually existing practice – a practice which is in fact a feature of capitalism, not any other social formation – can at the same time give rise to new forms of consciousness, ideas and capacities. The 'brotherhood of man' goes beyond the mere phrases of any reformer and becomes something real. The significance of this for Marx is obvious. The kind of social forms he envisages as necessary for communism emerge as an essential part of the struggles of the proletariat in the present. In this way, the possibility of communism, of people capable of the democratic management of society, emerges from within capitalism itself. As Lebowitz puts it:

> Just as every activity of the worker alters her as the subject who enters into all activities, similarly the process in which workers struggle for themselves is also a process of production, a process of purposeful activity in which they produce themselves in an altered way. They develop new needs in struggle, an altered hierarchy of needs.[39]

Thus the struggles of the proletariat contain within them the possibility of communism, and are themselves transformative activity. In this way the struggles of the proletariat are in some sense importantly prefigurative or anticipatory of communism. They can be seen as 'the prototype of truly human activity',[40] or 'in embryo the model of the future society'.[41] In workers' struggle they 'begin to create modes of existence which offer a virtuous alternative to the egoism characteristic not only of capitalist society more generally, but also of working class life within that society more specifically'.[42] Workers' struggles are a reaction to capitalism, the standpoint from which it is to be criticised, and the basis for an alternative.

However, any optimism that this provides a complete answer should be tempered here. To return to the language of needs, the 'need for society' involved in the struggles of the proletariat may have something in common with the solidarity involved in communism, but it is not identical to it. It is important to stress this: Marx cannot assert an *identity* between these two needs, any more than he can between hunger satisfied by a knife and fork and hunger satisfied by raw meat. The different contexts and practices in which they occur necessarily mean they are shaped and conditioned differently, even if they are somehow the same need 'at bottom'. Even more dramatically, the democracy

---

39   Lebowitz 2003, p. 181.
40   Löwy 2005, p. 104.
41   Löwy 2005, p. 91.
42   Blackledge 2012, p. 93.

necessary to organise, say, a strike may have something in common with the democracy required to organise collective control over production, but it is also quite different.

This problem can be put in general terms: for all that we might wish to identify certain practices (and their associated values, needs, desires, etc.) with the practices that make possible the society in which we want to live, the very fact that these practices are part of actually existing societies limits this identification. In each case, there remains a significant and unignorable gap between our awareness of the practice as it actually exists in the present and how it might operate in the future society. The source of this gap lies in the very fact that our consciousness is determined and delimited by our practice, and even practices that challenge capitalism remain to some extent marked by it. We do not have consciousness of communism because we have not lived it. For all that it is right to emphasise that the conception of revolutionary praxis is the solution to the question of how 'old subjects, the products of capital, go beyond capital', many of those that recognise this still underplay this gap.[43] Indeed, this gap is visible in the very metaphors used to describe the struggles of the proletariat in the quotations above: The embryo is not identical with the foetus, still less with the adult human, microcosms capture something important, but also leave out vital detail. The struggles may point beyond, but pointing somewhere is not the same as being there. The standpoint of the proletariat under capitalism may bear certain fundamental similarities to the standpoint of the future, but it cannot be seen as identical to it.[44] None of this would be a problem if we were able to read back from the human to the embryo, the macrocosm to the microcosm, from communism to struggle.[45] But we cannot read back, because we do not, yet, have an example of a completed process. We remain coated with the muck of ages, even as we begin to shake it off.

But if they are not identical, nor are they totally alien from each other. There is some similarity, some continuity, and it is this continuity on which we must pin our hopes for a different society. To this extent, Marx can be understood as

---

43   See, for example, my reviews of Hudis 2012 and Blackledge 2012, in Swain 2012b and Swain 2015.

44   It is important to distinguish here between the standpoint of communism understood merely as capitalism's transcendence, and more specific knowledge of what it would be like under communism. It is certainly possible to criticise capitalism as a historically specific form of social life, in order to reveal it as historically distinct and transient. It does not follow from this that we can adopt wholesale the standpoint of human beings under communism.

45   In a non-Marxist context, a similar question can be asked of Benjamin Franks' attempt to capture anarchist direct action as 'synechdochic' of a desired future (Franks 2006, pp. 134).

concerned with what is called prefigurative politics. However, as soon as this is said it must be qualified. The term prefiguration is not one Marx would have used. It is a term whose popularity has exploded in recent decades, especially among anarchist and autonomist political circles and various anticapitalist social movements. However, it is often an extremely undefined concept. At its most banal, it can be associated with Gandhi's injunction to 'be the change you want to see', an approach which suggests that all is required is merely choosing to live in the way that you want society to be organised.[46] The phrase is often traced back to Wini Breines' study of the American New Left in the 60s, in which Breines explicitly contrasts prefigurative politics with 'strategic' politics. Prefigurative politics is seen as 'an essentially anti-organisational politics characteristic of the movement, as well as parts of new left leadership, and may be recognised in counter institutions, demonstrations and the attempt to embody personal and anti-hierarchical values in politics'.[47] Sometimes prefiguration is discussed in terms of a means/ends relationship, in which political means must embody the ends they seek to achieve,[48] while others prefer to emphasise the experimental character of this politics, suggesting that any strict homology between means and ends is likely to be difficult to achieve or even understand.[49]

Some of these senses of prefiguration clearly do not apply to Marx. Firstly, he has already emphasised frequently that being the change we want to see is not possible: Reaching communism will be a long and hard task, it will require a process of change and development that cannot be fully anticipated in advance. It is not possible to, as it were, 'see the change and then be it', at least as long as this is understood as first having knowledge of the good society and then building it. Nor would Marx have been happy with drawing a distinction between his politics and strategic politics, at least if that meant ignoring state power and the difficult questions of politics.[50] Nor would he (and nor should we) accept a definition of prefigurative politics which question-beggingly builds in precisely what is to be explained – namely the emphasis on anti-hierarchical values.

However, Marx shares with certain kinds of prefigurative approaches the idea that the struggles of the present offer glimpses of possible future alternat-

---

46   See Farber 2014.
47   Breines 1982, p. 6.
48   Yates cites Graeber and Boggs as examples of this (Yates 2015).
49   Yates 2015, pp. 17–18.
50   See Chapters 3 and 7. It is also possible to doubt whether politics shorn of strategic questions is really politics any more. See Maeckelbergh 2011.

ive forms of life, while also recognising that these remain mere glimpses, and not a view of the whole alternative. Thus present action and events points towards a fuller or more complete form that is not yet entirely in view, but which shares some essential or structural features with it. This has affinities with the idea of figural interpretation that Erich Auerbach identifies as crucial to early Christian theology.[51] The core of this idea is that the content of the Old Testament is 'pre-figurative' of the events described in the New Testament, in particular the life of Jesus. Thus, for example, in Augustine, Moses is '*figura Christi*' – a prefiguration of Christ, whilst Noah's Ark is '*praefiguratio ecclesiae*' – a prefiguration of the Church.[52] This is sharply distinguished from a merely allegorical reading of the Old Testament. Rather, to say that the Old Testament is pre-figurative of the New is to say that the former describes real historical events, which are both *intimately connected* to and nonetheless *distinct* from the latter. Moreover, the full significance of the former only emerges in light of the latter, whilst the latter *completes* the former: 'Figural prophecy implies the interpretation of one event through another; the first signifies the second, the second fulfils the first'.[53] However, importantly, the New Testament is not itself the end of this process, but in turn anticipates and prefigures an as-yet-unrealised eschatological future that will complete it in turn.[54]

Perhaps this is of more instructive relevance to discussions of radical politics than we might initially think. Firstly, it follows from this that to prefigure something is not to be identical to it, any more than training for something is the same as doing it. To prefigure the future is to anticipate it, but not to actually live it. Secondly, to say that something is prefigurative of a future society takes on a new light when we think that it may only be truly said to be so *in the light of that future society*. Thus, whether a given social practice is *actually* prefigurative (in this sense) is not something that can be decisively answered until what it prefigures has come to pass. As Auerbach suggests, in a theological schema this can ultimately be resolved by the fact that the New Testament already exists, and the eschatological future already secured by scripture. For a materialist, however, such certainty is not available, and the future remains unwritten.[55] Perhaps a given social practice will be retained in the future, perhaps it will not, but we will only know when that time comes.

---

51   See Auerbach 1984.
52   Auerbach 1984, p. 38.
53   Auerbach 1984, p. 58.
54   Auerbach 1984, pp. 58–9.
55   But see Gordon 2018, for a reading of the figural approach that is sceptical it can avoid problems of historical certainty and determinacy.

That the full significance of the past is only revealed in the present is an idea that occurs occasionally in Marx's thought. It features in the letter to Ruge, when he remarks that 'It will then become plain that our task is not to draw a sharp mental line between past and future, but to *complete* the thought of the past',[56] and most famously when he remarks that 'Human anatomy contains a key to the anatomy of the ape', adding that 'the intimations of higher development among the subordinate animal species, however, can be understood only after the higher development is already known'.[57] The latter remark especially is sometimes seen as indicative of a problematic teleology. However, at its most straightforward it merely suggests that the full significance of the process can only be grasped at the end of it. Whether or not a practice is prefigurative of communism will only be answered decisively in communism (an idea with both Hegelian and iconoclastic and messianic roots).[58] Thus there is an important asymmetry between the relation of the present to the past and its relation to the future. As Wood stresses: 'Capitalism can provide the key to precapitalist society ... only because it actually exists and because it has given rise to its own historically constituted categories'.[59] No such luxury exists with communism.

On this model of prefiguration the aim is to prepare for the future, but also to be prepared to experiment, to look for the diverse forms of practice that might develop. It also means that whilst a certain practice may be the basis on which society can be re-organised, it may equally not be, and give way to a different one in the future. This, however, is not to say that this experimentation is to be blind, or completely directionless. After all, we are looking for practices that point beyond capitalism, and in the direction of the democratic management of the economy. Practices which stunt this capacity even more than wage labour are unlikely to be worth trying! Moreover, there is a place for theoretical study, in identifying particular groups of people in which these practices are likely to emerge, and whose struggles point in a particular direction.

It is worth pausing here to note that on this model it is the *struggle* of the proletariat that is central, rather than their *labouring*. This runs counter to a particular interpretation of Marx such that the transformative significance of the proletariat lies in the fact that they are *those who labour*.[60] It *is* true that

---

56   MECW 3 144.

57   *Grundrisse*, p. 105.

58   See Jacoby 2005, Benjamin 1968.

59   Wood 1995, p. 139.

60   For example, much of Hannah Arendt's criticism of Marx seems to rest on the claim that Marx 'held that labour was considered to be the supreme world-building capacity of man', and thus capable of re-shaping politics as well as nature (Arendt 1998, pp. 100–1).

Marx thought that labour – in the sense of a direct interchange with nature – is of fundamental importance for human life and human freedom. It is *also* true that Marx believed that the working class was the agent capable of overthrowing capitalism and creating communism. It does not follow from this that he thought they could do so because they are those who labour. In this context, comparison with the peasantry is instructive. In the *18th Brumaire* Marx differentiates the peasantry from the proletariat not in terms of whether or not their activity engages directly with nature, but rather on the degree of interconnectedness and organisation that their working relations permit. The peasantry, while identifiable as a distinct class, 'is formed by simple addition of homologous magnitudes, much as potatoes in a sack form a sack of potatoes'. Their lack of interconnection and co-ordination means that

> they are consequently incapable of enforcing their class interests in their own name, whether through a parliament or through a convention. They cannot represent themselves, they must be represented. Their representative must at the same time appear as their master, as an authority over them, as an unlimited governmental power that protects them against the other classes and sends them rain and sunshine from above.[61]

Thus the division of the peasantry means it cannot represent itself, and must rely on representatives who are at the same time masters. In contrast, because of the way its work is organised and the way in which it is driven to defend its interests, the proletariat is capable of developing forms of co-operation that allow it to represent itself.

This returns us to the central question of self-emancipation. A number of important points have emerged: Communist consciousness can only emerge as consciousness of revolutionary practice, a practice that emerges through struggles within capitalism. Through this revolutionary practice, people become 'fitted to found society anew' – they develop the capacities to manage society collectively, and to represent themselves without saviour leaders from outside.[62] This already indicates one reason to be suspicious of models of social change that do not emphasise self-emancipation – put bluntly, if you are going to prepare people for the democratic management of society, you had better grant them some opportunity for democratic management within

---

61   MECW 11, p. 188.

62   Or, to return to Marx's more Hegelian language, they exercise their democratic, constituting power unmediated by narrow representation.

their own struggles![63] However, the gap between the struggles of the present and their realisation in the future also suggests further reasons to stress self-emancipation. This is because it places a premium on experimentation and initiative, and necessarily downplays the importance of theoretical expertise and claims to authoritative knowledge of the future, a point I will return to in future chapters.

However, this still leaves important questions about the process of self-emancipation itself and how it develops and is encouraged. Not least, there is Marx's original question of how those who, like Marx, are committed to aiding processes of self-emancipation should act. Moreover, given that the development of communist consciousness is unlikely to be smooth and unitary, this raises the question of how different practices and experiences of struggle are shared and spread among different groups while still permitting their self-activity. How, in other words, to encourage self-emancipation without at the same time short-circuiting it?

4   Educating the Educator

To flesh this picture out further, it is useful to turn to Marx's own metaphor of education, something which appears not just in the *Theses on Feuerbach*, but frequently in his earlier writings. More broadly, concepts of social and human development and education are intimately entwined in the broader German traditions, both idealist and romantic, from which Marx emerges. Indeed, part of understanding any revolutionary process is understanding how ideas change and how people learn and internalise new practices and values. None of which is to say that this is a perfect analogy – the classroom and the barricades are not one and the same – but, I suggest, reflections on notions of educational development and in particular the role of educators within them can help shed light on analogous problems within politics.

The first example comes from Brecht De Smet, who has developed an account of critical pedagogy as part of a study of the Egyptian Revolution. De Smet (developing ideas from Vygotsky and Blunden), stresses the importance of *prolepsis*. *Prolepsis* is a context in which a developing subject projects themselves to a later stage of development, and acts as if they have already reached that stage. For De Smet, this process is central to understanding how the (Egyptian) working class forms itself as a collective subject. Proleptic learn-

---

63   Similarly, if your goal is to undermine the division between task-execution and task-definition, it is a bad idea to reproduce it in your movements and organisations.

ing 'anticipates or imagines competence through the representation of a future act or development as already existing'.[64] Prolepsis, in a sense, assumes that something is possible before it is, in order to help make it so. 'A classic example … is that of a child playing adult roles, projecting itself in a more advanced stage of its own trajectory'.[65] The exercise of certain 'external' activities also effects an internal transformation. Significantly, prolepsis can take two forms. *Auto-prolepsis* takes place when the subject themselves undertakes the projection in the form of self-instruction:

> Wildcat strike committees imagine grassroots and independent trade unions; workers' control over factories illustrate their potential of running the country without capitalists; and practices of participation, election and discussion within the movement foreshadow forms of participatory democracy.[66]

Heterolepsis, by contrast, involves the 'interpellation of a potential capacity of a subject by another actor'. Outside of the realm of politics, an example of this might be a parent speaking to their child as if they were an adult. Inside the realm of politics, it provides more substantial challenges.

This notion of prolepsis can help understand revolutionary praxis as a process of self and world transformation. The external performance of a particular activity also turns inward, transforming those involved in it. In De Smet's example (analogously to Marx's French artisans):

> The struggle of workers against company management produces the object of the strike or trade union committee, which is oriented externally, as a means to mediate the relations between workers and 'bosses'. But this instrument also turns inward, organising and structuring the collective actor, turning a volatile and amorphous collaboration of wage workers into a stable system of activity.[67]

This is complementary, rather than in contradiction, to the notion of prefigurative politics discussed in the previous section. This is because prolepsis must always be sufficiently close to the existing stage of development to be effective. If the projected state is too distant from the subject, any sense of learning

---

64   De Smet 2015, p. 91.
65   De Smet 2015, p. 52.
66   De Smet 2015, p. 91.
67   De Smet 2015, p. 90.

or development will fail. Thus *communism itself* (as a specific form of society) cannot be a proleptic projection (at least most of the time). It is far too distant a prospect for that – hard to describe and even harder to act out. Rather, prolepsis occurs by developmental stages. These stages need not be regular, or each take a specified period of time. There can be, as Lenin puts it, decades where nothing happens and weeks where decades happen. Moreover, it is possible at times for developments to outstrip expectations, and the proleptic projection itself to look pale in comparison. Moreover, while each stage develops from and completes the one that precedes it, the connection between each stage and the final end point remains speculative, and their full significance is only recognised at the end.

Autoprolepsis can be seen as self-emancipation in its purest form, in which the subject itself leads and drives its own development. This can be described analogously to Marx's own conception of free labouring activity discussed in the previous chapter: Workers as a collective subject collectively posit and realise their goals – goals which are set by themselves and recognised as such, rather than by an outside, hostile will. That this can, does, and will happen is a cornerstone of Marx's thinking. However, this still leaves the more complex question of *heterolepsis*. How can an agent from outside aid the development, rather than thwart it?

Negatively, De Smet identifies a number of pathologies – ways in which this process can be thwarted rather than advanced. Two of these stem from the fact that prolepsis is only effective if it takes place within what is called the zone of proximal development. They must be close enough to the particular developmental stage to be recognisable as achievable by the agent concerned. In political terms, being too far ahead of the appropriate stage of development can be described as *voluntarism* or, depending on its precise nature, *vanguardism*. This is an approach which either fails to motivate a sufficiently large number, or, through appearing to be simply ridiculous, fails to motivate anyone. On the other hand, the pathology of pessimism involves falling short of the level of development, underestimating the strength and scope of the movement, and thus failing to advance it further.

However, a different pathology is labelled (following Trotsky) 'substitutionism'. This is where a particular, different subject substitutes for and displaces the movement of the working class. This is precisely what is at stake in the *acherontic* or saviour-leader accounts, and in Marx's own notion of Bonapartism. While the previous pathologies were concerned with the relationship between proleptic projections and the relevant stage of development, the question of substitutionism seems to be about the spirit in which co-operation is engaged in. It is not just about whether or not a particular practice or proposal

is achievable, but about whether it is expressed in a way which ends up asserting ownership over the process, and thus displacing the agent themselves from
the centre of it.

As an appropriate mode of co-operation to avoid this, De Smet suggests
Blunden's definition of solidarity as

> a collaboration between different subjects that strengthens the subject-
> ness of the shared project and of each participant. Solidarity entails the
> freely offered submission of the provider of assistance to the beneficiary,
> in order to increase the agency of the other.[68]

This is in particular contrasted with colonising approaches, in which 'another
subject is helped by subsuming their activity into one's own project',[69] and
external reward ('commodifying') approaches, in which another subject is
treated only instrumentally.[70] For Blunden, 'solidarity is the opposite of philanthropic colonisation, because in assisting someone, the other remains the
owner of the project and is thereby assisted in achieving self-determination'.[71]
A similar idea is expressed by Tony Cliff, also in discussing substitutionism. Cliff
describes three possible models for thinking about the relationship between a
revolutionary organisation and the working class as a whole:

> [F]or lack of better names we shall call [them] those of the teacher,
> the foreman and the companion in struggle. The first kind of leadership
> shown by small sects is 'blackboard socialism' ... in which didactic meth-
> ods take the place of participation in struggle. The second kind, with
> foreman-worker or officer-soldier relations, characterises all bureaucratic
> reformist and Stalinist parties: the leadership sits in a caucus and decides
> what they will tell the workers to do, without the workers actively par-
> ticipating ... The third kind of leadership is analogous to that between
> a strike committee and the workers on strike, or a shop steward and his
> mates. The revolutionary party must conduct a dialogue with the workers
> outside it.[72]

---

68   De Smet 2015, p. 101.
69   Blunden 2010, p. 284.
70   De Smet suggests as examples 'political activism that recognises the proletarian project
      as a field for recruiting and journalism that perceives of strikes merely as news item' (De
      Smet 2015, p. 101).
71   Blunden 2010, p. 284.
72   Cliff 1960, p. 25.

The organisation must aim, then, to reach the third model, the ideal of a relationship of companionship in struggle. To do this requires flexibility and humility, a willingness to learn as well as to teach, and to take direction as much as to direct. This chimes closely with the 'solidarity' approach expressed by Blunden.

A different, but similarly instructive, conception of education can be found in the ideas of Jacques Rancière. In *The Ignorant Schoolmaster*, Rancière presents and develops the story of Joseph Jacotot, an eighteenth-century French pedagogue, who developed a system he called universal teaching. Universal teaching was a radical technique which achieved startling results. It was based on the assumption that it was possible to teach what we do not know, and that a teacher need not (and ought not) *explain* an idea to a pupil, but that pupils can learn it for themselves. Most strikingly, this emerged when attempting to teach Flemish students with whom he shared no language:

> To do so, the minimal link of a *thing in common* had to be established between him and them. At that time, a bilingual edition of *Telemaque* had been published in Brussels ... He had the book delivered to his students, and asked them, through an interpreter, to learn the French text with the help of the translation. When they had made it through the first half of the book, he had them repeat what they had learned over and over, and then told them to read through the rest of the book until they could recite it.[73]

This had, at least as the story goes, remarkable results. The capacity of the Flemish students to learn French simply through their own efforts surprised Jacotot, and led him to develop an entirely new theory of teaching. If they could learn in this way, then anyone could teach anyone.

For Rancière, what Jacotot had identified was the distinction between *explication* and *emancipatory teaching*. Explication by an expert operates on a presupposition of inequality from which it can never in fact escape. Explication, thus, is ultimately stultifying, since it is founded upon and ultimately reproduces hierarchies of intelligence: 'explication is the myth of pedagogy, the parable of a world divided into knowing minds and ignorant ones, ripe minds and immature ones, the capable and the incapable, the intelligent and the stupid'.[74] In contrast, intellectual emancipation presumes an absolute equal-

---

73   Rancière 1991, p. 2.
74   Rancière 1991, p. 6.

ity of human intelligences, putting inequality down only to manifestations of intelligence.[75] This assumption of intelligence provided a crucial starting point, which allowed for a radically different approach to teaching:

> [Jacotot] had a different notion of mutual teaching in mind: that each ignorant person could become for another ignorant person the master who would reveal to him his intellectual power. More precisely, his problem wasn't the instruction of the people ... His own problem was that of emancipation: that every common person might conceive his human dignity, take the measure of his intellectual capacity, and decide how to use it. The friends of Instruction were certain that true liberty was conditioned on it. After all, they recognised that they should give instruction to the people, even at the risk of disputing among themselves which instruction they would give. Jacotot did not see what kind of liberty for the people could result from the dutifulness of their instructors. On the contrary, he sensed in all this a new form of stultification. Whoever teaches without emancipating stultifies. And whoever emancipates doesn't have to worry about what the emancipated person learns. He will learn what he wants, nothing maybe.[76]

This passage indicates the crucial link that Rancière makes between this conception of education and political freedom. Emancipation can only arise on the basis of an assumption of equality which erodes the distinction between the expertise of the emancipator and the ignorance of the emancipated. 'Liberty is not guaranteed by any pre-established harmony. It is taken, it is won, it is lost, solely by each person's effort'.[77] Moreover, 'Equality is not given, nor is it claimed; it is practiced, it is *verified*'.[78]

There are various important differences between the Vygotskian account articulated by De Smet and Rancière's approach. There are times when Rancière looks like he comes close to endorsing approaches which others would probably think of as voluntarist. For example, Rancière suggests that:

> There cannot be a class of the emancipated, an assembly or society of the emancipated. But any individual can always, at any moment, be emancipated and emancipate someone else, announce to others the *practice* and

---

75   Rancière 1991, p. 27.
76   Rancière 1991, pp. 17–18.
77   Rancière 1991, p. 62.
78   Rancière 1991, p. 137.

add to the number of people who know themselves as such and who no longer play the comedy of the inferior superiors.[79]

If we take Rancière as suggesting that emancipation can be achieved at any given time, under any conditions, this appears to risk accusations of voluntarism (if, on the other hand, he merely means that anyone at any point can *begin* a process of mutual learning which is potentially emancipatory, but not necessarily that this process is completed, this charge might be avoided, though even then it may be contestable). Moreover, this passage also indicates Rancière's apparent suspicion of attempts to institutionalise emancipation – to have a society or organisation of the emancipated.

However, there are a number of ways in which both these educational approaches might help in understanding and developing the notion of self-emancipation in Marx. Firstly, both stress the importance of self-education, of learning through experience, as being central to the process of emancipation. This, it is worth stressing, is a practical matter. For Rancière, emancipation is the *practice* of equality, in contrast to the practice of stultification implied by instruction and explication. For De Smet, both forms of prolepsis involve acting as if one has achieved a stage of development not yet achieved. This conception of learning through experience is present throughout Marx, from his dismissive comments about the censor ('For him true education consists in keeping a person wrapped up in a cradle throughout his life, for as soon as he learns to walk he also learns to fall, and it is only by falling that he learns to walk') to the developed conception of revolutionary praxis.

Secondly, both approaches imply a critique of traditional, explication-based education, which cannot fail to reproduce hierarchical divisions, which has strong echoes of the third thesis on Feuerbach. Rancière's model of the stultifying educator, assuming expertise over those to be liberated, seems to be exactly what Marx has in mind here. Indeed, Rancière's own development of these ideas is connected to an attempt to re-assert Marx's 1845 critique of theoretical reflection against claims to the autonomy of theory, precisely because they too are uncritical of the role of 'intellectuals' and 'experts'.[80] It certainly seems to be an insight like this that led Marx to believe that emancipation could only be self-emancipation. Where they clearly agree is in the necessarily stultifying role of an attitude which believes it is possessed of superior insight, which insists on 'play[ing] the comedy of the inferior superiors'.[81] Emancipation must

---

79   Rancière 1991, p. 98.
80   See Rancière 2011, esp. Chapters 4 and 5.
81   Rancière 1991, p. 98.

be self-emancipation because adopting the privileged role of emancipator is to reproduce a hierarchical division which thwarts the possibility of genuine emancipation.

Thirdly, these approaches offer ways of grasping how those involved in this collaborative process of education might teach themselves *new* things. This is essential if we are to see how it might be possible to develop new social practices which are genuinely different from those which currently exist, and how a process of transformation might end up with something radically new, even something we cannot currently envision. This radical newness is even more prominent in Rancière, for whom the 'educator' takes little interest in what the educated actually learn. The proleptic approach is less radically open, but still emphasises the possibility and importance of going beyond the prolepsis to develop things that were previously unanticipated.

Finally, and perhaps most importantly, they suggest an approach on the part of those who are politically committed to emancipation – namely one that recognises that emancipation must always be self-emancipation, and that the only role for an 'emancipator' is as an aid to that process. For the proleptic approach the role of these is twofold – to help develop the appropriate 'projection', in order to advance the development of the working class, and to do so in a spirit of solidarity and openness, in order to avoid 'colonising' their struggles. Both of these require close engagement and participation in these struggles. For Rancière the role is even more minimal:

> The ignorant schoolmaster who can help her along this path is named thus not because he knows nothing, but because he has renounced the 'knowledge of ignorance' and thereby uncoupled his mastery from his knowledge. He does not teach his pupils *his* knowledge, but orders them to venture into the forest of things and signs, to say what they have seen and what they think of what they have seen, to verify it and have it verified.[82]

While this might appear like a deflation of the role of emancipator, an emancipator committed to their own redundancy, it involves real challenges and problems. Encouraging or ordering people to venture into the forest of signs, or struggle, is easier said than done. For one thing, it requires motivating people to action, without at the same time assuming leadership of them. For another, it requires them to believe they have the potential to 'learn', or transform soci-

---

82   Rancière 2009, p. 11.

ety, in the first place. For the very reason that this is not the 'normal' way in which either education or political change is thought about, it provides difficulties and challenges. Stultifying and dominating is easy – the alternative is hard, requiring patient work. Marx alludes to this when confronted with an actual working-class revolt:

> Confronted with the initial outbreak of the Silesian revolt no man who thinks or loves the truth could regard the duty to play *schoolmaster* to the event as his primary task. On the contrary, his duty would rather be to study it to discover its *specific* character. Of course, this requires scientific understanding and a certain love of mankind, while the other procedure needs only a ready-made phraseology saturated in an overweening love of oneself.[83]

This commitment poses a number of distinct practical problems, problems which I think it is appropriate to call ethical, to the extent that they concern the various ways in which those committed to a project of emancipation should act towards one another. At the very least, it requires a confidence in the capacity of others to learn, a willingness to encourage and to aid this learning, and a humility about one's own knowledge and expertise. Sometimes it may be possible, through analysis, participation and in a spirit of solidarity to offer specific proposals which might advance the development. Other times, not even these might be available, and perhaps what is necessary is something like Jacotot's radical confidence in the capacities of others. To say these questions are ethical is certainly not to say they are transcendental or universal principles or norms of action. They are problems and challenges immanent to the project of transcending capitalism and replacing it with a more democratic society, since self-emancipation is the only way out (or at least the only way out to something better). As such, the practical questions that flow from a commitment to self-emancipation are of the utmost importance. It is these questions that preoccupy the rest of this book.

---

83   *Early Writings*, p. 416.

CHAPTER 3

Historical Materialism and Self-Emancipation

> 'Men make their own history, but', this phrase echoes through the Marx-
> ist classics. The political aim of Marxists is to liquidate that 'but'. Their
> theoretical aim is to understand it.
>
> ALASDAIR MACINTYRE, 'Notes from the Moral Wilderness'[1]

∴

1   History and Prophecy

Any discussion of Marx's role as an engaged critical theorist cannot avoid discussing his theory of history. Many interpretations of Marx have suggested a
contradiction between his general theory of historical change and his commitment to self-emancipation, and thus that there is a contradiction between
his professed political commitments and his theoretical practice. This chapter
seeks to offer an interpretation that avoids this charge. In particular, historical
materialist theory plays two necessary roles in a process of self-emancipation –
helping reveal the historical character of capitalism and its laws and helping
guide the formation of strategies to overcome it. This is a conception of theory as fundamentally indexed to the goal of self-emancipation, rather than in
tension or outright contradiction with it.

There is a way of writing about Marx's theory of history which sees it as a
sort of cop out or defence mechanism.[2] The presence of a theory of history
is, on this reading, supposed to absolve Marx of the responsibility of presenting a positive ethical programme. A particularly vivid example of this can be
found in G.A. Cohen. According to Cohen, Marxism relied too heavily on a 'hard

---

1   MacIntyre 2009, p. 57.
2   I use 'theory of history' in the loosest possible sense here as, broadly, a set of generalisations
    about connections between historical events and processes. I will leave aside, for now, the
    question of the extent to which this can legitimately be called a theory, and what the precise
    nature of these connections are. For example, Callinicos 1995, makes the distinction between
    a 'theory of history' and a 'philosophy of history', suggesting that the latter is characterised by
    a teleology absent in the former. At this point I will make no such distinction, since to do so
    would beg precisely the sorts of questions this chapter is intended to discuss.

shell of supposed fact' and on 'bold explanatory theses about history in general and capitalism in particular'. These explanatory theses have, however, been proven false: 'Its shell is cracked and crumbling, its soft underbelly exposed'.[3] This metaphor sees Marx's project as some kind of armadillo, with tough socio-historical theory protecting the soft, squidgy (and slightly distasteful) underbelly of moral theory and obscuring it from scrutiny. On this view, Marx is vulnerable partly because this theory is at risk of being rendered false (and most of these commentators think it has), and partly because there seems to be something dishonest or illicit in this way of arguing. It is either a deliberate way of dodging important questions, or a move which has the unintended consequence of relegating difficult matters of morality to a secondary status.

I will not dedicate space here to considering whether or not historical materialism has been proven false. Rather, I am interested in the charge that there is something incompatible between a sincere commitment to self-emancipation and the means required to achieve it and a speculative theory that seeks to make predictive and explanatory claims about patterns of historical development. In particular, the question is whether the construction of a theory which predicts certain events and actions as historically determined, and perhaps even inevitable, is compatible with the demand that the process of emancipation remain the property of – under the conscious control of – the subject that must emancipate themselves. This is, it is worth noting, connected to but distinct from a broader debate about structure and agency (or indeed free will and determinism).[4] The problems I am concerned with are as much practical as they are conceptual – about how to develop theory that does not displace people themselves from ownership of their own struggles.

A clear example of the kind of criticism which is often made against Marx can be found in Eugen Kamenka's *The Moral Foundations of Marxism*. Kamenka suggests that Marx was never fully able to commit to the self-activity of the proletariat. Instead, he placed his faith elsewhere, in the inevitable movement of history. The proletariat were merely to act out their historical role, history was where the real action was:

> Marx would have liked to believe that the industrial proletariat was evolving such freedom, such enterprise [as would characterise communism], even under capitalism. But he was not prepared to stake much on the conception. History seemed a more powerful ally. The proletariat

---

3   Cohen 2001, p. 103.
4   See Callinicos 2009.

remained for him fundamentally a vehicle of history: not a class display-
ing enterprise, production and co-operation, but a class denied enterprise, production and co-operation, not a class that had freed itself from
the shackles of property, but a class denied property, a class whose whole
character consisted of nothing more than its exclusion from property,
than its suffering.[5]

According to this interpretation, Marx's commitment to proletarian self-emancipation is only skin deep. His real faith is not in people, but in history.

Kamenka argues that Marx saw his own society, and all of previous history,
as dominated by abstract laws outside of human control. The future society of
communism was to be one in which human beings were no longer dominated
by such abstractions, but were free to regulate society according to their own
rational will. However, this meant that the transition from the unfree society
to the free society was one which *had to be grasped according to the laws of the
unfree society*. The transition itself had to emerge out of the existing society.
However, if human beings were entirely dominated by abstract laws, then it
could not be on the basis of the free action of human beings within it, at least
not ultimately. It had to be explained according to the laws of history.

This meant that the role of someone who wanted to change the world was to
try and identify historical laws, in the hope that they would indeed prove that
the freedom of the future was going to emerge from the unfreedom of the past.
It is worth pausing at this point to reflect on whether someone committed to
this view of the world would even need to do this. If the transition to freedom
is really going to happen, why would you need historical research to prove it?
Or rather, once you've discovered this and become convinced of it, why would
you need to share it? At most it can play a re-assuring role for you and your
supporters, perhaps something to recite when you awake in a cold sweat won-
dering whether it is all worth it.

On this interpretation, Marx is like Isaac Asimov's fictional scientist Hari Seldon, the central figure of the *Foundation* novels. Seldon mastered the science
of psychohistory, something that could predict developments in history with
the same degree of accuracy as physics or chemistry: 'The laws of history are as
absolute as the laws of physics, and if the probabilities of error are greater, it is
only because history does not deal with as many humans as physics does atoms,
so that individual variations count for more'.[6] Using his powers of prediction,

---

5   Kamenka 1962, pp. 159–60.
6   Asimov 1952.

Seldon becomes aware of the likely collapse of the great empire in which he lives. Recognising he cannot prevent this collapse, he does his best to lessen its severity, and develops a plan to rebuild society, recruiting a collection of scientists in order to do it. Crucially, however, his plan must be hidden even from those who are to found the new society, and only revealed in increments. The central conceit of the stories is that each time the new society is imperilled, an individual emerges to make a vital decision, only for it to be revealed at the end that this is exactly what the plan predicted. This pattern is necessary because if people become aware of the predictions then they will not work – knowledge of the predictions introduces a new variable, potentially ruining the prediction itself. Asimov's fantastical example dramatises well the central problem: If you can predict the future with that much accuracy, you certainly don't need to tell anyone – and may even have reason not to.

This already indicates the kind of problems that arise for action, and for ethics, for this kind of approach. A traditional version of these problems can be found in Karl Popper:

> [The] strong activist tendencies of Marx's are counteracted by his historicism. Under its influence, he became mainly a prophet. He decided that, at least under capitalism, we must submit to 'inexorable laws' and to the fact that all we can do is 'to shorten and lessen the birth pangs' of the 'natural phases of its evolution'. There is a wide gulf between Marx's activism and his historicism, and this gulf is further widened by his doctrine that we must submit to the purely irrational forces of history.[7]

Here, Popper suggests two competing and incompatible tendencies within Marx, the activist and the historicist. To the extent that Marx was a 'historicist', believing in grand predictions about the movement of history, he could not be an activist, and *vice versa*. This is because the historicist sweep denies the significance of individual actions. Marx is saying: 'The world is changing of its own accord, whether you like it or not. So change it!' Thus he ends up engaged in a deep contradiction between two different aspects of his thought.

Moreover, this can be said to lead to an approach which evades concrete political and ethical questions. For example, Cohen criticises Marx for an 'obstetric' conception of history. He highlights Marx's claim, from the *1859 Preface*, that 'mankind inevitably sets itself only such tasks as it is able to solve'.[8]

---

7 Popper 1966, p. 397.
8 MECW 29, p. 264.

This, he suggests, is evidence of a political obstetricism, which sees the present as inexorably giving birth to the future. This has contributed to Marxism's blindness to difficult questions of ethics, politics and individual action:

> If you think of politics obstetrically, you risk supposing that what Lenin called 'the concrete analysis of a concrete situation' will disclose, transparently, what your political intervention must be, so that you do not expect and therefore do not face the uncertainties and hard choices with which a responsible politics must contend.[9]

On Cohen's view Marx's theory of history relegates active decision-making to, at best, a supporting role, and, at worst, no role at all. This means that activists become blind to important practical questions, and especially to the kinds of questions that might comprise an ethics: How should we act towards our comrades? How should we act towards the enemy?

Thus Marx stands accused of a practical contradiction which leads him into further practical problems. He cannot be, in Popper's idioms, a historicist and an activist. He must choose between historical materialism and political action. Indeed, if Marx is understood as constructing a predictive theory as powerful as those of the natural sciences – something like a steampunk psychohistory – then much of this criticism seems apt. While Popper is hardly a generous or sincere interpreter of Marx, his warning about the dangers of prophecy is not entirely without foundation. On this model, the role of the committed critical theorist appears to be to divine the future from the present, and at best concoct a plan to help get there faster. While sharing this plan with the masses might be a good idea (and even that is not obvious), any sense in which it is *their* plan begins to look tenuous. There is something problematic about someone who purports to be interested in radical self-determination adopting the role of prophet, of someone capable of seeing the future, and of handing it down to his followers. There is a problem both with the claim of privileged access to knowledge of the future, and also the attempt to then impose this vision on the masses.

---

9   Cohen 2001, p. 76.

2   False Starts

These kinds of objections were not unknown to Marx and subsequent Marx-ists. However, the attempts to deal with them by the generation immediately following Marx often entrenched the problems further. In this section I will consider two influential approaches to these questions, from two of the most significant post-Marx Marxists, Kautsky and Plekhanov.

Plekhanov's solution to this problem is to identify freedom with *knowledge of necessity*, a position that Engels also endorsed on some occasions.[10]

> Until the individual has won *this* freedom by heroic effort in philosophical thinking he does not fully belong to himself, and his mental tortures are the shameful tribute he pays to external necessity that stands opposed to him. But as soon as this individual throws off the yoke of the painful and shameful restriction he is born for a new, full and hitherto never experienced life; and his *free* actions become the *conscious and free* expression of necessity.[11]

Plekhanov, here, attempts to deal with the conceptual problem by saying that to act freely is to knowingly act according to the way in which history determines that you act. In a certain way, this allows you to become free by internalising the necessity, and making it your own project. This does permit a certain space for activism, and even free action. Once you know that you are doing the work of history, what you are doing becomes free. Knowing that your activity is on the side of history will inspire you to great deeds (and presumably finding out you are on the opposing side will lead to deep depression).

Plekhanov's position, however, does not seem to be Marx's. Plekhanov sug-gests that recognition of determination by necessity, heroically won by philo-sophical thinking, is sufficient for freedom. However, if the interpretation I have offered in Chapter 1 is correct, for Marx this recognition alone is not enough unless it also precipitates a transformation of the conditions of determina-tion. Determination by abstract laws of history and society must be replaced by conscious self-determination of the 'united individuals'. Recognition of neces-sity – both natural necessity and socially determined necessity – is necessary to achieve freedom, but it is not identical to it.

---

10   See O'Rourke 1974, for a discussion of this conception of freedom in Engels and Plekhanov, and its enduring significance in Soviet philosophy.

11   Plekhanov 1967, p. 18.

More significantly, however, Plekhanov's position does not seem to answer the practical problems addressed above. Indeed, seeing one's actions as doing the work of history is precisely the kind of mindset that Cohen believes leads to silence on important ethical questions. Moreover, the prophetic attitude seems to re-appear with a vengeance. Indeed, Plekhanov observes, with religious communities in mind, that 'history shows that even fatalism was not always a hindrance to energetic, practical action; on the contrary, in certain epochs it was a psychologically necessary basis for such action'.[12]

An attempt to deal more explicitly with the ethical question comes from Kautsky, who attempts to trace the development of ethics historically. Kautsky argues, effectively, that there is no particular problem of Marxist ethics, and that all that Marxism need do is combine the natural social instincts of man with a conception of 'scientific' socialism. This attitude towards morality comes out most clearly in Kautsky's approach to Kant's Categorical Imperative:

> The lofty moral law, that the comrade ought never to be merely a means to an end, which the Kantians look on as the most wonderful achievement of Kant's genius, and as the moral programme of the modern era, and for the entire future history of the world, that is in the animal world a commonplace. The development of human society first created a state of affairs in which the companion became a simple tool of others.[13]

Here the categorical imperative is defined as simply being a different formulation of the social instinct, common in all animals. Thus, whilst it is pitched as such, it is not so much a disagreement with the principle as a claim that there is nothing particularly special about it. It does not require a transcendental deduction or even any particular defence.

This social instinct forms the basis for morality, on Kautsky's account. The need to survive leads humans to organise socially, in certain particular ways, crucially leading to the development of class divisions. These class divisions are both necessary for the survival of humanity (at certain points in its history), and lead to conflict within humanity. This at once leads to an erosion of the social instincts between classes, and to their strengthening within classes. At the historical moment Kautsky is writing, the capitalism of the early twentieth century, this has developed to an extreme degree:

---

12   Plekhanov 1967, p. 11.
13   Kautsky 1918, p. 96.

the class struggle becomes the principal, most general and continuous form of the struggle of the individuals for life in human society; in the same degree the social instincts towards society as a whole lose strength, they become, however, so much the stronger within that class whose welfare is for the mass of the individuals always more and more identical with that of the commonweal.[14]

However, it is distinctive of humanity that they can fix these instincts into moral ideals, in the form of rules. Because these rules are developed according to specific forms of social organisation, they can quickly become a restraint: 'Thus something can happen in the human society that is impossible in the animal; morality can become, instead of an indispensable social bond, the means of an intolerable restraint on social life'.[15] This takes place in a process analogous to Marx's account of the relationships of production becoming a fetter on the forces of production: '[E]conomic development advances and creates new social need, which demands new moral standards' and so there develops a 'contradiction between the ruling morals of society and the life and action of its members'.[16]

This has differing effects on the two competing classes. For the ruling class it has the effect of a slide into immorality, of upholding certain virtues in public whilst flouting them in private. For the oppressed class it leads to an uproar of opposition, anger at injustice, 'an energetic will for something other than the existing'. This, however, is 'fundamentally only something purely negative, nothing more than opposition to the existing hypocrisy'.[17]

This negative sense of outrage, Kautsky argues, must be wedded to a scientific conception of socialism, from which it must be sharply distinguished: 'Thus even with Marx occasionally in his scientific research there breaks through the influence of a moral ideal. But he always endeavours and rightly to banish it where he can'.[18] The scientific deduction of the necessity of socialism is an essential complement of the moral outrage that arises due to class society. It is ultimately these kinds of considerations which will provide the basis on which a new society is based, because it indicates that a new society is necessary:

---

14   Kautsky 1918, p. 173.
15   Kautsky 1918, p. 187.
16   Kautsky 1918, p. 191.
17   Kautsky 1918, p. 195.
18   Kautsky 1918, p. 202.

Certainly not necessary in the fatalist sense, that a higher power will present them to us of itself, but necessary, unavoidable in the sense, that the inventors improve technic and the capitalists in their desire for profit revolutionise the whole economic life, as it is also inevitable that the workers aim for shorter hours of labour and higher wages, that they organize themselves, that they fight the capitalist class and its state, as it is inevitable that they aim for the conquest of political power and the overthrow of capitalist rule. Socialism is inevitable because the class struggle and the victory of the proletariat is inevitable.[19]

Thus Kautsky, like Plekhanov, offers a way of understanding how scientific knowledge of historical development – and its inevitable movement towards socialism – can be combined with the collective action of the proletariat. For him, it is about wedding this scientific knowledge to the instinctive revolt of the working class against their conditions.

However, in starkly distinguishing the consciousness of the working class itself from 'scientific socialism', Kautsky's schema risks – like Plekhanov – resolving conceptual problems at the expense of worsening practical ones. It is scientific socialism, and the scientists who construct it, that is in the driving seat. The workers themselves appear as mere recipients of knowledge, constructed by others, while the scientists appear as figures possessed of superior insight, capable of seeing further and better, and merely needing to share their plan with the workers, who will then energetically carry it out. In casting this stark separation, it seems all too easy to lapse into precisely the kind of positions Marx criticises in the *Theses on Feuerbach*. Who educates the scientific socialist?

Where both the criticisms and defences of Marxism discussed so far largely agree is in a conception of historical materialism as aspiring to scientific status – to something like Asimov's psychohistory. Indeed, many of the criticisms from figures like Popper and Kamenka are directed precisely at this assumption, which was just as widespread among defenders of Marx as critics. Kautsky and Plekhanov were arguably the most significant figures in Marxist philosophy between Marx's death and the outbreak of the First World War, and so their interpretations, often filtered through a particular Stalinist interpretation, acquired a status of orthodoxy which was just as significant for critics of Marx as for defenders of him.[20] Indeed, in 1958 Alasdair MacIntyre observed that, when it came to the character of historical materialist theory, 'in the definition

---

19   Kautsky 1918, p. 206.
20   Indeed, Cohen's own defence of Marx's theory of history is largely a defence of this

of what is at issue Stalin and Popper shake hands'.[21] To move forward in this discussion, it is necessary to challenge that shared assumption.

3   History as Constraint

In 1880 an ageing Marx published in a French magazine an appeal for a 'workers' inquiry', consisting of 100 questions to be put to workers on a range of different subjects, from how many workers were employed in their workplace, to the conditions of light, to 'the general physical, intellectual and moral conditions of life of the working men and women employed in your trade'.[22] This was prefaced by the following statement:

> We hope to find support for our cause among all urban and agricultural workers, who understand that they alone can describe the hardships they endure with the full knowledge of the matter; that only they, and not saviours sent by Providence, can vigorously apply remedies in the struggle against social evils from which they suffer; we count also on the socialists of all schools who, striving for social reform, must strive for an *exact* and *definite* knowledge of the conditions in which the working class, the class to whom the future belongs, works and begins to move.[23]

These do not seem to be the words or actions of someone who believed that the proletariat was to be led to victory by the iron laws of history. Rather, it suggests a keen sense of attention to social changes and developments within the proletariat.

This is motivated, I think, by Marx's desire to identify what is *possible*, to identify historical *constraints*. If asked to point to Marx's most famous general remarks on history two passages suggest themselves. From the *18th Brumaire*, the remark that:

> Men make their own history, but not of their own free will; not under circumstances they themselves have chosen, but under the given and inherited circumstances with which they are directly confronted.[24]

---

approach – privileging a particular reading of the 1859 Preface over many of Marx's other remarks.

21   MacIntyre 2009, p. 51.
22   See MECW 24, pp. 328–36.
23   MECW 24, p. 636n.
24   *Surveys from Exile*, p. 146.

And from the *1859 Preface*:

> In the social production of their existence, men inevitably enter into definite relations, which are independent of their will, namely relations of production appropriate to a given stage in the development of their material forces of production.[25]

These passages both indicate the sense of history as constraint. Certain features of our particular historical conditions, and the history that has gone before, constrain the actions that are available to us. We do not make history in conditions of our own choosing, we exist in conditions independent of our will, and no amount of willpower will change that.

Importantly, this is not just about action, but also about thought. As Wright points out,[26] it is often forgotten that the famous passage in the *18th Brumaire* quoted above immediately precedes *another* frequently quoted passage in Marx, which is as follows:

> The tradition of the dead generations weighs like a nightmare on the minds of the living. And just when they appear to be engaged in the revolutionary transformation of themselves and their material surroundings, in the creation of something which does not yet exist, precisely in such epochs of revolutionary crisis they timidly conjure up the spirits of the past to help them; they borrow their names, slogans, and costumes so as to stage the new world-historical scene in this venerable disguise and borrowed language.[27]

This, then, seems to be as much about the constraints of history on knowledge and consciousness as on action. The danger is that the past, in delimiting our horizons about what is possible, is always capable of pulling us back. Just when we think we are out – and on our way to founding society anew – circumstances pull us back in.

What role does this leave for individuals? Put simply, as much room as the constraints of history allow. Despite his other weaknesses, Plekhanov is correct to argue that 'The character of an individual is a "factor" in social development only where, when, and to the extent that social relations permit it to be such'.[28]

---

25   MECW 29, p. 263.
26   See Wright 2010.
27   *Surveys from Exile*, p. 146.
28   Plekhanov 1967, p. 41.

In this he means simply that different historical situations and social structures allow for different degrees of individual action. The individual actions of Napoleon might have made a difference in the way that the individual actions of a Polish peasant were unlikely to. This is not about Napoleon's personality, but his social position. The size of Cleopatra's nose might have mattered, but if it did it was because of her social position, and the power that position afforded her to influence others.

A couple of Marx's own examples help illustrate this. In a footnote in *Capital*, Marx responds directly to some criticisms of the *1859 Preface*:

> In the estimation of that paper, my view ... that the mode of production determines the character of the social, political, and intellectual life generally ... is very true for our own times, in which material interests preponderate, but not for the middle ages, in which Catholicism, nor for Athens and Rome, where politics, reigned supreme ... This much, however, is clear, that the middle ages could not live on Catholicism, nor the ancient world on politics. On the contrary, it is the mode in which they gained a livelihood that explains why here politics, and there Catholicism, played the chief part ... On the other hand, Don Quixote long ago paid the penalty for wrongly imagining that knight errantry was compatible with all economic forms of society.[29]

What enabled Catholicism or politics to be dominant at different periods was the way in which production was organised, the way that people gained their livelihood. Certain ways of life *fitted* and certain ways did not. This is clearly illustrated by the allusion to Don Quixote at the end. Knight errantry *was* a possible way of life in a particular historical period (though never a way of life possible for everyone). However, the entire point of Don Quixote as a novel is to demonstrate that *acting* like a knight errant in a society which does not recognise knight errantry as a practice *does not make you a knight errant*. The social practice simply has no significance. It does not fit.

A similar point is made by Marx in the *Grundrisse* about art and myth in the ancient world:

> [I]s Achilles possible with powder and lead? Or the *Iliad* with the printing press, not to mention the printing machine? Do not the song and the saga

---

29 *Capital Vol. 1*, p. 176n.

and the muse necessarily come to an end with the printer's bar, hence do not the necessary conditions of epic poetry vanish?[30]

There's a great deal going on in these passages, but the fundamental claim is that epic poetry, and certain conceptions of myth, have a particular social basis which disappears with the advent of new technology and the new social relationships that arise with them. Note, that Marx does not say that epic poetry is incomprehensible to us now: 'The charm of their art for us is not in contradiction to the undeveloped stage of society on which it grew. [It] is its result, rather, and is inextricably bound up with the fact that the unripe social conditions under which it arose, and could only arise, can never return'.[31] Whether or not Marx is right about epic poetry, the significance of this claim lies once again in the idea that certain human practices are only possible given certain stages of historical development. The art and myth of the Greeks are not incomprehensible, but they are inaccessible in the sense that we could never go back, never do them again in the same way.

The constraints that history puts on people's thoughts and actions also requires serious thinking about what sort of interventions are appropriate. For example, in 1850 a split took place in the Communist League. Those who believed that revolution was still on the cards went their separate ways from Marx and Engels (and the majority of the Central Committee). Here is how Marx expressed his disagreement:

> A national German approach has replaced the universal conception of the Manifesto, flattering the national sentiments of the German artisans. The will, rather than the actual conditions, was stressed as the chief factor in the revolution. We tell the workers: If you want to change conditions and make yourselves capable of government, you will have to undergo fifteen, twenty or fifty years of civil war. Now they are told: We must come to power immediately or we might as well go to sleep. The word 'proletariat' has been reduced to a mere phrase, like the word 'people' was by the democrats.[32]

Here 'the will' is quite consciously counterposed to the 'actual conditions', and the constraints of these actual conditions has implications for the kind of actions and rhetoric it was appropriate for the League to engage in.

---

30   *Grundrisse*, p. 111.
31   *Grundrisse*, p. 111.
32   *The Revolutions of 1848*, p. 341.

It is because Marx thought that history played this constraining role that he is so keen to study, understand and get to grips with it. Understanding the kinds of constraints history places on actions and thoughts *matters*. Marx's reasons for engaging in a study of history, and for developing a 'theory of history', are not about dodging questions of action, they are about acknowledging some central limitations on action. In particular, Marx takes it as a prerequisite of a course of action that it fits in a given historical period, that it is not just another version of Quixote's tilting at windmills. This, of course, is not Marx's only prerequisite, since he also demands that a course of action cuts *against* and points *beyond* the current historical circumstances. It is necessary, as the *Communist Manifesto* puts it, to identify measures 'which, in the course of the movement, outstrip themselves, necessitate further inroads upon the old social order'.[33] There is a great deal of behaviour that is fitted to capitalist society that does not point beyond it. However, action which claims to be revolutionary, but in fact is ahistorical and meaningless is no more a challenge to the existing order than a historical re-enactment society.

4   It's Been Coming! – Determination and Inevitability

So far so good. But critics of Marx are entitled to point to an elephant in the room. They will respond that Marx did not talk about history as merely constraining actions but as *driving* actions. 'Anyone', they will respond, 'can agree that historical circumstances restrain actions and we have to be sensitive to that fact; we hardly need Marx to tell us that'. Rather, what is distinctive about Marxism is a theory of history in the stronger sense, in which history drives actions in an impersonal, deterministic, perhaps even fatalistic, way. After all, Kautsky and Plekhanov didn't get their interpretations from nowhere! It is Marx's invocation of *determination* and *inevitability* in history, not merely of constraint, that leaves him open to the kind of interpretations I am trying to reject.

Given how much is written about Marx's attitude to history and the particular prominence that the 1859 Preface is given in so much Marxist literature, it is easy to forget that Marx's works of 1845–7 are primarily concerned with a rejection of certain kinds of historical schemas. It is precisely the post-Hegelian fashion for grand historical schemas which could both classify the past and pre-

---

33   *Communist Manifesto*, p. 104.

dict the future which Marx was reacting *against* when he outlined the limits of theoretical reflection in the *German Ideology*:

> At best its place can only be taken by a summing-up of the most general results, abstractions which are derived from the observations of the historical development of men. These abstractions in themselves, divorced from real history, have no value whatsoever. They can only serve to facilitate the arrangement of historical material, to indicate the sequence of its separate strata. But they by no means afford a recipe or schema ... for neatly trimming the epochs of history.[34]

And in the *Holy Family*:

> History does nothing, it 'possesses no immense wealth', it 'wages no battles'. It is man, real, living man who does all that, who possesses and fights; 'history' is not, as it were, a person apart, using man as a means to achieve its own aims; history is nothing but the activity of man pursuing his aims.[35]

Marx's own method is explicitly contrasted with one which imposes a grand schema onto the objects of analysis, rather than attempting to grasp the objects themselves and to generalise from them. The kinds of generalisations that Marx makes are to be understood as ways of arranging and grasping the historical facts, not as making firm claims about iron laws of history.

Later in their life, Marx and Engels show an awareness of the risks that such abstract schemas can pose. Engels remarks in a letter that 'The materialist conception of history has a lot of dangerous friends nowadays who use it as an excuse for *not* studying history'.[36] He was perturbed by the fact that 'too many of the younger Germans simply make use of the phrase historical materialism (and *everything* can be turned into a phrase) only in order to get their own relatively scanty historical knowledge ... constructed into a neat system as quickly as possible'.[37] In other words, they are acutely sensitive to others doing to their own writings what the young Hegelians had done to Hegel.

Moreover, one only needs to read Marx's attempts at writing actual history to see a different approach. The *18th Brumaire* and the *Civil War in France* are

---

34   *German Ideology*, p. 43.
35   MECW 4, p. 93.
36   *Letter to C. Schmidt*, August 5. 1890.
37   *Letter to C. Schmidt*, August 5. 1890.

two of the most significant works of nineteenth-century history. Both of them invoke the general conditions of economic crisis and stagnation in which the events occur as a backdrop, but that does not stop real, serious attention to the detail of the psychological motivations and interests of particular classes, class fractions and individuals, not to mention a grasp of the straightforwardly contingent and fortunate circumstances certain actors found themselves in. In the *Civil War in France* in particular, the context of a crisis of sovereignty in the aftermath of military defeat clearly plays a more immediate 'determining' role than the economic.[38]

What Merleau-Ponty says of later histories is just as true of Marx's own:

> A historical materialist history of the 1917 Revolution does not consist in explaining every revolutionary thrust in terms of the Retail Price Index at the moment in question, but of putting it back in the class dynamism and the interplay of psychological forces, which fluctuated between February and October, between the new proletarian power and the old conservative power. Economics is reintegrated into history rather than history's being reduced to economics.[39]

There is thus a certain irony when Popper asserts that:

> None of Marx's more ambitious historicist conclusions, none of his 'inexorable laws of development' and his 'stages of history which cannot be leaped over', has ever turned out to be a successful prediction. Marx was successful only in so far as he was analysing institutions and their functions. And the opposite is true also: none of his more ambitious and sweeping historical prophecies falls within the scope of institutional analysis.[40]

Yet if what I have suggested above is correct, then Marx is interested precisely in what Popper calls 'institutional analysis', in the sense of an understanding of institutions and practices on their own terms and in their relationships with other institutions and practices. Marx is concerned with the way certain institutional structures develop and proceed, and bases his generalisations on this kind of analysis (rather than *vice versa*).

---

38   See *The First International and After*, pp. 258–65.
39   Merleau-Ponty 2002, p. 198n.
40   Popper 1966, p. 393.

If this is the case, what does Marx mean when he says that the economic base determines the superstructure? Engels offers a famous clarification, which has often confused more than it has helped:

> According to the materialist conception of history, the *ultimately* determining element in history is the production and reproduction of real life. Other than this neither Marx nor I have ever asserted. Hence if somebody twists this into saying that the economic element is the *only* determining one, he transforms that proposition into a meaningless, abstract, senseless phrase. The economic situation is the basis, but the various elements of the superstructure – political forms of the class struggle and its results, to wit: constitutions established by the victorious class after a successful battle, etc., juridical forms, and even the reflexes of all these actual struggles in the brains of the participants, political, juristic, philosophical theories, religious views and their further development into systems of dogmas – also exercise their influence upon the course of the historical struggles and in many cases preponderate in determining their *form*.[41]

Thus Engels recognises that 'superstructural' elements can play an important role. Nonetheless, the economic base determines *ultimately*, but not *solely*.

This distinction between ultimate and sole determination has been mocked as a scholastic one, prone to collapsing.[42] However, Brenkert offers an extremely compelling way of understanding this difference:

> Consider ... a similar claim about the ultimately determining role which some element played in the formation and development of a person's character. There are clearly many forces and conditions which play a role in such a process. Still, it might be said that some early experience, or (more probably) set of experiences, played and continues to play an ultimately determining role in the person's character ... this basic experience (or set of experiences) plays a role of ultimate importance not simply in the long run, but also here and now. Further, it is not simply another force, and need not at all times be the most strong force, in the person's life. Still it is a force which organises all other forces about itself, subordinates them to itself, colours and gives the other aspects of the person's character the significance and meaning they have. It is like the theme in a piece

---

41   *Letter to J. Bloch*, September 21 1890.
42   For example by Kamenka 1962.

of music which may at times come to the fore or at other times recede into the background, but which is at all times the organising principle, that ties the work together.[43]

This notion of determination is not one which permits us to suggest that you can read off from the economic base any event or development. Nonetheless, it allows us to say that economic relations structure our lives, and place restrictions on them. Under capitalism, the basic economic elements – the commodity form, exploitation through wage-labour, division into antagonistic classes – form a background structure, which we often do not see until it suddenly bursts into relevance.

Althusser famously remarked that the economic determines in the last instance, but that 'the lonely hour of the "last instance" never comes'.[44] There is a sense in which this is true, in that there is no final showdown between forces and relations of production in which politics and human beings play no part. On Brenkert's model, however, you can identify a sort of 'last instance'. It is the moment analogous to where the determining early experience suddenly prevents you from doing something you intend to do, when you suddenly realise that for whatever reason you cannot do it. When 'just as they seem to be occupied with revolutionizing themselves and things' the past 'weighs like a nightmare'. It is in periods where the economy is most clearly constraining that its influence homes into view, as Merleau-Ponty notes:

> [A]s in the case of an individual life, sickness subjects a man to the vital rhythms of his body, so in a revolutionary situation such as a general strike, factors governing production come clearly to light, and are specifically seen as decisive. Even so we have seen just now that the outcome depends on how the opposing forces think of each other. It is all the more true, then, that during periods of depression, economic factors are effective only to the extent that they are lived and taken up by a human subject, wrapped up, that is in ideological shreds by a process amounting to self-deception, or rather permanent equivocation, which is yet part of history and has a weight of its own.[45]

This is similar to Eagleton's observation that, following the crisis of 2008, the word capitalism returned to common currency in a way it had not before, its

---

43 Brenkert 1983, p. 42.
44 Althusser 2005, p. 113.
45 Merleau-Ponty 2002, p. 199n.

central role in our lives revealed because its constraints and limits had become so violently apparent.[46]

The combination of this model with the remarks about constraint above also suggests a way in which it makes sense to talk about inevitability. In Engels's 1891 postscript to *The Civil War In France*, he observes something striking about the Paris Commune: Despite being dominated by Proudhonists and Blanquists, both of whom are, in their different ways, hostile to Marxism, the Communards had been forced to act largely in the way which Marx had recommended:

> But what is still more wonderful is the correctness of much that never-theless was done by the Commune, composed as it was of Blanquists and Proudhonists. Naturally the Proudhonists were chiefly responsible for the economic decrees of the Commune, both for their praiseworthy and their unpraiseworthy aspects; as the Blanquists were for its political commissions and omissions. And in both cases the irony of history willed – as is usual when doctrinaires come to the helm – that both did the opposite of what the doctrines of their school prescribed.[47]

Here he describes the way in which certain historical agents are forced to act in certain ways despite themselves.

This, however, needn't be understood strictly as any claim of historical destiny. Rather, these actions are the *consequences* of historical constraints. If there are certain constraints on our action then there are certain things we can and cannot do, and if we ignore this we are likely to fail in what we want to achieve. What underlies these remarks about the Commune is the idea that only certain courses of action were genuinely possible if they wanted to achieve their goals; in the case of the Commune, even the minimum goal of survival. This does not mean that there is only *one* possible course of action, but it does mean that certain courses of action are not available, at least without substantially revising our goals.

This suggests one sense in which it might be appropriate to talk about inevitability in Marx. Given the particular set of constraints on action, and the determining role that the economic structure plays, certain things are bound to happen, they are part of the structure of the situation. Once they have happened, we can say 'well that was always going to happen', much like a football commentator who after a goal declares 'It has been coming!'. They do not

---

46   Eagleton, 2011, p. xi.
47   MECW 27, p. 187.

mean that it was always going to happen in that second, at that moment, but nor would what they said be absurd if it had not happened. No given event might be inevitable, but particular *types* of events are inevitable. These are the types of events captured by words like 'crisis' and 'revolution'. Given the structure and antagonisms of certain social systems, these kinds of events are inevitable, in something like the sense in which goals are inevitable in football. This does not mean that they can be easily predicted or anticipated to an exact degree. And, like goals, they can be a long time coming.

5   History and Strategy

Continuing the football analogy can help here. We can think of the 'laws' of history Marx discusses by analogy with the rules and dynamics of a game. It is possible, as a disengaged viewer, to make a series of generalisations about the game of football, to adopt a third personal perspective to describe patterns of play. Given a particular arrangement and set up, given the background rules, it is even possible to make predictions. These are speculative, of course, but are grounded in an understanding of the dynamics of the game under examination, and thus are not entirely arbitrary. In order to make good predictions, one needs to be able to isolate and abstract, make generalisations, suggest 'laws', and define their scope. This can sometimes be expressed precisely in the kind of language that Marx employs. Commentators talk about players being 'forced' onto their weaker foot due to the pressure of opposition players. It is possible to make broad generalisations about use of space, about the moments in which goals are more or less likely, and about how to minimise and maximise possibilities. This is the sort of perspective which managers adopt to develop their strategies. It is the perspective of arrows and circles on a chalkboard. This strategy is based on a set of abstractions and generalisations which are based on a combination of the rules of the game and, far more importantly, a general sense of the patterns of play, the ways in which interactions between players, ball and space combine. And, perhaps the broadest generalisation is that, just like crises in capitalism, play for long enough and you will get a goal.

Yet, despite this, games are played in the moment. From the point of view of an individual player, every decision matters. They may have the strategy in their mind, and a certain sense of what they have to do to implement that strategy, but this hardly means they can plot out every kick of the ball in advance. Indeed, every action is important, and involves an act of decision (even if it might be experienced as 'instinctive' and might thus not be the result of deliberation). Having a strategy that is based on generalisations and tendencies does not replace urgent, active decision-making. If anything it elevates it. Football is played 'in the moment', and strategic generalisations are a part, but only a part, of this.[48]

This suggests we can understand Marx's historical generalisations as part of a strategic conception of history, as, with apologies for the pun, goal-directed. The football analogy captures something of what Daniel Bensaïd means when he argues that strategic thinking involves being constantly in the present:

> This is a suspended present, which is not a transition but a fork and bifurc-ation; a strategic present for those who stand still on the threshold of time. An art of time and contretemps, a strategy has as its temporal mode the present and its cardinal virtue 'presence of mind'.[49]

If Marx's generalisations and abstractions about history can be understood as forming part of a strategic project, then it is no mystery why he puts so much stress on the importance of individual action and intervention. Having a 'theory of history' is not a substitute for making difficult decisions, it is a necessary complement to it.[50]

Bensaïd offers a number of useful remarks on the elements of this strategic mode of thought. Strikingly, he talks about Marx's attitude in terms of a partic-ular kind of messianism. This is not the prophetic messianism Popper accuses him of, which predicts the future with unerring certainty, and makes a claim to privileged knowledge and insight.[51] Rather, it is a radically open messianism, which is alive to constantly shifting possibilities. Bensaïd identifies this kind of thinking in Walter Benjamin's remarks in his *Theses on the Philosophy of History*:

> We know that the Jews were prohibited from investigating the future. This stripped the future of its magic, to which all those succumb who turn to the soothsayers for enlightenment. This does not imply, however, that for

---

48   A similar point about the important role of perspective in questions of historical inevitab-ility is made in Tolstoy's epilogue to *War and Peace* (Tolstoy 1869). Of particular relevance to this discussion is the model of military command, in which he describes an inverse rela-tionship between the degree of theoretical reflection on actions and actual participation in them.

49   Bensaïd 2002, p. 87.

50   See Nilsen & Cox 2013, p. 12, for another account of Marxism as of strategic importance, as 'suggesting categories which are useful for empirical research and practical strategy, rather than watertight conceptual compartments'.

51   See also, for example, Tucker 1961.

the Jews the future was homogeneous, empty time. For every second of time was the strait gate through which the Messiah might enter.[52]

This is a messianism which is the very opposite of historical prophecy, which is characterised by openness to the possibilities of the future. As Bensaïd puts it, 'In Benjamin, political (strategic) anticipation appears as the precise negation of this ontological anticipation ... Messianic anticipation is never the passive certainty of an event foretold, but akin to the concentration of a hunter on the lookout for the sudden emergence of what is possible'.[53]

Of course, the analogy with games only stretches so far. Bensaïd identifies an important distinction between an infinite game and a finite game:

> A finite game has a precise beginning and end. It is played according to contractual rules within specified limits of time and space. It finishes with a decisive move, crowned with a victory or a title. An infinite game, in contrast, has neither beginning nor end. It knows no limits of space or number. Each of its rounds 'opens to players a new horizon of time'. Its rules can vary over the course of the game. It does not end in victory or defeat, but springs to life again in a perpetual process of birth and renewal that establishes a new field of possibilities.[54]

The class struggle is, as Bensaïd rightly identifies, closer to an infinite game than a finite game (though it is, of course, not a game at all). It does not have a fixed unchanging set of rules, it is not an endless rehearsal of the same set of procedures, 'there is no beginning, no limit, no endgame. Nor is there any referee to blow the whistle and send someone off, to ensure that the rules are observed, and to anoint the victor'.[55] This further emphasises the importance of openness to the future and the absence of certainties. It is even harder to talk about something as happening inevitably, since the very rules of the game, the nature of the constraints and determinations are themselves in flux, ongoing and changing. Politics 'is no longer a question of training for the repetition and mastery of a familiar pattern, but of being alert to the invention that replays an unfinished past in the future'.[56]

---

52   Benjamin 1968, p. 264.
53   Bensaïd 2002, p. 85.
54   Bensaïd 2002, p. 131.
55   Bensaïd 2002, p. 131.
56   Bensaïd 2002, p. 131.

All of this suggests another important reason why we need to know the rules of the game – to be able to change them. As well as helping us to form strategies, it brings into focus the rules themselves, and how they might be bent, broken, or even abolished. Studying the rules helps us recognise them as historical products – the offside rule is not a universal feature of kicking a ball about, but a historically created rule that has been adapted over time. Some rules can be changed without endangering the overall character of the game – passing back to goalkeepers, for example – others cannot help but transform it entirely – if everyone can pick it up with their hands, it's a different game. Knowing what the rules are and where they come from is essential to knowing *that they can change* and *how they need to change for you to achieve your goals*.

Something analogous can be said for the 'rules' identified by historical materialism. Knowing the way in which society works, and its historical genesis, is a necessary step to beginning to radically change it. Of course, it is not a sufficient step. Marx asserts this clearly in his discussion of commodity fetishism:

> The belated scientific discovery that the products of labour, in so far as they are values, are merely the material expressions of the human labour expended to produce them, marks an epoch in the history of mankind's development, but by no means banishes the semblance of objectivity possessed by the social characteristics of labour. [This] ... appears to those caught up in the relations of commodity production (and this is true both before and after the above-mentioned scientific discovery) to be just as ultimately valid as the fact that the scientific dissection of the air into its component parts left the atmosphere itself unaltered in its physical configuration.[57]

A fetish is not abolished merely because its origins are explained – it requires practical experience and living differently in order for it to actually disappear. Anyone who has ever listened to a radio phone-in about the introduction of video replays or goal line technology will know how hard it is to shift ideas that have been ingrained by generations of practice. Nonetheless, recognition of something as a historically specific product (rather than timeless feature of human life) remains an essential stage in changing it.

This approach suggests a radically different way of understanding the nature of Marx's theoretical generalisations. They are part of attempting to understand the present so as to change it. They are far from iron laws, rather they are

---

57   *Capital Vol. 1*, p. 167.

open to revision and reconsideration in relation to changing circumstances. And they only make sense as a complement to action, rather than as a substitute for it. This is theory fundamentally indexed to a goal of self-emancipation, rather than as a prophetic substitute for it. These two roles for historical materialist theory, helping recognise the historical specificity of the laws of society and formulating strategies within them, do not run counter to self-emancipation. They do not deny agency to the working class themselves, but rather help guide this agency. This is a conception of theory not as a substitute for activism, a la Popper, but as a complement to it.

Moreover, while this does not provide clear answers to ethical questions, it at least puts them back on the table. It shifts the focus onto analysis and understanding of practices and consciousness, and thus of a consideration of what kinds of practices are appropriate and possible in any situation, given the goal of social transformation. What practices genuinely both 'fit' and 'point beyond' at the same time? What pathways exist out of the present, how could things have played out differently in the past and how might we play them out differently in the future? These kinds of questions can, and indeed should, include questions of how we should act towards comrades, towards the enemy, which norms of behaviour we should adopt and so on.

It is important to stress here that knowledge of the 'laws of history', or rather of actual historical development and the specific forms of society it has given birth to, remains a vital part of emancipation. Understanding the world remains a necessary stage in changing it. In a sense this is a 'knowledge of necessity', but it is not a passive acceptance of one's fate – either for the better or worse. It is not a firm confidence in historical destiny, but knowledge that is to be used in the pursuit of a specific, human goal. Moreover, it suggests a different approach to how these theories are developed and distributed. They should take as their starting point, like Marx's *Workers' Inquiry*, the actual consciousness of the working class. These theories are not the special preserve of individual geniuses, whether scientist or soothsayer, but involve close, collective collaboration with actual social movements – for whom these theories must be intelligible and reflect their lives.

This, then, is how Marx can both be committed to self-emancipation and to developing historical materialism as a theory. Recall Webb's remarks I referred to in the Introduction, that Marx's problem was the problem of 'generating radical hope without foreclosing the future'. To treat historical materialism as an abstract science, capable of predicting the future with the same accuracy as physics or chemistry, risks precisely this foreclosure. However, to understand historical materialism as strategically indexed to self-emancipation itself, is to see it very differently. In this version, those, like Marx, who develop historical

Communism, Utopia and Vision

'Utopia negativa' is not exactly a rallying cry. Yet the positive utopian tradition of blueprints for the communal kitchens of the future has atrophied. It has suffered too many reversals; it has been eclipsed by too much history; and its imaginative sources have been drained. In an age of triumphalism and self-promotion, to advertise the future only adds to the clutter. Another utopian blueprint looks like just another billboard or video. The future, perhaps, can be heard, not envisioned.

RUSSEL JACOBY, *Picture Imperfect*[1]

∴

1   Introduction

If one way of a theorist foreclosing the future was adopting the role of prophet discussed in the previous chapter, another, for Marx, was to attempt to draw the future in great detail – to play the role of the utopian. That Marx criticised utopian socialists, and frequently used utopian as an epithet, is not in doubt. Whether he was at all consistent in this, and had any good reason to do so, is far more questionable. Indeed, Marx has the distinction of being accused simultaneously of being too utopian and not utopian enough. *Both* accusations appear in attempts to attribute the ills of the Soviet Union to Marx's thought. For some, it was a paradigmatically utopian vision, an act of social engineering to build an alternative against human nature, which could not avoid trampling over the rights of the individual.[2] For others, it was precisely the absence of attention to what this society was to look like that licensed a series of abuses and errors. Marx failed to prepare us for what communism actually looked like, and thus left a vacuum to be filled by whatever abuses one chooses.[3] As Ruth Levitas notes, 'Where utopia is concerned, the Cold War is still with us'.[4] Still

---

1   Jacoby 2005, p. 59.
2   Arendt 1951, Popper 1966, Talmon 1970, Gray 2007.
3   See Leopold 2007, Lukes 1987.
4   Levitas 2013, p. 171.

others argue that whatever Marx criticised the utopians for he could not in fact avoid doing himself: He was an 'accidental utopian'.[5] Or an even less generous interpretation might hold that Marx simply used utopian as a term of abuse against rivals in the Labour movement and beyond – an empty epithet to draw a false distinction.

Against these positions, this chapter argues that Marx had at least one good reason to criticise what he saw as the utopian approach, and this reason was rooted in his commitment to self-emancipation. Tracing Marx's attitude to various figures throughout his life, we can see a common thread involving suspicion of model-builders and demagogues, who would seek to present their alternatives to the masses and demand they are built.[6] While Marx attacks the utopians from several different angles, this is a constant presence in his writings, and informs a great deal of his practice.

One of the problems faced by this debate is the variety of ways in which utopia and utopian are used in discussion. There are meanings of utopia that come before Marx, and meanings that come after. The motivations of those writing utopias varies a great deal, from satire to entertainment to political change. The ambiguity in More's coinage of the term, between no-place and good-place, is often present – is the purpose of these utopias to build a future society, or to help us understand our own?

To begin with, it helps to distinguish three broad categories of utopia.[7] The first is simply the desire, hope, or belief that a society is possible that is better than the existing one. Included in this category is Mannheim's influential definition of utopia as involving ideas that are 'situationally transcendent' and 'when they pass over into conduct, tend to shatter, either partially or wholly, the order of things prevailing at the time'.[8] Similarly, the sense in which Ruth Levitas can talk of the colour blue as involving a utopian feeling, and as utopia being fundamentally linked to the virtue of hope, sits squarely in this usage.[9] The second is general discussions of alternative societies that are in various ways better than our existing one, or even merely sufficiently differ-

---

5   See, though approaching the point from very different angles, Webb 2000, pp. 2–3, Levitas 2013, p. 70, Elster 1985, pp. 251–8, and Geoghegan 2008, p. 34.
6   See Draper, 1990, Chapter 6.
7   While these distinctions address the three kinds of utopianism relevant to this discussion, they do not and cannot cover the wide variety of ways the term is used and discussed. For example, for reasons that will hopefully become clear, I pay no attention to dystopias as a category of utopias, despite their frequent inclusion. See Sargent 2010, Goodwin and Taylor 2009.
8   Mannheim 1936, p. 173.
9   Levitas 2013.

ent to bring into relief certain features of our own. This can take the form of fiction, modelling, or political treatises. It can be based on rigorous (social) scientific research, or idle speculation. These are, by intention at least, provisional and limited.[10] The third is the construction of detailed societies that claim to be best, either in the sense of ideal, or in the more limited sense of the best we can do, which Jacoby calls blueprint utopias.[11] These purport to offer a plan or blueprint for the good society, and thus (implicitly or explicitly) invite us to build it. On this model: 'utopias enrich our understanding of the world by offering a global, or total, view of ideal social organisation and operation, by contrast with the more partial, schematic views proffered by political theory ... utopianism takes an integrative rather than a partial view and attempts to make explicit the interconnections of the various elements of the ideal society'.[12]

Within these schematic categories, it is important to locate what I am saying about Marx. For Marx to be anti-utopian in the sense of rejecting the first version would be absurd. Clearly, Marx both felt himself to be committed to, and valued in others, the belief that society could be fundamentally different from what it actually was. It was, in a certain sense, his starting point and his end point – he started from the reaction of workers against capitalism, and sought to make firmer and clearer the sense that something better was possible. Marx was sceptical of the second kind of utopianism. He believed he had good reasons for this: In the main they were a distraction from the real movement developing under capitalism, from the growing strength of the proletarian movement moving inexorably towards communism. There was no need for idle speculation when it was happening before your eyes. Even if we concede these were good reasons *then*, we might worry they are not good reasons any more.

But it is the third that Marx was really worried about, namely the construction of blueprints, plans and ideals by theorists, politicians and schemers. These he thought not just a distraction from the real movement, but an active hindrance to it, 'silly, stale, and basically reactionary'. These thinkers believed

---

10 Levitas' own utopian approach seeks to stick resolutely to this category, insisting that utopian thought should 'develop alternative possible scenarios for the future and open these up to public debate and democratic decision – insisting always on the provisionality, reflexivity and contingency of what we are able to imagine, and in full awareness that utopian speculation is formed always in the double squeeze of what we are able to imagine and what we are able to imagine as possible' (Levitas 2013, p. 22).

11 Jacoby 2005.

12 Goodwin and Taylor 2009, p. 209.

themselves possessed of special insight into the best possible society, and demanded that such a society be built. The sole role for the masses in this schema is to build it. It is this particular argument that this chapter focuses on. I will argue that Marx's rejection of this method is directly linked to a concern for self-emancipation, and that this should also give us good reason to reject it too. In part, I will illustrate this through comparison with a practice in contemporary political theory known as ideal theory.

The end of the twentieth century saw increasing demands that Marxists and other critics of capitalism outline their alternative. From the right came the increasingly shrill insistence that there is no alternative, something that the collapse of the Soviet Union reinforced and the economic crisis seems to have done little to shake. Many on the left have since stressed, for understandable reasons, the importance of describing that alternative in reasonable detail, insisting it is a task that cannot, and should not, be avoided.[13] This can be seen as an intervention into that debate, in particular to sound a note of caution. My aim is to make explicit an argument that I take to come from Marx, but one that I think would be valuable whatever its source. It is not intended to shut down discussions of alternatives, or to denigrate the work of those who dedicate themselves to constructing them, either in thought or practice. However, it does involve identifying some real risks and challenges, ones that Marx saw, and ones we should keep in view today.

2   Communism as Vision

Of course, Marx does have an alternative to capitalism – it's called communism. But we do not learn very much about it. As discussed in Chapter 1, it is certainly possible to piece together from Marx's writings a number of features of communism – there would be an end to the division of labour, there would be worker control over the labour process, there would, perhaps, be the possibility of something like Albert's balanced job complexes. At the core of these proposals is the transcendence of capitalism in a way that maintains its productive powers, but subjects them to collective control, and thus overcomes capitalism's dehumanising features.

That it is possible to piece together Marx's proposals and put them together should not, however, distract us from an essential point: Marx did not see describing and articulating the details of the communist system as a press-

---

13   See, e.g., Lebowitz 2003, Wright 2010, Ollman 2005, Hudis 2012.

ing political task.[14] (Berki observes that you could probably produce a 50 page volume from Marx's explicit remarks on communism, as if this is a large number, but the MECW is 50 volumes!)[15] If he did, the document he wrote which he named a manifesto would have said far more about it, instead of offering only a series of general demands, which were modified within months at the outbreak of revolution in 1848. Marx would not have limited his most detailed description of communism to critical notes that were never published. For all that 'from each according to his ability, to each according to his need' is an inspiring slogan, if Marx intended it as the regulating principle of an entire society it may have been wise for him to include it somewhere other than in a series of notes.[16]

Nor does piecing these proposals together amount to what people generally expect when they ask for a description of an alternative society, much less a detailed one. Marx's description has no institutional depth. It does not tell us what the institutions that are to ensure democratic management look like. It does not tell us how people get to decide when and if they can fish, hunt and criticise, let alone clean toilets, look after the children or cook the food. Just as there is no description of institutional form, there is only the haziest account of the character of everyday life (again, we fall back on hunting, fishing, criticising). Compare with Weitling, who Engels mocks for describing how cutlery will be chained to tables.

While communism is taken to embody certain ethically valuable features (most obviously freedom and democracy), the institutional forms in which these values are manifest are absent. We should presume that Marx believed there would have to be institutional forms, even if they are just for the administration of things, but he does not appear interested in telling us what these are.[17] Moreover, beyond the commitment to freedom and democracy, communism is remarkably free of other values. There are a few remarks about reciprocity (See Chapter 1), and about living according to our nature (See Chapter 6), but we are not told what our nature is, beyond what we already know about being productive animals, who individuate ourselves within society.

Thus communism is Marx's alternative, but it is a rather empty one. It is one which is perhaps best characterised in terms of what Berki calls 'vision':

---

14   See Hudis 2012 and Ollman 1977 as examples of how this can be done.
15   Berki 1983, p. 14.
16   For that matter, he might also have suggested it be 'inscribed on a banner' *before* the higher phase of communism, rather than only in it.
17   See Avineri 1968, p. 246.

> A person who stands on a hilltop or on a beach and looks to the distance, with erect head and, in order to enjoy and appreciate the infinite horizon in front of him, with his eyes suitably narrowed, has vision. He sees far, far ahead, and he sees large things: majestic peaks, undulating pastures, misty waves, in the distance while being relatively oblivious of, relatively blind to, the details of objects and of things: pebbles, crags, bird-feathers, immediately around him.[18]

Communism as an alternative society tends, in Marx, to take this form. It is big picture vision, rather than close detail. It sees the outline of things, the sharp contrasts between the big objects. What he does not see is the small detail, the detailed forms and shapes, the fine-grained interrelations between the objects. Rather, it is a world of broad brush strokes and sharp contrasts.

Moreover, this vision is primarily defined negatively. It is in terms of the abolition and removal of various social ills, and the institutional structures that cause them. We will remove the division of labour between design and execution. We will abolish private property in the means of production. We will abolish the sexual division of labour. As Engels writes:

> What we can now conjecture about the way in which sexual relations will be ordered after the impending overthrow of capitalist production is mainly of a negative character, limited for the most part to what will disappear. But what will there be new? That will be answered when a new generation has grown up: a generation of men who never in their lives have known what it is to buy a woman's surrender with money or any other social instrument of power; a generation of women who have never known what it is to give themselves to a man from any other considerations than real love, or to refuse to give themselves to their lover from fear of the economic consequences. When these people are in the world, they will care precious little what anybody today thinks they ought to do; they will make their own practice and their corresponding public opinion about the practice of each individual – and that will be the end of it.[19]

---

18 Berki 1983, p. 4. For Berki, this is explicitly contrasted with communism as insight, as the real movement, which, of course, we can see develop as we live it. According to Berki, Marx's entire work is best understood in terms of a fruitful but ultimately futile attempt to reconcile these two perspectives on communism.

19 MECW 26, p. 189.

To this extent, Marx can be identified with those who Russel Jacoby calls iconoclastic utopians (in explicit contrast with blueprint utopians). These thinkers are a generation of Jewish-German radicals, suffused with traditions of both revolutionary communism and German romanticism. This is a utopianism that 'dreamt of a superior society but who declined to give its precise measurements',[20] that 'listens for, but does not look into the future ... [t]hat pines for the future, but does not map it out'.[21] To the extent that communism is any kind of utopia at all, it is a negatively defined utopia, a utopia of absences and gaps, of outlines and contours. It is a not-here, rather than a there.

The rest of this chapter is taken up with two questions: Why does Marx insist on remaining at the level of vision, and is he able to maintain a coherent criticism of capitalism while doing so? The first requires an account of Marx's critique of the utopians, the second a consideration of the role of alternatives in criticism.

3 Whose Ideals, Whose Society?

For Marx, the charge of utopian was not merely an epithet, it described a way of doing politics that was necessarily doomed to failure. As such, it did not merely pick out a particular group of thinkers, but a general political method against which it was important to be on constant guard. A wide range of figures appear to fall foul of the charge of utopianism in Marx's career. Indeed, this often indicates the point at which Marx believes that a given thinker has ceased to appropriately represent the workers' movement, and in fact now merely presents their own peculiar, and deficient, project. Thus, for example, in 1844 Proudhon is referred to favourably when compared to Marx's German contemporaries: 'Not only does Proudhon write in the interests of the proletarians, he is himself a proletarian ... His work is a scientific manifesto of the French proletariat and therefore has quite a different historical significance from that of the literary botch work of any Critical Critic'.[22] However, Proudhon himself falls foul of the charge of utopianism in his later works,[23] and in 1865 Marx again describes Proudhon's work as 'extremely deficient and at times even schoolboyish' for his

---

20   Jacoby 2005, p. 16.
21   Jacoby 2005, p. 145.
22   MECW 4, p. 41.
23   For example, 'M. Proudhon's theory of values is the utopian interpretation of Ricardo's theory'. MECW 6, p. 124.

attempt to derive his principles 'a priori, instead of deriving science from a crit-ical knowledge of the historical movement, a movement which itself produces the material conditions of emancipation'.[24] In 1845 Engels expresses a similar attitude to Fourier, endorsing his focus on the actual lives of working people and noting that 'French nonsense is at least cheerful, whereas German non-sense is gloomy and profound'.[25] Here he describes Weitling as the only German communist worth engaging with, but later he too is mocked for engaging in uto-pian experiments and expending energies on debating whether or not knives and forks ought to be chained to tables.[26] The endorsement occurs precisely because he is seen as emerging from and reflecting the weavers' revolt, while the condemnation comes only when he has ceased to do this, and is merely presenting abstract models.

These criticisms are part of Marx's general hostility to those who would play the role of 'saviour leader' within the workers' movement, and connected to his confidence in the capacities of the movement itself. Such an approach is already signalled in the 1843 Letter to Ruge:

> Hence, nothing prevents us from making criticism of politics, particip-ation in politics, and therefore real struggles, the starting point of our criticism, and from identifying our criticism with them. In that case we do not confront the world in a doctrinaire way with a new principle: Here is the truth, kneel down before it! We develop new principles for the world out of the world's own principles. We do not say to the world: Cease your struggles, they are foolish; we will give you the true slogan of struggle. We merely show the world what it is really fighting for, and consciousness is something that it has to acquire, even if it does not want to.[27]

These arguments are then echoed in the *German Ideology*, in which Marx and Engels announce their break from the critical philosophy of the past, which contains the famous assertion that 'Communism is for us not a state of affairs which is to be established, an ideal to which reality [will] have to adjust itself. We call communism the real movement which abolishes the present state of things'.[28] The *Communist Manifesto* asserts that 'The theoretical conclusions of the Communists are in no way based on ideas or principles that have been

---

24   MECW 20, p. 29.
25   MECW 4, p. 615.
26   MECW 38, p. 56.
27   MECW 3, p. 144.
28   *German Ideology*, p. 57.

invented, or discovered by this or that would-be universal reformer'.[29] Over twenty years later, writing about the Paris Commune, Marx would argue that the working class of Paris 'can afford to smile at the coarse invective of the gentlemen's gentleman with the pen and inkhorn, and at the didactic patronage of well-wishing bourgeois-doctrinaires, pouring forth their ignorant platitudes and sectarian crotchets in the oracular tone of scientific infallibility'.[30]

In *Socialism, Utopian and Scientific*, Engels summarises 'the Utopians' mode of thought' that had 'for a long time governed the socialist ideas of the nineteenth century':

> The solution of the social problems ... the Utopians attempted to evolve out of the human brain. Society presented nothing but wrongs; to remove these was the task of reason. It was necessary, then, to discover a new and more perfect system of social order and to impose this upon society from without by propaganda, and, wherever possible, by the example of model experiments. These new social systems were foredoomed as Utopian; the more completely they were worked out in detail, the more they could not avoid drifting off into pure phantasies.[31]

In a letter of 1877 Marx, concerned that such features were creeping back into the workers' movement through Lassalle's followers, harks back to debates with utopian socialism, criticising 'the play of the imagination on the future structure of society' and dismissing it as 'silly, stale and *thoroughly reactionary* [my italics]'.[32] Silly, stale, and thoroughly reactionary sums up remarkably well Marx's various criticisms of the utopian approach. The first two of these charges (silly and stale) are widely discussed and well examined. The third (thoroughly reactionary), and in particular the element of it I will focus on, have received far less attention.[33]

The first, 'silly', charge, is that the ideas proposed by the utopians were unscientific. Specifically, they failed to demonstrate how they might emerge out of existing society, and to appeal to any agent that was capable of real-

---

29   *Communist Manifesto*, p. 95.

30   *First International and After*, p. 213.

31   MECW 24, p. 290.

32   MECW 45, p. 284.

33   Paden 2002 offers a similar, but alternative, taxonomy to divide up the various ways in which Marx might be thought to criticise the utopian socialists. Paden divides these into tactical, strategic, materialist, humanist and metaethical critiques. Loosely, the strategic, materialist and humanist critiques can be grouped under the first category, the tactical into the second, and the metaethical in the third.

ising them. This idea has probably received the most attention when it comes
to discussing Marx's critique of the utopians. Indeed, it is the version most
commonly offered by Marxists themselves. The argument suggests that Marx,
uniquely, is capable of demonstrating that his alternative (communism)
emerges organically from within capitalism. The growth of the proletariat as
a self-conscious, organised class, the development of the productive forces, the
increasingly crisis prone nature of capitalism, all point in a certain direction,
and Marx is merely following these pointers towards their obvious destination.
Marx certainly does make these sorts of criticisms.[34] He does think it a severe
deficiency, and rather silly, if a vision of the future cannot be demonstrated
as the product of the present. However, this is not his only, or arguably even
main, reason for rejecting the utopian method. Firstly, many utopians did offer
accounts of transition, use scientific methods, and base their visions in notions
of human nature – it was just that they did so on grounds that Marx found
implausible.[35] But this is a disagreement over facts, rather than over method.
Moreover, if this was his *only* difference with the utopians, then why did Marx
refrain from offering his own vision in any detail? If he was confident that communism was grounded in a plausible story of transition, he need not have done
so. He could have offered his own version of Utopia, down to the last detail.
The fact that he does not suggests that there was more to his criticism than the
question of transition.[36]

The second, stale, charge is similarly familiar. This is that the utopian approach is fundamentally out of date. Utopian speculation may once have had
value, but it is now worthless:

> The significance of Critical-Utopian Socialism and Communism bears an
> inverse relation to historical development. In proportion as the modern
> class struggle takes shape, this fantastic standing apart from the contest,
> these fantastic attacks on it lose all practical value and all theoretical jus-
> tification.[37]

This is because their visions now leave them out of step with the real movement. The working-class movement itself was growing, was tending towards a
confrontation with the bourgeoisie, and tending towards victory in that con-

---

34   See, for example, *First International and After*, pp. 261–3.
35   See Paden 2002, pp. 68–9.
36   Webb 2000, p. 31.
37   *Communist Manifesto*, p. 117.

flict. Anything that did not contribute directly to the struggle was (potentially at least) a sectarian distraction. The question of what the alternative is would fundamentally work itself out, perhaps because mankind only sets itself problems it can solve. The very fact that capitalism was coming under question showed that it was solvable.[38]

Note that this charge seems to encompass both the second and third categories of utopia I outlined above. It does not appear to discriminate between idle speculation and ideal speculation, between the consideration of provisional proposals and the construction of ideal models. Both, if Marx is correct, can be seen as distractions from the real movement. This particular angle of attack is commonly identified in accounts of Marx's critique of the utopians, but it is also the weakest, and so understandably does not convince many. Even if we accept, with Marx, that the workers' movement was inexorably moving towards something, with some basic awareness (vision) of what it is, this position is now harder to sustain.[39] The testing out of alternatives, in both thought and practice, seems a far more pressing concern for contemporary anti-capitalists, and far less obviously a distraction from the 'real action'.[40]

That said, there is perhaps a more sympathetic reading of Marx here. If Marx is read as saying that any old talk of alternatives is a distraction from the real movement, then it is he, not his opponents, who sounds like a dogmatist. But there is another way of taking what Marx is saying, which is that there is no *special role for theory* in designing alternatives. This is, perhaps, because the workers' movement is in fact full of alternatives. There is no special need for well-meaning philanthropists or philosophers to articulate alternatives, because the workers themselves argue over and address them every day. Here it is worth returning to the French workers described in *The Economic and Philosophical Manuscripts*. We might imagine that these beer halls abound with alternatives, both in terms of nascent, prefigural social relationships, and in actual, boozy discussion. Perhaps we should take Marx as saying not that *these* discussions detract from the real movement – they are the real movement. What detracts is experts who believe it is their special task to do so.

However, Marx does not merely stick at saying the utopian approach is out of date. He says it is reactionary. This goes further, suggesting that it is not merely irrelevant, but actively thwarts radical change. Here, I think, we should take Marx as being concerned especially with the third category of utopias I

---

38   See Paden 2002, pp. 72–5.
39   See Singer 1993, Leopold 2007.
40   Against this position, see Webb 2000, p. 158.

described above, the blueprint utopias. This is what Marx has most decisively in mind when criticising the utopians: the practice of building blueprints for future societies, and setting them up as plans to be built.

Marx's first concerns about these kinds of blueprints are epistemic. Marx believes that our ability to know the details of alternative societies are strictly limited. The evidence for this worry is most clear in Marx's criticism of Bray in the *Poverty of Philosophy*. Here Marx is concerned precisely that attempts to mentally reconstruct an alternative society end up merely reproducing elements of this society:

> Mr Bray does not see that this equalitarian relation, this corrective ideal that he would like to apply to the world is itself nothing but the reflection of the actual world; and that therefore it is totally impossible to reconstitute society on the basis of what is merely an embellished shadow of it. In proportion as this shadow takes on substance again, we perceive that this substance, far from being the transfiguration dreamt of, is the actual body of existing society.[41]

Returning to the metaphor of vision, the more you attempt to fill in the fine detail, the specific individuals and their everyday lives and social relations, the more you end up filling in gaps with features of existing society. Far from getting at the ideal society, you merely end up reproducing the old society in shadow.

A slightly different epistemic concern with blueprints is their tendency towards fixity. Ricoeur characterises this in terms of the shift from fiction to picture:

> [I]t may be that the specific disease of utopia is its perpetual shift from fiction to picture. The utopia ends by giving a picture of the fiction through models. Saint-Simon, for example, proposed that there be three houses of parliament, and he diagrammed the hierarchy of their rule. One chamber would be the house of invention, another the house of reflection or review, and the third the house of realisation or execution. Each house was composed of specific numbers or specific groups. The house of invention, for example, had three hundred members: two hundred engineers, fifty poets or other literary inventors, twenty-five painters, fifteen sculptors or architects, and ten musicians. This accuracy and this obsessive

---

41   MECW 6, p. 144. See also *Surveys from Exile*, pp. 122–3: '[F]undamentally [utopianism] only idealises the existing society, takes a picture of it free of shadows and aspires to assert its ideal picture against the reality of this society'.

relation to special configurations and symmetries is a common trait of written utopias. The utopia becomes a picture; time has stopped. The utopia has not started but rather has stopped before starting. Everything must comply with the model; there is no history after the institution of the model.[42]

Marx can be understood as being worried about something similar, that if a vision becomes a fixed picture it risks freezing a process of emancipation, rather than renewing it. As Evgeny Zamyatin put it, 'Utopia is always static'.[43] This risk of fixity might apply even to more provisional proposals, initially not intended as blueprints. The more detail included, the more likely a vision freezes.

However, these epistemic concerns are only part of the critique of utopian blueprints. Even independent of these problems, there is a second question relevant to self-emancipation.[44] This angle of criticism only emerges when we consider who is supposed to design the blueprint. The blueprint is, paradigmatically, the product of an individual thinker, with a claim to special knowledge of the ideal society. This thinker designs the blueprint, and relegates the role of everyone else to building it and living within it.[45]

In this context it is interesting that when the *Theses on Feuerbach* were first published after Marx's death (as an appendix to *Ludwig Feuerbach and the End of Classical German Philosophy*), Engels used the specific example of Robert Owen in order to gloss the third thesis (Engels's additions in italics):

---

42   Ricoeur 1986, p. 295.

43   Jacoby 2005, p. 35.

44   While the idea that the principle of self-emancipation formed a critique of the utopians is reasonably widespread among socialist activists (Draper 1971), attempts to develop, defend or criticise it in academic literature are scarce. Webb 2000 and Paden 2002 are clear exceptions to this.

45   This interpretation has strong affinities with what Paden calls, drawing on Cornel West, the metaethical criticism of the utopian socialists. This is that the mistake of the utopians was that they proposed first-order utopias, based on specific social arrangements, whereas the principle of proletarian self-determination demanded, in effect, second-order utopias 'that include a set of framework institutions to institutionalize this free and effective discursive process' (Paden 2002, p. 87). Ironically, this emphasis on utopia as framework suggests an affinity with Robert Nozick's conception of utopia (Nozick 1974, Part III). In some ways, the arguments offered in this section build on this critique. However, there are two reasons I avoid Paden's terminology here. Firstly, a 'second-order' utopia, if it is to be reasonably substantive, is still at least potentially subject to the same question of who gets to design it that can be asked of a first-order utopia. Secondly, I prefer to emphasise that this is not 'merely' a 'meta' question, but a practical question of how to do good political theory, and, therefore, good politics.

The materialist doctrine that men are products of circumstances and upbringing, *and that, therefore, changed men are products of other circumstances and changed upbringing*, forgets that it is men who change circumstances and that the educator must himself be educated. Hence, this doctrine is bound to divide society into two parts, one of which is superior to society (*in Robert Owen for example*).[46]

Now, it is not at all clear that in 1844 Marx did have Robert Owen in mind (see Chapter 2), but the fact that Engels felt that Owen was an example of what Marx describes here is important. It suggests that the 'who educates the educator' question that Marx poses there can be similarly posed towards the designers of blueprints. They too risk splitting society into two parts, the blueprint designers and the builders.[47]

So what, one might respond? If the blueprint builders have designed a perfect society, or at least the best one we can design, what is the problem with just getting on with building it and living within it? One answer is Marx's epistemic doubt that they can really access the best society. But another is that this approach appears to run counter to self-emancipation, specifically because it excludes the overwhelming majority from questions of institutional design. It gives us no say in the form of the society we are to live in.

To further illustrate what I think Marx is getting at here, it is useful to compare the utopian approach he is criticising with a prominent approach in contemporary political theory, generally known as ideal theory. Ideal theory sees the main role of political theory as being the construction of ideals, against which existing society can be compared, and then found wanting. This approach has been criticised on similar epistemic grounds to Marx's critique of utopians – as tending to ideologically reinforce existing society[48] – but here I am more interested in the process by which the ideals are designed.

Comparing Marx's opponents with these particular thinkers is likely to be controversial. After all, those most interested in ideal theory are liberal political philosophers in the late twentieth and early twenty-first centuries. These seem to be worlds away from Fourier, St. Simon and Owen. Nonetheless, I want to suggest there are some significant shared features, and an examination of the method and presuppositions of ideal theory can help better understand what

---

46   MECW 5, p. 7.

47   For more on the relationship between utopianism and sectarianism, see Draper, 1990, Chapter 1.

48   See, e.g., Finlayson 2015, Young 1990, Mills 2005, Geuss 2008.

concerns Marx about approaches that see developing a blueprint as a necessary and fundamental stage of political critique and transformation. Moreover, the widespread influence of ideal theory in contemporary political theory suggests (at least if this comparison is valid) that this remains a live debate. Indeed, there is a strong case for saying that Marx's critique applies better to these thinkers than to many contemporary thinkers who are happy to embrace the term utopia, but remain suspicious of blueprints.[49]

Ideal theory is an approach that sees the construction of ideals as a priority. The methodology here involves reflecting on the ideal arrangements of society, deriving certain principles that would operate in that society, and then applying those principles as standards by which to judge society as it actually is. The ideal thus provides the intellectual resources that enable you to do political critique. A paradigmatic example of this approach can be found in Rawls's *A Theory of Justice*:

> A complete conception defining principles for all the virtues of the basic structure, together with their respective weights when they conflict, is more than a conception of justice; it is a social ideal. The principles of justice are but a part, although perhaps the most important part of such a conception. A social ideal in turn is connected with a conception of society, a vision of the way in which the aims and purposes of social cooperation are to be understood ... Fully to understand a conception of justice we must make explicit the conception of social cooperation from which it derives.[50]

Here Rawls is clear that there are two key features of his model of criticism, (1) the ideal vision, and (2) the principles that are associated with it. These principles are more or less universal, and are conceived of as generally ordering society in a 'just' manner. Having established these principles based on an ideal conception of society, current society is then found wanting in one way or another (or, as some interpret Rawls to suggest, happily vindicated).

It is then, from this position, possible to generate certain kinds of recommendations. Ideal theorists diverge on the character of these recommendations. For some, these recommendations are to be understood as just as ideal

---

49   Though not my main purpose, this also might give some reasons to be sceptical of attempts to combine or supplement Marxism with liberal theories of justice that are deeply influenced by ideal theory. See, for example, Callinicos 2006, Reiman 2012.

50   Rawls 1999, p. 9.

as the vision itself, while for others, the ideal vision is used as the basis for then generating non-ideal recommendations. Nonetheless, where these approaches agree is on the central and ineliminable role of the ideal vision in their project. Whatever the character of the recommendations, they only make sense against the background of an ideal vision of society – as Simmons puts it:

> A good policy in nonideal theory is good only as transitionally just – that is, only as a morally permissible part of a feasible overall program to achieve perfect justice, as a policy that puts us in an improved position to reach that ultimate goal. And good policies are good not relative to the elimination of any particular, targeted injustices, but only relative to the integrated goal of eliminating all injustice.[51]

How reasonable is it to compare this to the utopian method that Marx criticises? Defenders of ideal theory will certainly bridle at the idea. To the extent that these emerge from an Anglo-American liberal tradition they appear to be sharply at odds with the utopian tradition, and influenced by some of its biggest critics. Many will respond that it is a mistake to conceive of the ideal as something to be built. Rather, they are to function as something closer to regulative ideals, to which society must aspire but never expect to reach.[52] Thus rather than demand the building of the ideal society, they merely insist that society be adjusted towards it in a piecemeal fashion. There is, however, fairly substantive disagreement on this position within ideal theorists. Those most influenced by Rawls do, in fact, follow him in speaking of ideal theory as 'realistically utopian: that is, as probing the limits of practicable political possibility'.[53] In any case, even where the ideal is not intended to be a real possibility, it is still assumed to be both available to and necessary for political theory. On the other hand, it might be objected that I have simply confused two senses of ideal – the ideal as product of reflection, and the ideal as 'the best'. This will not do. The ideal theorists' models are not merely the product of ideals, they also make a claim to be the *best*. It is true they are not oceans of lemonade or fantastical science fiction worlds, but they are ideal constructions designed to think about what the best circumstances would be.

The core feature shared by these two different traditions is that described by Engels in the quotation above. A new and more perfect system of social order is evolved out of the human brain, and imposed upon society by propaganda. Sig-

---

51   Simmons 2010, p. 22.

52   These thinkers generally follow Cohen (see e.g. Cohen 2008, Chapter 6) in rejecting that such ideals must necessarily be fact-sensitive.

53   Rawls 1999, p. 4 See also Simmons 2010, and Valentini 2009.

nificantly, this more perfect system is *prior to* and *necessary for* social change. Hendrix distinguishes between two kinds of priority of the ideal, temporal and logical.[54] To assert the logical priority of the ideal is to simply say that in order to do political theory there must be an ideal, but that we needn't know what that ideal is. The ideal theory is analogous to unified field theory in physics – there must be one, but we do not know what it is, and we can do more specific scientific inquiry without it.[55] To assert the temporal priority, on the other hand, is to assert that developing the ideal must come first in a temporal sequence. Before we know what the ideal is, we cannot do political theory.

Considering the temporal priority helps us close in on Marx's worry. The temporal priority of the ideal suggests something like the following: The ideal is designed, through reflection and insight; then it is compared to reality; then recommendations are developed on the basis of it. In other words actual political activity, campaigns, social movements, political programmes, are understood to act in light of the ideal, coming after it, and moving towards it. In this sense, the ideal can be seen as pre-political, a prerequisite for politics, rather than political itself.

But if this is the case, the design of the ideal itself will necessary exclude most political actors. Note that this is built into the structure of the ideal building. If the ideal is necessary for politics, it cannot come about through politics. It is important to stress here too that it is an *ideal*, not a provisional, heuristic model, subject to revision and reconsideration. It is a claim about the features the good society would embody. We thus start to see why the *Theses on Feuerbach* are relevant here. In institutionalising the division of labour between those who design the ideal and those who are to live in and build it, this method necessarily excludes people who are to live in that society from its institutional design. And this is a problem for Marx, precisely because the construction of an alternative society must be the act of those who are going to live in it. If these people are denied active participation in the design of these institutions, then this denies both an important dimension of freedom itself, and vital practical experience in preparing them for democratic self-determination.

To understand why this is such a problem, we should look to the kinds of things that an ideal has to contain if it is to function properly as the basis for political critique. It has to have a fairly comprehensive vision of the structures of society. To take a paradigmatic example, in Rawls it contains the institutions of private property and the family. The more of these sorts of questions that

---

54   Hendrix 2012.
55   Hendrix 2012, p. 134.

are placed in the ideal, rather than precisely being *up for debate*, the narrower the scope becomes for actual participation in design. In this structure, as Lorna Finlayson suggests,

> the political philosopher stands to people at large in the same relation as a stranger who, entirely unsolicited, drew up detailed blueprints for a suggested improvement to your home ... Their response to a shout of 'It's not up to you!' is to draw up another proposal, this time a proposal as to the decision-making procedures and distribution of authority that should obtain among members of your family when it comes to matters of home improvement. You would say, 'You really don't get it? *It's not up to you*'.[56]

What this suggests is that the method of ideal theory, and of at least the versions of utopianism that share its assumptions about the priority of the ideal and the role of theory in developing it, is structurally in tension with a commitment to self-emancipation. This is something, I argue, that Marx recognised; and it explains his hostility to ideal theories and his reticence to offer his own blueprints. As Webb puts it:

> [The principle of proletarian self-determination] informed pretty much everything Marx ever said about the formal organisation of communism. More importantly, perhaps, the same principle forced Marx to remain silent when it came to conceptualising the future far more often than it prompted him to describe it. Whilst, that is, the principle led him to proclaim that the proletariat would require a national plan to regulate production and thus bring it under their conscious control, it was also this principle which prevented him from saying anything about what this would actually involve.[57]

Two further points are worth making about this criticism. Firstly, this problem is particularly acute for Marx because of the breadth of his conception of democratic self-management. At the core of this is the question of our attitudes to the central institutions of society – for Marx, democratic control had to go 'all the way down', and thus the 'it's not up to you' charge was one that he felt particularly acutely. Secondly, however, to the extent that this tension is built into the very method of ideal theory, even more limited accounts of self-determination

---

56   Finlayson 2015, p. 66.
57   Webb 2000, pp. 68–9.

ought to be wary of it.[58] Indeed, a great deal of contemporary liberal political theory combines the methodology of ideal theory with a substantive commitment to freedom as self-determination or autonomy. If these two poles turn out to be in tension, it is something that should not merely interest Marxists.

4   Utopia Negativa

Those, then, are Marx's reasons for seeking to maintain communism at the level of vision, refusing to fill in its gaps and specify its institutions in the form of blueprints. They are reasons intimately connected to a commitment to self-emancipation, and they are, in my opinion, rather good ones. However, many of those who accept at least the broad outlines of this critique will likely respond that, despite all this, the development of blueprints remains the lesser evil. This is because, for either conceptual or practical reasons, such blueprints are necessary for a radical critique of capitalism. For the conceptual critics, critique without such blueprints is at best blind and at worst incoherent. For the practical critics, the experience of the Soviet Union and the absence of any systemic alternative or hegemonic counter-movement to capitalism means that even if Marx's hostility to blueprints was once justified, it can no longer be. Rather, such blueprints become an urgent necessity. In this section, I will argue against both positions, though perhaps less forcefully against the latter. Our world is crying out for alternatives; we still should not think of these as blueprints.

4.1   *Recognising the Bad*

The first set of worries I will address are conceptual ones. These suggest that there is something flatly incoherent about criticising capitalism without a reasonably detailed alternative in mind, such that to do so involves some sort of fundamental contradiction or intellectual failing. For example, Berki remarks that

> It would not only be foolish but totally meaningless to criticise 'ruthlessly' if you didn't know why you were doing it, and you could not have a clear

---

58   See, for example, Dworkin 1988, p. 10, for whom what matters is a shared practice of justification, or Christman 2009, pp. 239–40, for whom autonomous agents should not be 'understandably alienated' from their institutions and principles. These are weaker than Marx's requirements for democratic control, but they may still fall foul of the worry, depending, of course, about whether we see the opportunity (or not) to participate in design as a necessary feature of justification or understandable alienation.

conception of your grounds or reasons, unless you had *some* notion of that which your 'ruthless criticism' – perhaps indirectly – is intended to help come into being. Marx knows as well as any sane person that you cannot criticise groundlessly and that it is incoherent to talk about a 'movement' that doesn't go anywhere, has no intelligible destination, whose motion is comparable to that of a person stamping the ground desperately in front of an 'Engaged' lavatory door.[59]

This idea that one cannot criticise groundlessly, and that these grounds are necessarily connected to the alternative you seek to build, is intuitively powerful. However, it is unclear precisely what it is supposed to involve. One possibility is the demand that a good political criticism must be *constructive*, i.e. that as well as knocking down what exists it should always also offer an alternative that is possibly better (and thus, presumably, requires a degree of detail to determine that it is so). It is worth noting, however, that this standard is not applied to other spheres of criticism.[60] No one thinks pointing out a logical flaw in an argument is invalid or incoherent if no better argument is offered. Even in many ethical questions this is not the case: 'For example, when faced with a group of youths who are pouring petrol over a cat and are about to set it on fire, I do not need to make positive suggestions about how they could spend their afternoon in order to intervene and to criticise them for what they are about to do'.[61] Moreover, as Finlayson argues, the way in which this different standard is applied in political criticism often has a pernicious ideological function, since the expectations of what a real, possible, or practical alternative is, is often bound up precisely with the standards of existing society. There can thus be something importantly liberating about not offering an alternative, and 'merely' ruthlessly criticising.[62]

However, rather than being a question of constructiveness, this could be a point about recognition. Without an awareness of a good alternative, we simply have no capacity to recognise or be motivated by society's existing wrongs. On

---

59   Berki 1983, p. 41.
60   See Finlayson 2015, Freyenhagen 2013.
61   Freyenhagen 2013, p. 218.
62   See also Ollman 2005: '[utopianism], though it addresses *our* ideal future, carries out the debate on *their* terrain. Instead of forcing capitalists and their "paid hirelings" to defend what is intolerable and unnecessary in present-day society, it allows them to sit back and pick holes in whatever sounds untidy or unlikely in our hopes for the future. It does capitalists the immense favour of letting them go on the offensive, rhetorically speaking'.

this assumption, without offering us a more detailed picture of the good society, Marx gives us no basis to recognise or be motivated by the badness of capitalism. However, this too is dubious. Demonstrating this involves a defence of what Freyenhagen has called 'epistemic negativism', the claim that knowledge of what is bad is not dependent on knowledge of what is good, and 'meta-ethical negativism', that we can account for the normative force of the bad without invoking what is good.[63] To make the case for this I will offer two examples of modes of criticism which (at least apparently) do not depend on appeal to what a good alternative might look like. I do not suggest that these are the only ways of making such an argument. However, I suggest that they are each reasonable, and in fact fairly everyday ways of doing so, with nothing particularly mysterious about them.

The first might broadly be understood as a claim about *comparative ills*. Richard Wilkinson and Kate Pickett's book *The Spirit Level* makes a powerful case for the claim that social inequality is bad for human beings. This is a substantive claim about what is bad, which enables us to criticise societies which are more unequal. However, these conclusions are reached not by the description of an ideal society in which people are equal, but by *the comparison of existing societies which are more or less equal* and identifying that there is a strong correlation between inequality and a wide range of physical, mental and social ills:

> It has been known for some years that poor health and violence are more common in unequal societies. However, in the course of our research we became aware that almost all problems which are more common at the bottom of the social ladder are more common in more unequal societies. It is not just ill-health and violence, but also ... a host of other social problems. Almost all of them contribute to the widespread concern that modern societies are, despite their affluence, social failures.[64]

This conclusion is reached through comparison. Countries like Sweden and Japan are more equal, and suffer from fewer of the problems they identify than those, like the USA and UK, with vast inequalities.

There are two points to stress about this argument. Firstly, that the substantive claim that inequality is bad for us is not generated by comparison with an ideal, hypothetical society, but with a comparison between *existing* soci-

---

63   Freyenhagen 2013, pp. 209–31.
64   Wilkinson & Pickett 2009, p. 18.

eties, none of which is presented as perfectly equal or just, with reference to specific bads. Secondly, and more significantly, this claim is not dependent on the *endorsement* of those actually existing alternatives as a model. In the recommendations they offer towards achieving greater equality Wilkinson and Pickett do not recommend that the UK and the USA 'become exactly like Japan and Sweden', and for good reason. Whilst these societies are more equal, there are other ways in which we might not want to be like them. Most notably, both countries have high rates of suicide, whilst Japan has gender inequalities which appear deeply problematic. Moreover, the way in which equality is achieved in these countries is very different – on the one hand through state interference, on the other through entrenched cultural practices. The strategy which Wilkinson and Picket in fact recommend to achieve greater equality – supporting worker-owned companies – is different again.

At no stage in this process is a model of an ideal alternative proposed or assumed. Rather, there is a comparison between a range of different actually existing but imperfect societies, through which it is possible to identify and isolate a particular shared negative feature – inequality – and suggest that strategies are pursued to avoid it. None of this requires a *specific* alternative which is either hypothetical or aspired to.[65]

The second possibility for criticising without an alternative is criticising with reference to an archetypal bad. The idea here is that something is condemned because of the features it shares with something which is indisputably bad. You see an idea of this sort in Adorno's famous new categorical imperative, to arrange human thought and action so that 'Auschwitz will not repeat itself, [that] nothing similar will happen'.[66] But this kind of argument is hardly the preserve of critical theorists. Consider the following passage from Virginia Woolf:

> [The Society of Outsiders] will dispense with personal distinctions – medals, ribbons, badges, hoods, gowns – not from any dislike of personal adornment, but because of the obvious effect of such distinctions to constrict, to stereotype and to destroy. Here, as so often, the example of the Fascist States is at hand to instruct us – for if we have no example of what we wish to be, we have, what is perhaps equally valuable, a daily and illuminating example of what we do not wish to be. With the example then, that they give us of the power of medals, symbols, orders and even, it

---

65   See Sen 2009, pp. 87–113 for an alternative defence of comparative criticism.
66   Adorno 1973, p. 366.

would seem, of decorated ink-pots to hypnotize the human mind, it must be our aim not to submit ourselves to such hypnotism.[67]

The Society of Outsiders which Woolf recommends will eschew medals and distinctions precisely because of the way in which they have seen them used in Fascist societies. The Fascist state is employed precisely in this passage as a kind of archetypal bad. We don't know what the society we want will look like, but we know what it *won't* look like.

This archetypal bad can help criticism in two ways. Firstly, in the sense Adorno uses it, it gives us something to orient *away from*, which can sometimes be just as useful as having something to orient towards. Secondly, like with Woolf's medals and ribbons, to the extent that we can identify shared features between this archetypal bad and our own societies, it gives us reasons to condemn those features. As I will illustrate in the next chapter, Marx himself makes frequent use of this strategy when he compares capitalism to earlier forms of class society, especially slavery. These reasons are *defeasible* reasons, since it is often not sufficient to point to such shared features in order to condemn them. They may have other redeeming qualities. Nonetheless, such a comparison does give *a* reason to condemn, and potentially a very powerful one.

On this line of thought there are some things that are so clearly, transparently worthy of condemnation that to give reasons or an alternative is not only unnecessary, but may even be monstrous in itself. The thought is that anyone who asks you to give reasons why, for example, the Holocaust or torture is bad, has completely misunderstood just how bad they are. Society needs to be completely transformed, and the very fact that you can't see it only demonstrates how much this is the case. As the Manic Street Preachers put it, 'if you need an explanation, then everything must go'. This is the sort of reaction that ought to be generated in response to a question like 'But what's the alternative to Auschwitz?' If you cannot see with your own eyes that Auschwitz is monstrous, then no amount of argument or ideal alternatives seems likely to help. This is one of the thoughts evoked by Brecht's poem 'The Buddha's Parable of the Burning House':

Lately I saw a house. It was burning. The flame
Licked at its roof. I went up close and observed
That there were people still inside. I entered the doorway and called

---

Out to them that the roof was ablaze, so exhorting them
To leave at once. But those people
Seemed in no hurry. One of them,
While the heat was already scorching his eyebrows,
Asked me what it was like outside, whether there was
Another house for them, and more of this kind. Without answering
I went out again. These people here, I thought,
Must burn to death before they stop asking questions.
And truly friends,
Whoever does not yet feel such heat in the floor that he'll gladly
Exchange it for any other, rather than stay, to that man
I have nothing to say.

4.2   *Filling in the Gaps*

For many, though, the most significant objections to Marx's anti-utopianism are not conceptual but practical. It is not about whether it is conceptually possible to criticise, but about whether, in fact, such criticisms are capable of motivating and guiding political action. Thus Stemplowska suggests that:

> [O]ne of the roles of normative theory is to recommend more or less straightforwardly achievable change in the circumstances we find ourselves in, but another is to judge what we have already achieved against a final landmark of where we ought to be. Indeed, being concerned with the latter is part and parcel of accepting that there are good reasons for a given society to change in the first place.[68]

The Brecht poem offers a partial, but not entirely adequate response to this. For some, at some periods of history, in some locations, this is not a question that requires a detailed alternative. It is akin to leaping from a burning house, and if the alternative is unspecified then so be it. Thus motivation needn't only come from an orientation towards the good, but can also involve moving away from the bad. This suggests that a detailed alternative is not always necessary, rather we require the recognition that things are bad and the expectation that they could be better – even in the very limited sense of no longer being on fire!

Yet this is not a complete answer, since we are not always in such dire straits that a leap into the unknown is enough. Even if in terrible circumstances we

---

68   Stemplowska 2008, p. 332.

might be motivated without much sense of the alternative, under more toler-
able, more 'normal' circumstances we will require more. Daniel Singer asks if

> it is still possible to build such projections after the terrible Soviet exper-
> iment and the dramatic collapse of great expectations? Yes and no. In a
> sense, a project is now more indispensable than ever. After all that has
> happened, people may still be driven by their conditions to rebel, but they
> will not enter a coherent movement, will not join a potentially hegemonic
> bloc capable of long term action without knowing the goal and the route
> to be travelled, the end and the means.[69]

Thus, on this account, even if people are motivated by initial reactions to negative conditions, they must be presented with a coherent vision of an alternative
if they are to be won to any kind of long-term political project.

It is important to be clear what the specifics of this criticism are. As I suggest above, Marx is particularly concerned with the construction of blueprints
and ideals. This, of course, does leave room for other kinds of alternatives to
be discussed – namely alternatives that do not aspire to the status of blueprints or ideals. There are many ways of considering how society could be
different that do not involve detailed plans. For one thing, if we return to
Ricoeur's characterisation of the risk of slipping from fiction to picture, perhaps the solution may be to stay at the level of fiction. Perhaps fiction is a
better medium for the consideration of alternatives than political treatises.
Moreover, as Webb observes, people think about alternatives in a host of different ways:

> I think it almost self-evident to say that the ways in which people ima-
> gine improvements being made to their lives are almost never 'utopian'.
> Most people think in terms of winning the lottery, or in terms of sexual
> conquests, and rarely in terms of lucid descriptions of imaginary states.
> And yet writers keep claiming that utopias are comparable to dreams;
> that they embody our hopes, desires and aspirations in much the same
> way. This then leads critics ... into the false belief that those who oppose
> utopianism are somehow opposed to all forms of hope and are secretly
> plotting some wild scheme to eradicate dreams from the world.[70]

---

69   Singer 1993, p. 253.
70   Webb 2000, p. 166.

Another, very different way of talking about how society might be different is through the proleptic proposals discussed in Chapter 2, especially those that take the form of *demands*. These are not ideals, or complete pictures of society; rather they propose narrowly specific ways in which the society might be different. Moreover, they gain their strength precisely because of the way in which they remain neutral about these 'big' questions. It is possible for people with diverse views about what an ideal society will look like to 'get behind' a specific demand. But even these limited demands are a way of considering how society might be different, and moreover they have a logic of their own – in other words, they can overspill their initial content, and provide new questions and challenges. As discussed in Chapter 2, one of the ways in which such demands or proposals can thwart self-emancipation is through being proposed in the wrong spirit – i.e., in a way which usurps the agency of the workers themselves – but another is in their specific content, through being so specific that a proposal is incapable of motivating large numbers of people. In this sense, content can determine form, turning what appears to be a provisional proposal into a fixed blueprint.[71]

Moreover, for all that Marx's vision of communism is limited, it does suggest one very specific way in which things can be better: The abolition of the capitalist mode of production and its replacement by democratic control. Berki suggests that such a formal, procedure-focused account cannot hope to either motivate or guide us:

> what we are asked to believe is that it is adequate to define communism as mere external social organisation (of production and intercourse) and that it is enough to refer to the substantive values which this organisation is intended to foster merely in terms of 'satisfaction of needs' and 'free development' ... Nothing in the first place follows at all from the particular kind of social organisation as to the quality of human relationships and life in general that it can necessarily be said to engender and maintain ... Marx could never cogently argue that this communist society ('organisation' only!) will be *better* in any definite sense – ethical, existential, eudaimonic – than capitalist society.[72]

---

71   I will return to the question of demands in Chapter 7; however, it is worth noting at this
       point that, after a period in which demands were thoroughly out of fashion in the anti-
       capitalist movement because they appeared to legitimise the powerful, new attention is
       being paid to this question.

72   Berki 1983, p. 73.

This, however, assumes that these formal features – free development, democratic control, etc. – are completely devoid of ethical content. It is true that they make few substantive claims about 'the good life', or the kinds of truly human relationship that will operate within these formal structures. However, just because this vision is formal does not mean that it is normatively insignificant. A more free society is better than a less free one, and social arrangements that encourage freedom are preferable to ones that don't.

However, Berki's question about more substantive values is one that deserves an answer. While Marx is entitled to say that a purely formal account of communism is still, to this extent, better, it still contains important gaps when it comes to how we might build society itself. Even if we accept that it is legitimate to criticise capitalism, and that people will be motivated to attempt an alternative, we still do not know what they should do to build it. Or rather, we do not know enough. Most of what we know takes the form of either negative proposals – abolish this, overthrow that – or piecemeal proposals. We do not know what positive values will fill this new world, or what kind of people will inhabit it, much less the kinds of norms that will regulate their behaviour. But if we do not know that, how are we able to link these proposals into a coherent political project? We may not need to know the final destination now, but we need to at least know the direction of travel, and have a sense that we are getting *closer* to something.

The answer, at least the only one apparently available to Marx, is that the vision can only take shape as part of the movement itself. A sense of how this might work is offered by Levitas, for whom utopia is not a blueprint, but a method. This method can be broken down into three modes. Firstly, there is the archaeological mode, which involves 'piecing together the images of the good society that are embedded in political programmes and social and economic policies'.[73] This is premised on the idea that 'most political positions contain implicit images of the good society and views of how people are and should be, the latter often elided in statements about human nature'.[74] It is possible

---

73   Levitas 2013, p. 154.
74   There are some affinities between this argument and Hendrix's claim that we should accept the logical priority of the ideal while eschewing its temporal priority. Both share the idea that an implicit conception of the good underpins political practice, but that this should be approached at best indirectly, and not specified prior to engaging in politics. However, to the extent that Hendrix remains in the territory of 'the ideal' he suggests a unitary conception, while Levitas's approach is open to multiple, more context-specific ideas. More generally, Levitas's metaphor of archaeologist and architect seem closer (to me at least) to the work of clarifying a good society than Hendrix's scientists beavering away at a unified field theory.

to excavate these implicit images from political movements, slogans and campaigns. Following from this is the ontological mode, which focuses on 'what kind of people particular societies develop and encourage. What is understood as human flourishing, what capabilities are valued, encouraged and genuinely enabled, or blocked and suppressed, by specific existing or potential social arrangements'.[75] Finally, bridging this, is the architectural mode, 'the imagination of potential alternative scenarios for the future, acknowledging the assumptions about and consequences for the people who might inhabit them'.[76]

This dynamic of archaeology, ontology, architecture operates in the opposite direction from the classic blueprint utopias. It does not move from the ideal to the actual, but from actual political movements to the construction of alternatives, starting with society as it is. Moreover, the analogy with archaeology stresses both the fragmentary quality and the *effort* that goes into finding and identifying these implicit images. As Freyenhagen stresses, identifying the good society is not merely about holding a mirror up to the bad.[77] It requires excavation, with oddly shaped pieces that leave gaps when re-assembled. Similarly, calling the final phase architectural is intended to imply a degree of craft or art, where we are confronted with the materials we have, rather than the materials we want.[78] It is 'less and more than a model or blueprint: Less, in being a provisional hypothesis about how society might be, offered as part of a dialogue, neither intending nor constituting a forecast, recognizing itself as in part a present future. More, in inviting both reader and writer to imagine'.[79]

But the emphasis on archaeology and architecture imply something else. First of all, there has to be something to excavate and reconstruct. This method can thus be seen as *political* in the way that I described ideal theory as *pre*-political. While ideal theory sees the ideal as a precursor to politics, politics itself is a precursor to Levitas' method. It needs to be done in close attention to social movements as they actually are. Moreover, sometimes there will be more material than others. Sometimes political movements will throw up a vast array of ideas and practices to be examined, considered, dusted off and fitted

---

75   Levitas 2013, p. 177.

76   Levitas 2013, p. 154.

77   See Freyenhagen 2013, pp. 214–20 and Chapter 6 of this book.

78   Both of these metaphors chime with Tomba's reading of the role of the historical materialist, who is represented as an archaeologist excavating geological layers to 'show the not-yet that has remained encapsulated in the already-been' (Tomba, 2013, p. 176) and as a painter, painting with the palette of colours that flash up in moments of historical transition and crisis (Tomba, 2013, p. 64).

79   Levitas 2013, p. 199.

together to form a guiding vision for the future, and sometimes there will be nothing much to say. Any vision of an alternative, its degree of detail and specificity, will be dependent on the strength, creativity and confidence of those movements.

This suggests a clear alternative to the blueprint utopian method. It begins with the wrongs of society, and the reaction of people to those wrongs. It places emphasis on the hope (though not necessarily blind optimism) that things can be better, and on encouraging that hope. Part of this involves developing arguments that link the particular ills to specific features of society – to identify that they are not historically necessary, and in fact could be overcome. Finally, it involves close participation with those movements that arise to challenge these ills in order to develop and draw out possible visions of that better future. This, I suggest, is precisely how Marx intended to proceed, and I think it is not only defensible, but far closer to the process of actual politics than any blueprint or ideal approach. It is a process that begins by identifying negative features of society (social bads) and people's reactions to them. In the next two chapters I turn more directly to the substantive bads involved in capitalism, and how they can be incorporated into this negative approach, forming the starting point for both criticism and articulating alternatives.

CHAPTER 5

Exploitation, Justice and Freedom

The essence of exploitation is not that the working wage represents only a part of the value of the newly created product but that the surplus is taken away from the worker by force and that the process of capital accumulation is alien to his interests, while the unproductive sectors serve to maintain and strengthen the role of the bureaucracy (or bourgeoisie) over production and over society, and thus in the first place, over the labour and social life of the working class.

JACEK KUROŃ and KAROL MODZELEWSKI, 'Open Letter to the Party', 1965[1]

∴

1   Introduction

Exploitation has become one of the most debated and argued over concepts in Marx's work. Indeed, there are almost as many interpretations of exploitation as there are Marxists. As a concept, exploitation goes right to the heart of both Marx's normative and economic critiques of capitalism. It is the central wrong done to the working class in capitalist production, the wrong on which capitalism is founded, *and* it is the key to explaining both the source of profit in capitalism and how the capitalist class emerges as the dominant class in terms of both wealth and power. These two dimensions often become merged, such that people think defeating the economic component (through, for example, debunking the labour theory of value) is sufficient to render irrelevant the normative component, and vice versa. In what follows, I focus on the normative component. I offer an interpretation of exploitation as a wrong suffered by the working class in wage-labour, which gives reason and motivation for them to resist it. Moreover, I suggest that this interpretation is compatible with the approach suggested in the previous chapter, in which it is possible to identify wrongs without references to substantive goods, and use the responses to these wrongs as part of a process of clarifying and developing an alternative to them.

---

1   Kuroń & Modzelewski 1982, pp. 72–3.

Marx argues that capitalism is a system of exploitation in which the capitalist class profits from the labour of the working class, by paying it less than the value it creates in the production process. The capitalist is able to do this because they purchase the labour-power of the worker, and in doing so are able to control the entire labour process, in order to produce as much value as possible. Moreover, while the worker is free to sell their labour-power to whomever they choose, they must sell it to some capitalist, since they have no other means of meeting their needs. The worker 'is compelled by social conditions to sell the whole of his active life, his very capacity for labour, in return for the price of his customary means of subsistence, to sell his birthright for a mess of pottage'. However, this compulsion takes the form of a 'voluntary agreement' (though it takes centuries to get to this point), and, just as importantly, an equal exchange. This is because what the capitalist buys is labour-power, not a particular quantity of labour, and the capitalist buys it at its value, since the value of labour power is not to be found in what it produces, but in what is required to produce it, i.e. the wages necessary for the worker to live and continue to be able to function. Thus, the sale of labour-power, which is the central transaction on which capitalism is based, is an equal exchange, which is 'a piece of good luck for the buyer, but by no means an injustice towards the seller'.[2]

It is important to clarify what is meant by focusing on exploitation as a normative bad. Firstly, it is to say that Marx believes capitalist exploitation involves doing a wrong to the worker – indeed, it is a wrong on which the entire system is founded. Some interpreters prefer to see exploitation as a purely descriptive concept, only of interest to economic theory. For some of these thinkers, we ought to look elsewhere in Marx for the moral resources to criticise capitalism, perhaps to alienation (the subject of the next chapter). For others, this is consistent with Marx's general scepticism towards ideas of morality and ethics – any reasons to condemn capitalism come from its inefficiency or crisis-prone nature, rather than strictly moral considerations. Certainly, there are some reasons to be sympathetic to this idea. One is Marx's own assertion that capitalist exchange is voluntary and equal, referenced above. Another is that the first appearance of the word exploitation in *Capital* gives an entirely technical, economic definition: 'The rate of surplus-value is therefore an exact expression for the degree of exploitation of labour-power by capital, or of the worker by the capitalist'.[3]

---

2 *Capital Vol. 1*, p. 301.
3 *Capital Vol. 1*, p. 326.

However, when looking at the way in which Marx uses the term exploitation more broadly, it becomes difficult to maintain this interpretation. It is true that the language of exploitation (*Ausbeutung*) begins to appear in Marx's work in the *Economic and Philosophical Manuscripts* at precisely the point where he becomes interested in political economy. Here, however, it does not have this precise technical definition. Rather, it appears to have a fairly ordinary-language meaning, or at the very least it is taken for granted: landlords exploit peasants, and capitalists exploit workers. In the *Condition of the Working Class in England* Engels uses it in a similar sense.[4] It also occurs in the everyday sense of using or utilising. In the *German Ideology*, the words *Exploitation* and *exploitieren* almost entirely replace the German word *Ausbeutung*, and appear frequently, in a number of contexts.[5] In particular, there is a criticism of Stirner's treatment of utility, which Marx characterises as a 'theory of mutual exploitation':[6]

> The verbal masquerade only has meaning when it is the unconscious or deliberate expression of an actual masquerade. In this case, the utility relation has a quite definite meaning, namely that I derive benefit for myself by doing harm to someone else (*exploitation de l'homme par l'homme*).[7]

All of this gives the impression that Marx is familiar with a fairly everyday usage of the idea of exploitation, as using something or someone in a certain way to gain advantage, and expected people to be familiar with the usage, and, moreover, with the idea that exploiting someone was, in general, a bad thing that involves doing a wrong.

This suggests a problem with attempting to separate Marx's notion of exploitation from the everyday. There is a tendency in some of the literature on this subject to suggest that there is 'Marxist exploitation' and 'everyday exploitation', and that these are completely distinct senses. For example, Richard Arneson writes: 'Quite obviously exploitation in the Marxian technical sense does not imply exploitation in the ordinary evaluatively charged sense of the

---

4   See, for example, MECW 4, pp. 498–500 and 506–7.
5   Both terms appear in *Capital*. The rate of exploitation is *Exploitationsgrad*, but later Marx talks about the antagonism between *der ausbeuter und dem Rohmaterial seiner Ausbeutung* (see Section 3 of this chapter).
6   *German Ideology*, pp. 431–8.
7   *German Ideology*, p. 433.

term. (In this ordinary sense, exploitation involves mistreatment.)'[8] However, this seems to me to be a flawed approach. As I show below, Marx denounces capitalist exploitation in part by comparing it to other forms of exploitation. He uses all sorts of normatively laden terms to describe exploitation under capitalism. At least part of what he is doing is appealing to our intuitive conceptions of exploitation to demonstrate that capitalism is a particular form of it. It is clear that some kind of condemnation is involved in Marx's account of exploitation. To say that x exploits y is to *already say* that there is some sort of taking advantage which is beneficial to the exploiter and detrimental to the exploited, and that this is involved in the *relationship itself*. Moreover, there are clear parallels between Marx's sense and the everyday sense.[9] For example, in discussing exploitation Marx is referring to the *use* of others. One of the things that is meant by saying that capitalists exploit workers (and even more clearly when slave-owners exploit slaves) is that the capitalist *uses* the worker, and even more crucially uses their labour (or labour power).

This suggests that any understanding of Marxist exploitation ought to at least have some affinity with the way in which we talk about exploitation in everyday situations, and ought to accord with at least some of our intuitions about what is wrong with exploitation more generally. Moreover, it ought to be capable of properly capturing the phenomenon of exploitation as we experience it, of accurately describing what we think is going on in situations of exploitation.

It is also worth making a point about economics, and about the labour theory of value. Because my interpretation of exploitation focuses on domination and taking advantage, it is formally independent of that theory. I am in no particular rush to abandon the labour theory of value, but this account of exploitation does not depend on it. Moreover, there is at least one good reason for not connecting the wrongness of exploitation too closely to the labour theory of value. For Marx, the rate of surplus-value is a precise expression of the degree of exploitation, but it seems very unlikely that this means that the more surplus-value is acquired the *worse* the exploitation is, at least if this is to be the sole measure. This is because on this measure some workers with the best pay and conditions – software engineers, say, or workers in a high-tech engineering or chemical plant in Switzerland – become the most exploited. It does not seem correct to say that they therefore suffer the *worst* exploitation. This is not to say that this measure is irrelevant – there are all sorts of ways in which it can

8   Arneson 1981, p. 203 See also Elster 1985, pp. 166–8.
9   See Wood 2004, pp. 242–6.

be seen as important (in economic theory, in questions of which workers have more strategic power etc.), but it is not all there is to exploitation.

2   Exploitation and Justice

Part of the reason for the depth of controversy about exploitation is how close it lies to the interpretive debate about Marx and justice. This debate, the cause of a great deal of spilled ink, has its roots in Marx's apparent inconsistencies towards the wage relationship under capitalism.[10] Marx both denounces it and appears to say it is perfectly just. Two passages are particularly relevant here. The first is the transition between Chapters 7 and 8 of *Capital Vol. 1*, in which Marx invited us to shift our focus from the sphere of exchange to the sphere of production. In the sphere of exchange, the capitalist and worker are equals, and no injustice is done – it is only in the sphere of production where we can see the capitalist clearly as master. The second is the *Critique of the Gotha Programme*, in which Marx both appears to offer some principles that look suspiciously like distributive justice, while also criticising a focus on distribution and apparently restricting it to a bourgeois horizon of right.[11]

These lend themselves to two competing interpretations. Firstly, that Marx did not and could not condemn capitalism as unjust, since justice was a concept that made sense only within this horizon of bourgeois right – i.e. within capitalist relations of production. Capitalism could thus only be unjust according to its own standards (which it frequently is – capitalism is full of people swindling, cheating and extorting each other rather than exchanging 'at value'). Whatever was worthy of condemnation about capitalism, whatever shifting to the realm of production is supposed to reveal, it is not a matter of justice. Rather, it is a matter of freedom, or some sort of non-moral good.

The alternative is that, in fact, capitalism was unjust, but had the powerful appearance of being just. Shifting to the realm of production thus gives the lie to this appearance, and reveals the truth – justice in exchange rests on injustice in production. These accounts tend to point to Marx's frequent use of the language of theft and plunder when discussing the wage relationship. The capitalist class does the working class an injustice by stealing from it, by taking something that they are not owed or do not deserve. On the other hand, Marx's own disavowal of the language of justice is explained either rhetorically or psy-

---

10   See, e.g., Wood 1972, Geras 1985, Tucker 1961 and Nielsen 1989.
11   MECW 24, p. 87.

chologically, most famously in Cohen's assertion that Marx believed capitalism was unjust but he did not believe he did.

This debate over justice in general then has consequences for the specific debate over exploitation. It was natural for those who believed Marx was concerned with justice to interpret exploitation in these terms, while others rejected it, generally preferring to identify what is wrong with exploitation as a matter of domination, coercion or force – and thus as concerned with questions of freedom.[12] However, this coincides historically with a trend that Young identifies to increasingly narrowly define justice as a matter of the distribution of goods, and as being concerned with *theories* of justice, which 'typically derive fundamental principles of justice that apply to all or most societies, whatever their configuration and social relations, from a few general premises about the nature of human beings, the nature of society and the nature of reason'.[13] Thus, particularly in the hands of the analytical Marxists, the pursuit of a justice-based account of Marxist exploitation became increasingly a question of either an unjust distribution (either of starting distributions of assets or final distributions), or of an unjust transaction.[14] This coincided too with various attempts to develop non-Marxist accounts of exploitation that are primarily either distributional or transaction-based.[15] Paradoxically, this focus tended to move ever further from the wage relationship itself, and indeed from even conceiving of exploitation as a direct relationship between exploiter and exploited, shifting focus instead to the conditions that make possible the act, rather than the act itself.[16]

In what follows I argue against justice-based interpretations, and in favour of one that stresses the importance of domination, and in particular the taking advantage of vulnerability and powerlessness. I do this for three reasons:

---

12   Examples of the latter are Holmstrom 1977, Schwartz 1995, Reiman 1987. Examples of the former are Arneson 1981, Roemer 1988 and Laycock 1999. It's worth noting that this division does not map cleanly onto the controversy over whether Marx is concerned with justice *whatsoever*. For example, Reiman argues that exploitation is a matter of force and coercion, but that it ought to be integrated into a criticism of capitalism as unjust.

13   Young 1990, pp. 2–4.

14   The argument that Schwartz calls the canonical account is an example of an approach which is concerned with an unjust transaction. Something like this is defended by Warren 1994 and considered a correct interpretation of Marx but rejected by Cohen 1990. It is in part apparent failings with this approach that led Arneson, Roemer and others to shift their focus to distributive justice.

15   See in particular Steiner 1984.

16   Roemer 1985 is the clearest example of this (see also Przeworski 1985, pp. 223–31). Vrousalis 2013 is an example of the opposite view.

Firstly, I consider it closer to what Marx actually says. As I elaborate on below, when Marx asks us to shift our attention from the realm of circulation to the realm of production, he demonstrates how the wage relationship allows the capitalist to dominate the process of production, and in turn dominate the worker themselves, using this domination in order to take advantage of them, in ways that perpetuate this domination. Secondly, it is straightforwardly closer to what is generally meant by exploitation – using (someone) to gain an advantage. Finally, to the extent that the justice accounts demand a 'theory' of justice, they are in opposition to the methods I discussed in the previous chapter. They require knowledge and articulation of an ideal distribution, against which capitalism is found wanting, and thus risk the charge of utopianism.

Arneson offers a particularly clear account of this kind of model:

> As I see it, the normative idea in Marx's conception of exploitation has its origin in his vision of a cooperative economy which is organised with tolerable efficiency and which produces a given stock of goods for the satisfaction of people's desires at a cost of a given amount of human drudgery. Each person deserves a fair (equal) share of economic goods in exchange for the willingness to contribute a fair (equal) share of economic goods in exchange for the willingness to contribute a fair (equal) share of the drudgery that is required to produce those goods ... There are various ways by which an economy can deviate from this ideal standard in its treatment of people. Exploitation is one important form of mistreatment. To be exploited is roughly to be forced to perform drudgery to an unfairly great extent, and to receive in return an unfairly small share of goods, where this forcing is brought about via an inequality of power favouring some economic agents over others.[17]

According to this interpretation, exploitation is entirely about an unjust distribution of advantages and burdens, measured according to shortfall from a cooperative ideal.

Arneson's description brings out clearly the extent to which these accounts appear to be dependent on precisely the kind of ideal theory approach I discussed in the previous chapter. Indeed, it is striking that in explicating his account of exploitation as depending on an unfair distribution, Arneson immediately moves to a comparison with an ideal distribution (for him this is merely

---

17   Arneson 1981, pp. 212–13.

the same thing, in 'another idiom').[18] This, I think, is true: it is very difficult to criticise a distribution as unfair except by comparison with a fair one.
However, if the points I made in the previous chapter are correct then this
counts strongly against such an approach. Indeed, I think Marx recognises this
when he rejects criticising capitalism in distributive terms. The *Critique of the
Gotha Programme* contains a famous critique of the inadequacy of any notion
of equal right or entitlement for delivering genuine emancipation. Such things
remain constrained by the horizon of bourgeois right.[19]

It is worth noting that this entire controversy only makes sense if what is
meant by justice is something more specific than simply questions of right or
wrong. Indeed, one of the ways in which this debate gets distorted is the sense
that justice, in this sense, exhausts normative political theory. There is a marked
tendency in some writings to assume that any substantive social wrong must
ultimately boil down to a question of (in)justice. Increasingly, it becomes taken
for granted that to say something is unjust and to condemn it are synonymous. For example, Nielsen, in attacking Wood's arguments that Marx rejects the
language of justice, suggests that this debate might merely be a 'trivial verbal
one'.[20] Since Wood accepts that Marx condemns capitalism as severely unequal
and exploitative he 'must agree ... that capitalism is indeed, in the plain untechnical sense of the term, an unjust social system'.[21] Perhaps it is a symptom of
too much political philosophy, but it is entirely unclear to me what the 'plain,
untechnical sense' of justice is. Of course, if justice is defined differently, either
less narrowly concerned with distribution, or more specifically concerned with
domination, democracy and power, capitalist exploitation may be more easily
integrated into a justice account. Young herself, for example, wants to hold on
to the word justice but stresses that domination and oppression should be the
primary terms in which it is thought of.[22] However, in the main discussions of
justice remain dominated by distributive language, and in particular by Rawls
and the various variations and developments of his core approach.[23] In any

---

18   Arneson 1981, p. 212.
19   See MECW 24, 87. See also Geuss 2008, pp. 76–9.
20   Nielsen 1989, p. 173.
21   Nielsen 1989, p. 170.
22   Young 1990, p. 9. See also Gould 1978 and Draper, 1990, p. 27, for whom "The point of Marx's
      attacks on the modern mythology was not to forbid appeals to justice (or even Justice) but
      to anchor such appeals in class struggle. The appeal to justice has always been a staple
      of any social movement, but it is meaningful only if the movement bases its concept of
      justice on its social struggle, instead of basing its social struggle on an abstractionized
      conception of justice." p. 27.
23   For example, when Callinicos argues that Marxism ought to develop a theory of justice, it
      is to Rawls, and the distributive paradigm, that he looks.

case, there is a real difference between saying something is wrong because it is unjust and saying it is wrong because it denies freedom (or indeed because it is heretical, illiberal, evil, lacks solidarity or many other terms of condemnation).

Thus, in denying that exploitation is a matter of justice, I am arguing three things: Firstly, it is not a question of an unfair, unjust or unequal transaction or exchange. Secondly, it is not a matter of distribution, either of starting point or outcome. Thirdly, it is not based on fundamental and universal principles that are derivable independently of given social conditions and integrated into a complete and over-arching *theory*.[24]

3 Mutato Nomine de te Fabula Narratur[25]

Marx believed that capitalism was a system based on the systematic domination of the labour of one class by another in order to control the products of that labour, in particular to control the social surplus produced by it. In this respect, capitalism was identical to every other historically existing class society:

> Only the form in which this surplus labour is in each case extorted from the immediate producer, the worker, distinguishes the various economic formations of society – for example between a society based on slave labour and a society based on wage labour.[26]

The transition to capitalism may have radically transformed many social relationships, and created some radically new ones, it may have 'drowned the most heavenly ecstasies of religious fervour, of chivalrous enthusiasm, of philistine sentimentalism, in the icy water of egotistical calculation', but it remained for all that, a system for the social domination of labour, of 'brutal, shameless, naked exploitation'.[27]

Under feudalism the character of exploitation was clear as day:

---

24 Young 1990, p. 3.
25 'The name is changed, but the tale is told of you!' A quotation from Horace's satires, used by Marx in *Capital Vol. 1*, p. 378.
26 *Capital Vol. 1*, p. 325 (my translation). 'Nur die Form, worin diese Mehrarbeit dem unmittelbaren Produzenten, dem Arbeiter, abgepreßt wird, unterscheidet die ökonomischen Gesellschaftsformationen, z.B. die Gesellschaft der Sklaverei von der der Lohnarbeit'. *MEW*, Vol. 23, p. 226. See also pp. 1027–8.
27 *Communist Manifesto*, p. 82.

> The necessary labour which the Wallachian peasant performs for his own maintenance is distinctly marked off from his surplus labour on behalf of the boyar. The one he does in his own field, the other on the seignorial estate. Both parts of the labour-time [necessary and surplus] thus exist independently, side by side with each other.[28]

Here the boyar, by virtue of his ownership of the land and dominion over them, can force the peasants to perform a period of surplus-labour. The difference between the two periods is clearly marked off by the fact that they take place in different geographical locations. Thus the peasant can see that the work he does for the boyar is not his own, and he would not do it were it not for the threat of expulsion or death. Under capitalism, this becomes less clear because the capitalist asserts control over the entire labour process, and acquires control over it through 1. their prior ownership of the means of production; and 2. their purchase of the labour-power of workers. In this the necessary portion of the labour becomes mixed with the surplus, and the entire transaction appears as a wholly voluntary one.

Nonetheless, Marx frequently asserts that capitalism was *as much* a system of exploitation as those systems which had gone before it (if not more). This is a crucial, albeit secondary, part of the role of *Capital*, and a more important part of Marx's political economy in general, especially the more popular pieces. The rampant bourgeoisie did not tire of asserting that there had been something profoundly wrong with the feudal exploitation it had done away with. Marx's concern was to demonstrate their hypocrisy in this denunciation. Marx very much agrees with the Magistrate he quotes in *Capital*: 'We declaim against the Virginian and Carolinian cotton planters. Is their black market, their lash, their barter of human flesh more detestable than this slow sacrifice of humanity which takes place in order that the veils and collars may be fabricated for the benefit of capitalists?'[29]

In his more theoretical pieces Marx also stresses the continuities between capitalism and its predecessors alongside its differences. The appendix to the first edition of *Capital* makes this point clearly:

> It follows that two widely held views are in error: There are first those who consider that wage labour, the sale of labour to the capitalist and hence the wage form, is something only superficially characteristic of capitalist

---

28 *Capital Vol. 1*, p. 346.
29 *Capital Vol. 1*, pp. 353–4.

production. It is, however, one of the essential mediating forms of capitalist relations of production, and one constantly reproduced by those relations themselves. Secondly, there are those who regard this superficial relation, this essential formality, this deceptive appearance of capitalist relations as its true essence. They therefore imagine that they can give a true account of those relations by classifying both workers and capitalists as commodity owners. They thereby gloss over the essential nature of the relationship, extinguishing its *differentia specifica*.[30]

The second error is the one which is of particular concern here. What Marx calls the *essence* of capitalist production relations, its *differentia specifica*, is *not* the free exchange of commodity-owning equals in the form of wage labour. Rather it can be 'distinguished only formally from other more direct forms of the enslavement of labour and the *ownership of it* as perpetrated by the owners of the means of production'.[31] In this passage it is non-capitalist forms which are described as more direct (whereas, as we saw, in the *Communist Manifesto* it is capitalism which is presented as 'naked' exploitation), but the core argument is the same. There is no essential difference between wage-labour and feudal bondage in respect of their being systems of exploitation.[32]

This suggests that one of Marx's intentions in describing capitalism as exploitative was to demonstrate an important continuity between it and other forms of society that were already generally accepted to be exploitative. Indeed, this is the very purpose of the newspaper quotation above, to highlight a fundamental similarity between capitalism and slavery, in order to identify as hypocritical and misguided those who would condemn slavers but defend capital. Moreover, this gains much of its rhetorical force from the fact that slavery was broadly (though not of course universally) considered to be uncontroversially bad.

Indeed, the analogy with slavery, and the language of freedom, emancipation and domination is a constant feature of Marx's writings about capitalism. Towards the end of the chapter on the working day in *Capital*, Marx surveys the prospects for the organisation of the working class to overcome their exploitation in various countries, and has a stark warning for the American working

---

30   *Capital Vol. 1*, p. 1064.

31   *Capital Vol. 1*, p. 1063.

32   As Schwartz puts it, 'Marx is not only contrasting capitalist exploitation with earlier forms. He is indicating basic continuities in virtue of which "exploitation" has a univocal sense in all class societies' (Schwartz 1995, p. 173).

EXPLOITATION, JUSTICE AND FREEDOM

class: 'Labour in a white skin cannot emancipate itself where it is branded in a black skin'.[33] Of the worker who emerges more clearly at the end of this section he says:

> The contract by which he sold his labour-power to the capitalist proved in black and white, so to speak, that he was free to dispose of himself. But when the transaction was concluded, it was discovered that he was no 'free agent'. That the period of time for which he is free to sell his labour-power is the period of time for which he is forced to sell it, that in fact the vampire will not let go 'while there remains a single muscle, sinew or drop of blood to be exploited' [Here Marx quotes Engels].[34]

Similarly, '[Labour-power's] enslavement to capital is only concealed by the variety of individual capitalists to whom it sells itself'.[35] 'The system of wage labour is a system of slavery, and indeed a slavery which becomes more severe in proportion as the social productive forces of labour develop, whether the worker receives better or worse payment'.[36] Finally, '... the instrument of labour appears as a means of enslaving, exploiting, and impoverishing the worker; the social combination of labour processes appears as an organised suppression of his individual vitality, freedom, and autonomy'.[37]

Engels, too, echoes these terms in his analysis of the growing working class:

> The only difference as compared with the old, outspoken slavery is this, that the worker of today seems to be free because he is not sold once and for all, but piecemeal by the day, the week, the year, and because no one owner sells him to another, but because he is forced to sell himself in this way instead, being the slave of no particular person, but of the whole property-holding class.[38]

---

33 *Capital Vol. 1*, p. 414.
34 *Capital Vol. 1*, p. 416.
35 *Capital Vol. 1*, p. 764.
36 *Capital Vol. 1*, p. 310. This might be evidence for thinking, in contrast to my earlier point, that Marx did in fact think that labour which produced more surplus-value is worse off. However, the only factors referred to here are the *amount* of labour which is forced and coerced, as a factor of its intensity and duration, rather than its value. Being made to work harder and longer is plausibly to be more severely exploited, even on my account.
37 *Capital Vol. 1*, p. 638.
38 MECW 4, p. 379.

Whilst this semblance of liberty may involve 'some real freedom on the one hand' it is for the worker 'unchanged at bottom'.[39] Similarly 'Under the brutal and brutalising treatment of the bourgeoisie, the working man becomes precisely as much a thing without volition as water, and is subject to the laws of nature with precisely the same necessity; at a certain point all freedom ceases',[40] and finally 'the philanthropic Tories were right when they gave the operatives the name white slaves'.[41]

All of these comparisons suggest that, whatever was wrong with exploitation for Marx, it was not, primarily, a matter of distribution. Indeed, the comparison with slavery is twice used by Marx to mock the idea that better distribution, in the form of higher wages, would mitigate exploitation. Firstly, in *Capital*, he argues that

> these things no more abolish the exploitation of the wage-labourer, and his situation of dependence, than do better clothing, food and treatment, and a larger *peculium*, in the case of the slave. A rise in the price of labour, as a consequence of the accumulation of capital, only means in fact that the length and weight of the golden chain the wage-labourer has already forged for himself allow it to be loosened somewhat.[42]

And later, in the *Critique of the Gotha Programme*, Marx mocks Lassalle's approach to fair distribution:

> It is as if, among slaves who have at last got behind the secret of slavery and broken out in rebellion, a slave still in thrall to obsolete notions were to inscribe on the programme of the rebellion: Slavery must be abolished because the feeding of slaves in the system of slavery cannot exceed a certain low maximum![43]

The implication of this point is clear: There is something absurd about locating the wrongness of slavery in the amount of food the slaves get, rather than the manifest domination and degradation they suffer. It may be less *absurd* in the case of the worker, but it is no less misguided. Perhaps this comes across most clearly in the closing lines of the *Communist Manifesto*. A glib point, perhaps,

---

39   MECW 4, p. 379.
40   MECW 4, p. 425.
41   MECW 4, p. 474.
42   *Capital Vol. 1*, p. 769.
43   MECW 24, p. 92.

but the workers of the world have nothing to lose but their *chains*, not nothing to lose but their iniquitous compensation for the value of their labour.

These points also count against the idea that exploitation is best understood as an unfair or unjust transaction, such that it is a wrong in the same class as theft.[44] I have already referred to passages above where Marx rejects the idea that there is anything unfair in what the capitalist pays to the worker, but this remains a widespread interpretation. Indeed, this is part of what Justin Schwartz (rightly) calls the 'Canonical View' of Marxist exploitation. The basis of this is that the worker receives less in wages than the value of what she produces. Thus there is an unequal transaction. Of course, not all unequal transactions are unjust. For example, Steiner points out that donating £100 for a plate of food at a charity dinner can be described as an unequal transaction, in the sense that what is received is less than the value of what is given.[45] Marx himself attributes the idea that all transactions must necessarily be seen as a kind of 'mutual plundering', in which the question of 'who wins' is foregrounded, to the bourgeois economists, and explicitly contrasts it with producing 'as human beings'.[46]

The passages above already highlight one limitation of this approach – even a worker who receives far more for their labour will remain tied and subjected to a capitalist. However, it is also important to stress how much this misdescribes what takes place in the wage-relation. For it is *not* the case that the worker sells what she produces to the capitalist in exchange for her wages. Rather, she sells her labour-power, her capacity to labour, her time. This she sells (at least in perfect conditions) at its market value. This appears to be an exchange of equals (which is precisely Marx's point). It is not that the labourer exchanges her *products* for a mess of pottage, it is that she exchanges her *life activity*. It *is* the case that once the labour-power has been bought the capitalist will do everything within his power to ensure that as much labour is performed in the period it has been bought for. The overriding goal is to ensure that labour-power produces more than its own value – if it produces less, the capitalist has failed. But none of this means that there was an unequal transaction initially.[47]

---

44   Steiner, for example, locates exploitation somewhere on a spectrum between theft and fair exchange.

45   Steiner 1984.

46   *Early Writings*, pp. 275–7. See also *German Ideology* 432–3.

47   See Wood 2004, p. 251, and Brenkert 1983, pp. 133–6, for more on this argument. It is worth noting that this is not formally incompatible with an account, like Reiman's, that sees exploitation in terms of forced unpaid labour (Reiman 1987). If Marx is correct, and the consequences of the sale of labour-power is that the worker is paid less than the value of the actual labour performed, then some of that labour could be appropriately described

It would be clearer that there was an injustice if you add in the additional claim that the worker is entitled to the products of her labour (or perhaps the equivalent value of them). In this case, capitalist exploitation appears as an elaborate trick to acquire the products of labour which rightly belong to the labourer themselves. However, this does not appear to be a claim that Marx ever made, at least not in any general sense.[48] Whilst Marx did endorse a labour theory of value, he did not endorse a Lockean labour theory of property.[49] Moreover, this also seems to misdescribe the process of exploitation under capitalism. It is not the case that there is a transfer of the products of labour to the capitalist within the labour process. There is no moment where the worker owns their products before the capitalist then seizes them. Rather, they belong to the capitalist the moment they are created. Much of the language of 'transfer' of value tends to obscure this fact – formally, no product is 'transferred' from the labourer to the capitalist – the capitalist has it all from the beginning.[50]

Nor is it correct to think that capitalist exploitation necessarily involves the enrichment of the capitalist at the expense of the worker. This is an intuitive way of thinking about it, especially if we think in terms of a finite amount of resources to be distributed, but it in fact badly misconstrues the situation. To the extent that the alternative is starvation or unemployment, the worker *gains* from selling their labour-power. They are in a better-off position than they were before. Indeed, as I will return to below, this is a feature of much of what we would consider exploitation in everyday language. The exploited come out of the process better off than they were before, as does the exploiter. As Wood puts it, 'this is just what we should have expected. For it goes along naturally with being vulnerable and in a weak bargaining position that you have more to lose by not being exploited than your exploiter has to lose by not exploiting you'.[51]

---

as unpaid. However, to the extent that there is something wrong with this, it is essential that this unpaid labour is forced, that it is analogous to slavery. Unpaid labour is not in itself wrong; forced unpaid labour is.

48   He does say that in the lower stage of communism people will receive rewards according to their labour (MECW 24, 86–7). However, this is neither a standard for capitalism, nor a goal in itself. It is a standard for a stage still marked by the society it has emerged from, and one which should be superseded.

49   An example of an argument in favour of exploitation resting on such a principle can be found in Van Parijs 1993, Chapter 5.

50   This is where I differ from Schwartz, for whom exploitation is to be understood as forced surplus transfer. Whilst Schwartz is correct to lay the stress on the role of force, and the consequent denial of freedom, he is wrong to see the transaction as one of transfer.

51   Wood 2004, p. 252.

But there *is* something wrong in the enrichment of the capitalist in the labour process, and to see what it is we have to look to the discussion of co-operation in *Capital*. Here Marx stresses the importance of the gap between the individual sale of labour power, and the productive co-operation in the workplace:

> The worker is the owner of his labour-power until he has finished bargaining for its sale with the capitalist, and he can sell no more than what he has – i.e. his individual, isolated labour-power. This relation between capital is in no way altered by the fact that the capitalist, instead of buying the labour-power of one man, buys that of 100, and enters into separate contracts with 100 unconnected men instead of with one. He can set the 100 men to work, without letting them co-operate. He pays them the value of 100 independent labour-powers, but he does not pay for the combined labour-power of the 100. Being independent of each other, the workers are isolated. They enter into relations with the capitalist, but not with each other.[52]

However, in the workplace, the workers cease to be individual bearers of labour-power, and through their co-operation are able to be significantly more than the sum of their parts. But this co-operation only occurs once they 'have ceased to belong to themselves'. It is capital which sets them to work, and thus

> the productive power developed by the worker socially is the productive power of capital. The socially productive power of labour develops as a free gift to capital whenever the workers are placed under certain conditions, and it is capital which places them under these conditions. Because this power costs capital nothing, while on the other hand it is not developed by the worker until his labour itself belongs to capital, it appears as a power which capital possesses by its nature, a productive power inherent in capital.[53]

There has been no unfair exchange here, the capitalist has bought labour-powers at their values, and brought them together to make something more productive. However, as a function of this relationship, the capitalist has to exert control, either directly or through managers, over the production pro-

---

52   *Capital Vol. 1*, p. 451.
53   *Capital Vol. 1*, p. 451. See also Lebowitz 2003, pp. 83–7.

cess: 'That a capitalist should command in the field of production is now as indispensable as that a general should command in the field of battle ... The work of directing, superintending and adjusting becomes one of the functions of capital, from the moment that the labour under capital's control becomes co-operative'.[54] There are two reasons for this function – firstly the need to organise co-operative production, to ensure maximum productivity, and secondly (and moreover), to control the workers themselves. This is because 'as the means of production extend, the necessity increases for some effective control over the proper application of them, because they confront the wage-labourer as someone else's property [*fremdes Eigentum*]'. Indeed, it is not just the means of production, but the productive activity itself that 'confronts them, in the realm of ideas, as a plan drawn up by the capitalist, and, in practice, as his authority, as the powerful will of a being outside them, who subjects their activity to his purpose'.[55]

In these passages, Marx describes control by the capitalist as 'a function of the exploitation [*Ausbeutung*] of the social labour process, and is consequently conditioned by the unavoidable antagonism between the exploiter [*Ausbeuter*] and the raw material of his exploitation [*dem Rohmaterial seiner Ausbeutung*]'. What is the character of this antagonism, then, if it is not a matter of unfair distribution or exchange? It is that separate, isolated individuals are compelled by social conditions to enter into individual contracts with the capitalist, who is then able to take advantage of their separation and isolation in order to enrich himself. Moreover, this process of enrichment extends the domination of the capitalist over the worker, with this domination growing over time. Indeed, at the heart of this seems to be a fairly mundane definition of exploitation, such that the capitalist exploits the worker by taking advantage of their vulnerability, and in doing so, establishes conditions of domination that maintain and reproduce that vulnerability.

4   The Wedges of Hephaestus

The sense of exploitation at stake here is a fairly ordinary one, and similar in structure to many canonical cases of exploitation: Consider the famous example of *The Port Caledonia and the Anna*, in which a boat suffering difficulties asked for help from a nearby tug-boat. The captain of the tug asked for

---

54   *Capital Vol. 1*, pp. 448–9.
55   *Capital Vol. 1*, pp. 449–50.

£1,000, far more at that time than the cost of the boat and the help, or he would refuse help. The other captain agreed to pay the money for the tug. Or an airline that charges you £60 to print a boarding pass at the airport that you could have printed elsewhere for 50p. Once you are already at the airport, bags packed and ready to go, you do not have much choice but to pay. Or finally, Nicholas Vrousalis's more stripped-down example of a person trapped in a pit: 'A finds B in a pit. A can get B out at a little cost or difficulty. A offers to get B out, but only if B agrees to pay a million euros or to sign a sweatshop contract with A. B signs the contract'.[56] Note that in all of these examples, the exploited does not end the interaction worse off. Many people will, on balance, value actually getting their flights more than keeping £60, and the captain of the sinking ship will value both his life and his ship at above £1,000; and B will similarly likely value her escape (and life) more than signing a sweatshop agreement. If they were to refuse the agreement, then they would *not* be better off, they would be stuck at sea, down a pit, or in Stansted Airport.

In each of these cases, we feel that there has been some sort of taking advantage, of powerlessness or vulnerability. One response to this might be that what is worthy of condemnation is not, in fact, the taking advantage, but the powerlessness itself. Thus, in fact, we are back to a distributive account, except with power rather than resources. Unequal distributions of power are worthy of condemnation, but we should 'hate the game, not the player'.[57] There are a number of inadequacies with this response, however. First of all, it is highly questionable whether things like power or freedom can be incorporated into a distributional account without either badly misunderstanding their nature or missing important dimensions of them.[58] However, more broadly, we should imagine ourselves in the examples above and ask whether it would be an adequate response. In most cases, I suggest, it would not be. In the case of the budget airline, *they have designed the rules*. In the other two cases, however, we still would feel mistreated in some way. If this does not convince, consider one further example, outside of purely economic transactions: Wertheimer spends a great

---

56   Vrousalis 2013, p. 18.

57   Arneson, for example, argues that '[W]hat bothers Marx about capitalism is not simply that it supplies too little of this nice non-moral value. Rather the problem is the skewed distribution of freedom which a market economy enforces, and the superiority which Marx claims for socialism is supposed to lie in socialism's tendency to correct this maldistribution' (Arneson 1981, p. 220). It is striking that the clause requiring an imbalance of power between exploited and exploiter is introduced in a somewhat *ad hoc* fashion. But even this is not sufficient, since what is required is not just an imbalance of power but an attempt to take advantage of that imbalance of power.

58   Young 1990, p. 32.

deal of time talking about the sexual exploitation of patients by psychother-apists.[59] This is appropriately described as exploitation, and clearly involves doing a wrong to the exploited (even if, like in some of the cases Wertheimer describes, they do not believe it does). In these cases we are not angry about any initial power imbalance (indeed, these are a structural part of the relation-ships), or any distributional outcome (on whatever perverse matrix we might measure that). We are angry about the actions of the exploiter, because they have abused their power, degraded their patient, and failed to treat them prop-erly.

This is the core of what is wrong with exploiting a *person*. We take advantage of some vulnerability. Wood offers an account of exploitation in these terms. He describes two forms of exploitation: Exploitation in which we make use of a fea-ture of another person in order to gain some benefit (b[enefit]-exploitation) and exploitation understood as making use of a weakness or vulnerability (a[dvantage]-exploitation):

> As their names are meant to imply, a-exploitation and b-exploitation form a complementary pair, and a-exploitation comes before (is the basis of) b-exploitation. That is, when we exploit a person, or something about a person, we make use of some ability, activity or property of the person (we b-exploit it) as a means to some end of ours. But what makes this use possible, and distinguishes exploiting the person or the thing about them from mere use of it, is the fact that the person or thing about them is put at our disposal by the fact that they are vulnerable to us in some way. We a-exploit this vulnerability, and that is what makes it possible for us to b-exploit the person's activity or ability (or whatever) that we are b-exploiting.[60]

Of course, that people are vulnerable may be a particular quirk of fate (get-ting lost at sea, falling down a pit), a social relationship that is in some sense unavoidably unequal (like the patient-therapist relation), or a set of social rela-tions that are historically specific and possible to change (like capitalism).

This notion of taking advantage of vulnerability can also be linked back to the conception of freedom discussed in Chapter 1. There I suggested that Marx shared important affinities with self-determination-based accounts of freedom, which stress the importance of (collective) control over the (subject-

59   See Wertheimer 1996, Chapter 6. See also Bohmer 2000.
60   Wood 2004, p. 246.

ive and objective) conditions of our own action. Lacking this sort of control renders us vulnerable to particular kinds of exploitation. Thus exploitation can be seen, in these terms, as a kind of inappropriate reaction to conditions of unfreedom. It serves to reinforce and benefit from this unfreedom, rather than overcome it.

There are a number of ways that this is even more acute in the situation of wage-labour under conditions of capitalism than it is in the examples described. Firstly, the capitalist class is the architect of the conditions the workers find themselves in:

> Of course, the pretensions of capital in its embryonic state, in its state of becoming, when it cannot yet use the sheer force of economic relations to secure its right to absorb a sufficient quantity of surplus-labour, but must be aided by the power of the state – its pretensions in this situation appear to be very modest in comparison with the concessions it has to make, complainingly and willingly in its adult condition. Centuries are required before the 'free' worker, owing to the greater development of the capitalist mode of production, makes a voluntary agreement, i.e. is compelled by social conditions to sell the whole of his active life, his very capacity for labour, in return for the price of his customary means of subsistence, to sell his birthright for a mess of pottage.[61]

The class of workers does not, in fact, exist by accident, but was created through a historical process and is maintained by legal and institutional structures, with bodies of armed men invoked as a last resort.

Secondly, the conditions of capitalist production, as well as reproducing the dependence of the worker, involve systematic domination. Marx argues that this is built into capitalist production, precisely because of the nature of labour-power as a commodity. Having purchased labour time, the capitalist endeavours to squeeze as much labour as possible in that period. As a result of this, 'that a capitalist should command on the field of production, is now as indispensable as that a general should command on the field of battle'.[62] This particular aspect of unfreedom in exploitation can, as Schwartz rightly notes, be understood entirely in terms of what is commonly called 'negative freedom'.[63] Whatever other aspects of unfreedom is involved in capitalist exploitation, for

---

61   *Capital Vol. 1*, p. 382.
62   *Capital Vol. 1*, p. 448.
63   Schwartz 1995, pp. 175–6.

the period of time that labour is sold the worker is not negatively free to do what she pleases. This period of unfreedom is also one in which the worker's very body is subject to very direct physical constraints and hardships. *Capital* is full of examples of this, where Marx emphasises the way in which the body itself is repetitively constrained, contorted and directed in ways that distort it and deplete its strength.[64]

Thirdly, the appropriation of the surplus-product by the capitalist raises important democratic questions, linked to the question of freedom as self-determination.[65] The consequence of capitalist exploitation is that the surplus product ends up in the hands of the capitalists. Yet the surplus-product is nothing but more and future conditions for agency. Decisions over what to do with the surplus product are major social decisions, and whether to use it to invest in social housing, provide for the poorest, go to the moon, make large donations to political parties, or simply to work less, are substantively political. It is a major consequence of capitalist exploitation that many of these decisions remain stubbornly outside of the control of most people. This is a further unfreedom which results from exploitation, one which is just as important from the point of view of collective self-determination.[66]

Finally, the exploitation of wage-labour is not a one-off thing, but constantly reproduces the conditions of domination. In the tug-boat example, the rescuer may have taken advantage of the condition of the other vessel, but he restored it to safety, and the relationship of dependence ended then and there. The condition of workers under capitalism is closer to that of the man in a pit who signs a sweatshop contract – they become bound to the capitalist in a relationship of dependence, 'more firmly than the wedges of Hephaestus held Prometheus to the rock'.[67]

From the point of view of the exploited, there is nothing complicated or mysterious about what is wrong with all of this. That one has a vulnerability that is being taken advantage of is reason enough to want to remove that

---

64   Tomba offers an account of *Capital* that particularly stresses these forms of bodily domin-
       ation and damage (although Tomba is content to call this an injustice, he also stresses that
       the perspective that recognises this is "the test bed for disputing Rawls's theory of justice"
       (Tomba, 2013, p. 91)).
65   See Przeworski 1985, pp. 237–8.
66   Some (e.g Arneson 1981) have rightly argued that labour which does not (for contingent
       reasons) produce a surplus is still exploited, and therefore that there is nothing distinct-
       ively problematic about surplus acquisition over and above the exploitation of labour in
       general. However, these points make clear that there is something significant about sur-
       plus acquisition for freedom, even if only indirectly.
67   *Capital Vol. 1*, p. 799.

vulnerability, and challenge those who take advantage of it. Indeed, as Wood points out, it is precisely from this perspective that Marx invites us to see capitalist exploitation. It is not from the abstract position of the would-be social reformer, interested in tinkering with the system from a position of neutrality, but from the position of the exploited themselves. For them, the direct experience of exploitation will be the experience of vulnerability to and domination by capital, and of having that situation systematically reproduced in order to benefit someone other than themselves.[68] Moreover, this point of view is not an irrelevant or marginal one; it is the point of view of large sections of society, if not the majority. From this point of view, we do not need any extra, special reasons why such people should act to resist exploitation and the relationships of domination and vulnerability that make it possible. As Wood puts it 'looked at in this way, the idea that exploitation is bad raises no moral issues at all – no more than it raises a moral issue why a starving person should want food or *a person in chains should want to cast them off*'.[69]

None of this depends on an ideal, distributive or otherwise, against which capitalism is to be found wanting. It is of course true that the exploitative approach adopted by the capitalist compares rather poorly to the production as human beings that Marx imagines will take place under communism. We may well want to denounce the capitalist with a wide range of moral language, and imagine that under communism people will act better. But whatever alternative we might want to suggest (and even if we have no such alternative),

> the exploitation is not welcome to the victim. The victim is bound to desire both that the vulnerability had not been taken advantage of, and also that it had not been there to take advantage of in the first place. Victims of exploitation therefore always have reason to try to prevent someone's taking advantage of their vulnerabilities, and even more reason (at least as long as they live among fellow creatures whom social relations have rendered essentially hostile to them) to rid themselves of these vulnerabilities if they possibly can.[70]

---

68   Wood 2004, p. 259.
69   Wood 2004, p. 258, my italics. We may also want to be able to say, as Wood does, that there is something reprehensible about adopting the role of the exploiter, of taking advantage of a situation of powerlessness rather than remedying it (and perhaps that there is something different that is wrong with not acting at all). However, whatever is reprehensible here needn't be a matter of justice.
70   Wood 2004, p. 262.

Marx sometimes makes remarks that seem consistent with this. For example, in the *Grundrisse* he suggests that:

> The recognition [*Erkennung*] of the products as its own, and the judgement that its separation from the conditions of its realisation is improper – forcibly imposed – is an enormous advance in awareness [*Buwusstsein*], itself the product of the mode of production resting on capital, and as much the knell to its doom as, with the slave's awareness that *he cannot be the property of another*, with his consciousness of himself as a person, the existence of slavery becomes a merely artificial, vegetative existence, and ceases to be able to prevail as the basis of production.[71]

Here the point is that (proper, correct) recognition of the situation is sufficient to give workers a reason to resist, just as recognition of slavery gives the slaves reason to resist. No additional moral content is required, beyond awareness of one's situation.

One argument against this idea, that workers always have a reason to condemn and resist exploitation and to limit their vulnerability to capital, is the notion that capitalist exploitation has, at some stages, been historically necessary. Since Marx argues that capitalism is historically necessary (which he did), he must be committed to the idea that at some times in history struggling against exploitation was irrational, that there was no reason to struggle against it. Thus, if we merely focus on the point of view of the exploited, we are unable to distinguish between cases of rational and irrational struggle against exploitation.

Here, contra many commentators,[72] I think we ought to bite the bullet and take Marx at his word, which is that certain class societies are *both* historically necessary *and* reprehensible and worthy of condemnation. Moreover, this is precisely *because* he is concerned with the viewpoint of the exploited. It is hard to understand Marx's admiration of figures like Spartacus and Thomas Münzer if he believed that historically necessary exploitation should not nonetheless be actively struggled against. The paradoxical sense of this might be slightly alleviated when we consider that were it not for the exploited reacting against it, we would not be able to find out whether a certain kind of exploit-

71 *Grundrisse*, p. 463.
72 For example, Schwartz argues that Marx only condemns unnecessary exploitation, and suggests that 'his evident hatred of exploitation even in [necessary] circumstances might be explained by a plausible conviction that they involve much unnecessary as well as some necessary exploitation' (Schwartz 1995, p. 166).

ation is or is not historically necessary, and also not drive society forward so that it might cease to be so. It is only because some in society experience it as something to react against that its historical necessity is even a question; and any steps to overcome this necessity tend to be taken because people struggle against it in this way. From the point of view of the exploited, exploitation is always something to react against, even if it is, in some sense, historically necessary. This gives an additional meaning to Connolly's slogan that gives this book its name: There are none better equipped to decide what is a fetter.[73]

If workers are vulnerable to capital, the root of this lies in their separation and isolation from one another. It is the fact that they each appear as the individual bearer of labour-power, and deal with the capitalist as an individual, that enables and facilitates their exploitation. It follows, then, that once this exploitation is recognised, the workers have a reason to reduce this separation – to form associations and work together. As Lebowitz observes, 'only by struggling to reduce their degree of separation can workers achieve their goals'.[74] This leaves us where we began in Chapter 2 – workers are driven towards forming co-operative organisations and associations which defend their interests, and these organisations represent a lasting gain of class struggle. Moreover, if this vulnerability is to be eliminated, rather than merely mitigated, then these organisations – or some version of them – must ultimately challenge the relations of production themselves, i.e. the capitalists' control over the means of production.

Thus the unfreedom of exploitation presents the starting point for a reaction against it, and from this reaction it is possible to identify a course of action towards an alternative. We move from a substantive bad, exploitation and the unfreedom it necessarily involves, to the outlines of an alternative, which can then be fleshed out as the movement itself develops. For Marx, however, the negative consequences of domination in labour went beyond immediate recognition of constraint and domination. He believed that being unable to determine one's own activity had profoundly negative consequences for human wellbeing in general. In addition to the immediate sense that unfree-

---

73   One way of reading what I am arguing here is as the inverse of Schwartz's point that 'since freedom is a good, unfreedom is an evil' (Schwartz 1995, p. 165). Schwartz argues that freedom has an advantage over certain other norms in that it is overwhelmingly considered good; the burden of proof is on those who would argue against its goodness, not on those who must argue for it. My approach starts from the experience of unfreedom as negative, as a basis for arguing that freedom is positive.

74   Lebowitz 2003, p. 87.

CHAPTER 6

Alienation, Human Nature, Human Good

1 Introduction

For Marx, capitalism was not just exploitative, it was alienating. It involved a systematic denial of opportunities for self-realisation through practical activity, and this had devastating consequences for those who lived under it. As Ollman puts it, alienation is 'the intellectual construct in which Marx displays the devastating effect of capitalist production on human beings, on their physical and mental states and on the social processes of which they are a part'.[1] Thus alienation is a concept that captures the various ways in which, to put it simply, *capitalism is bad for us*. Marx's theory of alienation has been the basis of a wide variety of debates and controversies, but my particular concern in this chapter is with the relationship between it and concepts of human nature and essence. The discussion here proceeds analogously to the previous chapter. There the concern was that to talk about exploitation it was necessary to have a substantive distributive theory of justice. Here, the concern is whether it is possible to talk about alienation without a similarly substantive vision of human nature, of what it is to be a truly realised human.

In Chapter 1, I described how Marx suggested that labour, under certain historical conditions, could involve a kind of distorted objectification, in which instead of our productive activity helping us realise our freedom in the world, we come to see that activity as something fundamentally separate from us, and the environment in which it takes place as a fundamentally hostile world. In his early writings, Marx discusses the unfolding of this process in four dimensions.[2] Firstly, workers are alienated from the products of their labour, from the world of objects which surround them, and therefore from the natural world more broadly. Their products appear not as objects of their own free creation, but as things into which they pour their energy, only for another to profit from it: 'The worker places his life into the object; but it no longer belongs to him, but to the object'.[3] This, however, is only possible if the labour which

---

1 Ollman 1976, p. 131. See also Mészáros 1970, and Sayers 2011.
2 This is a thumbnail sketch of an interpretation of alienation I have written extensively about elsewhere. See Swain 2012a.
3 *Early Writings*, p. 324.

produced such objects also appeared as an alien force, external to the worker themselves, capable of being separated off and used for the purposes of others:

> Just as in religion, the spontaneous activity of the human imagination, the human brain and the human heart detaches itself from the individual and reappears as the alien activity of a god or of a devil, so the activity of the worker is not his own spontaneous activity. It belongs to another, it is a loss of self.[4]

This separation denies any possibility for free, consciously directed activity. This denial involves, at least in these early passages, a kind of dehumanisation, a denial of the human capacity for free creation, which Marx articulates in terms of species-being or essence [*Gattungswesen*]. Such unfree activity is not merely deplorable as a denial of freedom, but it also has significant negative consequences for health and wellbeing, both physical and psychological. This is what Marx means when he says that the worker 'does not confirm himself in his work, but denies himself, feels miserable and not happy, does not develop free mental and physical energy, but mortifies his flesh and ruins his mind'.[5] Workers under capitalism are thus estranged not just from their activity and the product of their activity, but from *themselves*.

Finally, this shapes relationships between human beings: 'Every self-estrangement of man from himself and nature is manifested in the relationship he sets up between other men and himself and nature'.[6] As discussed in Chapter 1, Mészáros describes this in terms of the notion of 'second order mediations'. Through the sale of labour-power, capitalism introduces a particular kind of secondary mediation into the relationship between human beings and nature, which in turn affects the relationships between individual human beings:

> Man's productive activity cannot bring him fulfilment because the institutionalised second order mediations interpose themselves between man and his activity, between man and nature, and between man and man ... [I]f man's self-mediation is further mediated by the capitalistically institutionalised form of productive activity, then nature cannot mediate itself

---

4 *Early Writings*, p. 326.
5 *Early Writings*, p. 326.
6 *Early Writings*, p. 330.

with nature and man cannot mediate himself with man ... [M]an is confronted by man in a hostile fashion in the antagonism between Capital
and Labour.[7]

This alienation is a general phenomenon, not merely experienced by the
worker. The capitalist too, has their activity shaped and dominated by forces
that appear outside of their control. Marx does, however, appear to identify a
difference between the capitalist and the worker:

> The propertied class and the class of the proletariat present the same
> human self-alienation. But the former class finds in this self-alienation
> its confirmation and its good, *its own power*; it has in it a semblance of
> human existence. The class of the proletariat feels annihilated in alien-
> ation; it sees in it its own powerlessness and the reality of an inhuman
> existence.[8]

The idea of alienation, then, appears to form a fundamental part of Marx's
arsenal of critical concepts. Capitalism *dehumanises*, in a very literal sense. Yet
this language is controversial, both in interpretations of Marx, and in general
debates about the role of essentialism and theories of human nature in political
projects. These controversies reflect real concerns about the radical potential
of such theories, but are also marked by a complex diversity of meanings and
interpretations that makes progress difficult. Many interpreters see in Marx an
account that is heavily indebted to Hegel and Aristotle, and which sees particular things, including humans, as having essences which define their proper role
and use.[9] This is generally linked, as I will discuss further below, to a conception
of the good life, such that living well is understood in terms of living according
to one's nature or essence (the position, sometimes ascribed to Marx, known as
perfectionism).[10] Thus to be alienated is, on this reading, to fail to live according
to our human nature and is, by definition, bad.

But such notions of human nature or essence have become increasingly controversial within political theory. There have been several drivers of this. Liberal theory has increasingly emphasised the importance of allowing people to
define their own conception of the good, rather than presupposing one based

---

7   Mészáros 1970, p. 83.
8   MECW 4, p. 36. See also *Capital Vol. 1*, p. 990.
9   See e.g. Fromm 1961, Blackledge 2012, Meikle 1985.
10   See Hurka 1993, Lukes 1987, Wall 2012.

on supposed human features. Post-structuralist theory has tended to undermine unitary accounts of the subject, stressing the fragmentation of the self,
undermining the idea that there is a simple subject which can be said to be
'alienated' or otherwise, and even questioning the value of a unified, unalienated self. Historical treatments have emphasised how bound up conceptions
of the human are with specific forms of domination and exclusion, and such
ideas are increasingly seen as depending upon either a naïve humanism which
erases difference, or on some historically specific and exclusionary criteria.[11]
For example, Young suggests that 'any definition of a human nature is dangerous because it threatens to devalue or exclude some acceptable individual
desires, cultural characteristics, or ways of life'.[12] Moreover, pinning political
projects on notions of human nature seem to leave us as 'hostages to fortune'
when it comes to empirical evidence.[13]

Within specifically Marxist debates, Althusser famously argues that Marx
broke decisively with any conception of essence as part of a break with teleolo-
gical theories of history, and that he was correct to do so.[14] Laclau and Mouffe
deepen this criticism, levelling accusations of essentialism at any attempt to
identify the interests of certain historical subjects as fundamental to history.
Most obviously, this occurs in a critique of the classical conception of the role
of the working class in Marxism. In particular, what Laclau and Mouffe reject
is the idea that there are any fundamental needs or interests which exist prior
to their articulation in political terms.[15] These criticisms often have something
more specific in mind than the general human essences that the advocates of
essentialism discuss, meaning it is not always easy to identify precise points of
difference. Whether or not, for example, the essentialism that Miekle endorses
and the essentialism Laclau and Mouffe reject are the same can be hard to dis-
cern.

In any case, these various developments have led cumulatively to an intellectual climate understandably hostile to notions of human nature, essence or
purpose. This climate is such that Axel Honneth can write (in a foreword to a
study of alienation) that 'Philosophical developments of the past decades on
both sides of the Atlantic have put an end to such essentialist conceptions; we
now know that even if we do not doubt the existence of certain universal features of human nature, we can no longer speak objectively of a human 'essence',

---

11   See e.g. Phillips 2015.
12   Young 1990, p. 37.
13   Phillips 2015, p. 40.
14   Althusser 2005.
15   Laclau and Mouffe 2014.

of our 'species powers', or of humankind's defining and fundamental aims'.[16] Yet if alienation depends on such a concept, then, it seems, we can no longer speak of alienation either. Alienation itself is a sitting duck.

The aim of this chapter is to argue that the concept of alienation need not fall with this critique. This is in part because there are aspects of this critique that deserve to be taken seriously, in particular the sense that conceptions of human nature are either vapid or exclusionary in some ways. However, it is worth stressing that this is also a particular problem for my treatment of self-emancipation. To return, briefly, to the ideas at the end of Chapter 4, I discussed Levitas's account of utopia in terms of ontology, archaeology and architecture, with the emphasis on actively constructing and reconstructing alternative societies. It was there emphasised that this activity should not be foreclosed or short-circuited by pre-political conceptions of the good society, but that it should be seen itself as a political process. Yet if the force of a charge of alienation depends precisely on some kind of universal human nature or essence, this seems to undo all of this argumentation. Instead, it seems, all that is required is to identify the essence from which we are separated, and to attempt to undo this separation (ontology overwhelming archaeology and architecture).[17] What space, then, for self-emancipation?

In response to these concerns, I argue that alienation should be seen as resting not on substantive claims about the human essence, but on a claim about the negative consequences of a particular mode of living. This does make a claim about human beings, but it is primarily a negative one, a specific claim about what is bad for us. As such, it stands and falls on its value as much as a descriptive concept as a normative one – its value is in its contribution to understanding and explaining the specific ills of capitalism. While this claim must figure in both attempts to criticise capitalism and to articulate alternatives to it, it does not depend on any substantive conception of the human that is identifiable in a pre-political manner. To the extent that it makes sense to talk about an 'essence to be realised', this is something to be known in its realisation. This, then, is not the discovery or unfolding of an identifiable nature,

---

16   Honneth 2014, p. vii.

17   It is for this reason that Rancière suggests the logic of emancipation is distinct from that of alienation, since 'Emancipation could then only appear as a general re-appropriation of a good lost by the community ... Emancipation could only occur as the end-point of the total process that had separated society from its truth' (Rancière 2009, p. 43). Jeaggi, while defending her own interpretation of alienation, rejects Marx's for precisely the reason that it appears as a re-appropriation of something previously lost (Jaeggi 2014, p. 39).

but an active participation in the construction of a human identity. Alienation, in this sense, becomes a term for the denial of this active participation, and its devastating consequences.

2   **Marx and Human Nature**

Conceptions of both essence and human nature appear reasonably often in Marx's writings, though, like his alternative to capitalism, they are rarely addressed directly in systematic terms. Most famously, the *Economic and Philosophical Manuscripts*, which also contain Marx's most explicit use and detailed exposition of the notion of alienation, invoke a notion of *species-being*.[18] Here, Marx argues that alienated labour necessarily also alienates human beings from their species, since it alienates them from their essential human activity. This essential human activity is represented as conscious, purposive and transformative action (labour), which is seen as distinguishing human activity from mere animal activity. The element of consciousness is particularly important, since it makes possible a moment of reflection in which humans can reflect on themselves within a world they have created: 'In tearing away the object of his production from man, estranged labour therefore tears away from him his species-life, his true species-objectivity, and transforms his advantage over animals into the disadvantage that his inorganic body, nature, is taken from him ... It estranges man from his own body, from nature as it exists outside him, from his spiritual essence, his human essence'.[19]

By the time Volume 1 of *Capital* was written, the language of essence had largely disappeared from Marx's work. Indeed, there Marx insists that 'Individuals are dealt with here only in so far as they are the personifications of economic categories, the bearers of particular class interests and relations'.[20] This might suggest that any idea of a core 'self' from which we can be alienated is a mere mystification. However, even here, many of the themes from the *Economic and Philosophical Manuscripts* reappear. In particular, many of the passages discussed in Chapter 1 of this book about the contrast between humans and non-human animals in terms of purposive, creative activity closely map passages in the earlier manuscripts. Notably, too, in Marx's treatment of cooperation we see a conception not of species-*essence*, but of species *capabilities*

---

18   *Early Writings*, pp. 326–30.
19   *Early Writings*, p. 329.
20   *Capital Vol. 1*, p. 92. See also p. 179.

[*vermögen*]: 'When the worker co-operates in a planned way with others he strips off the fetters of his individuality and develops the capabilities of his species'.[21]

Still, much of Marx's work remains marked by a deep suspicion of any general claims about the human being. Most famously, there is the sixth *Thesis on Feuerbach* where he says that 'the human essence is no abstraction inherent in each single individual. In its reality it is the ensemble of the social relations'.[22] This is often seen as marking an important shift away from a way of thinking in terms of fixed human essences to a historical approach, which recognises 'human nature' as a historical and socially conditioned product. Indeed, the *German Ideology* contains several polemical criticisms of this kind of idea. To take just one, Marx asks 'what sort of man is this, "man" who is not seen in his real historical activity and existence, but can be deduced from the lobe of his own ear or from some other feature which distinguishes him from the animals? Such a man "is contained" in himself, like his own pimple'.[23] Similarly, the *Grundrisse*, alongside more apparently 'essentialist' language, also includes several passages where the idea of general, non-historical human nature seems to be called into question:

> The human being is in the most literal sense a *Zoon politikon*, not merely a gregarious animal, but an animal which can individuate itself only in the midst of society. Production by an isolated individual outside society – a rare exception which may well occur when a civilized person in whom the social forces are already dynamically present is cast by accident into the wilderness – is as much of an absurdity as is the development of language without individuals living together and talking to each other.[24]

Moreover, even when Marx seems happy to talk about some kind of human nature, he does not tell us very much about what living according to it involves, at least beyond the general, visionary and formal claims about communism. Even at his most apparently essentialist in the *Economic and Philosophical Manuscripts* he does not offer a particularly substantive account of what it means to enact our species-being, beyond the exercise of conscious, collective and purposive activity. The *kind* of activity remains relatively unspecified, rather it is the form that matters.

---

21   *Capital Vol. 1*, p. 447. See Basso 2015, pp. 115–35.
22   *Early Writings*, p. 423.
23   *German Ideology*, p. 539.
24   *Grundrisse*, p. 84.

Perhaps the closest Marx comes to offering more substantive content is probably in a famous passage in the *German Ideology*:

> [A]s soon as the division of labour comes into being, each man has an exclusive sphere of activity, which is forced upon him and from which he can't escape. He is a hunter, a fisherman, a herdsman, or a critical critic, and must remain so if he does not want to lose his means of livelihood; while in communist society, where nobody has one exclusive sphere of activity but each can become accomplished in any branch he wishes, society regulates the general production and thus makes it possible for me to do one thing today and another tomorrow, to hunt in the morning, fish in the afternoon, rear cattle in the evening, criticise after dinner, just as I have a mind, without ever becoming hunter, fisherman, herdsman or critic.[25]

There is some reason to think that this piece is more ironic than it is often understood as being.[26] However, taken at face value it might be seen as representing a substantive ideal of a developed human nature, and, if so, perhaps an overdemanding and rather unrealistic one.[27] However, Marx's emphasis on the division of labour, and the phrase 'in any branch he wishes', suggests an alternative reading, where this is merely an example of a freely lived life (and a rather prosaic one reflecting the attitudes of a nineteenth-century German).

What are we to make of this apparent rejection of universal human nature alongside frequent claims about the human animal? The first point to observe is that Marx is clearly dismissive of a kind of 'common sense' attitude towards human nature, which fixes a particular, historically specific kind of human behaviour and seeks to naturalise it. Czesław Miłosz observes this phenomenon neatly:

> The man of the East cannot take Americans seriously because they have never undergone the experiences that teach men how relative their judgements and thinking habits are. Their resultant lack of imagination is appalling. Because they were born and raised in a given social order and

---

25   *German Ideology*, p. 53.
26   See Carver 1988, who points out that the only words actually written by Marx in the original are the probably sarcastic references to critical critics.
27   Blackledge, for example, suggests this is 'plainly utopian in the negative abstract sense of the term' (Blackledge 2012, p. 58).

in a given system of values, they believe that any other order must be 'unnatural', and that it cannot last because it is incompatible with human nature.[28]

In this context, one particular revealing passage can be found in a footnote to Volume 1 of *Capital*:

> To know what is useful for a dog, one must investigate the nature of dogs. This nature is not itself deducible from the principle of utility. Applying this to man, he that would judge all human acts, movements, relations, etc., according to the principle of utility would first have to deal with human nature in general, and then with human nature as historically modified in each epoch. Bentham does not trouble himself with this. With the driest naïveté he assumes the modern petty bourgeois, especially the English petty bourgeois, as the normal man.[29]

On the one hand, here Marx is making a familiar criticism of the Benthamite approach naturalising the status quo – assuming that bourgeois nature is human nature. On the other hand, he also suggests that if this was in fact appropriate, it would be necessary to identify human nature in general, and human nature as modified in each particular epoch. Many interpretations have suggested this is precisely Marx's approach – to isolate human nature in general, and consider it in its historical modifications.[30] However, both the sarcastic references to dogs and the conditional 'would have to' should caution against such a straight reading. Marx is saying what Bentham would have to do, not (necessarily) what he is concerned with doing.

If Bentham wanted to follow Marx's advice, how might he go about it? One way of thinking about this is in terms of what Clifford Geertz calls the stratigraphic model:

> In this conception, man is a composite of 'levels', each superimposed upon those beneath it and underpinning those above it. As one analyses man, one peels off layer after layer, each such layer being complete and irreducible in itself, revealing another, quite different sort of layer underneath. Strip off the motley forms of culture and one finds the structural and functional regularities of social organisation. Peel off these in

---

28   Miłosz 1980, p. 29.
29   *Capital Vol. 1*, pp. 758–9n.
30   See, e.g. Ollman 1976, Tabak 2012, Fromm 1961.

turn and one finds the underlying psychological factors – 'basic needs' or what-have-you – that support and make them possible. Peel off psychological factors and one is left with the biological foundations – anatomical, physiological, neurological – of the whole edifice of human life.[31]

On this model, then, 'human nature' is something like what is left once we have peeled off certain historical and social layers. Human nature is that which is basic to human beings, once they are removed from any particular context of society.

This kind of account faces a real problem, namely that it is unclear what it has to say that is in any sense *interesting*. There is a strong risk that whatever claims about the pre-social human that will result from this will be of such a general nature as to be largely banal. This is Geertz's worry, who believes that these kinds of generalisations will be unable to say anything much about human beings. We peel away layer after layer, but what we get is not the pure, genuine human within, but nothing at all, until it falls completely out of our hands. This seems to be precisely Marx's thought in the *Theses on Feuerbach* – the human essence is not to be found by stripping off layers of social relations, rather, it is in the layers themselves. Stripping off these layers may allow us to identify certain basic needs – shelter, nutrition, etc. – and these needs are certainly not trivial.[32] To take the concrete example of hunger, it remains the case that capitalism's failure to provide basic nutrition for hundreds of thousands across the world stands as a savage indictment of it. However, to talk about alienation and the denial of self-realisation – rather than merely the failure of capitalism to feed us – seems to require needs that are more complex and substantive than this. Indeed, Marx distinguishes explicitly between our merely animal needs and our human needs – which are necessarily social.

This emphasis on the social character of needs raises the possibility of an alternative way of thinking about human nature, which can broadly be called historicist. The most significant and systematic attempt to defend such a model is offered by Sean Sayers, who stresses the way in which human nature goes through a process of dynamic change across history. Human nature is not a fixed constant which can be isolated or identified, but is necessarily something in a process of development, and historically shaped by the development of the productive forces and the way in which they are employed.[33] Sayers bases

---

31   Geertz 1993, p. 37.
32   See Geras 1983 for an argument that this could form the basis for a socialist morality.
33   See Gould 1978.

his conception on the relationship between the development of human needs and human powers. As human powers develop, so do needs. 'Needs and powers are two different, negative and positive, sides of the same process – the growth of human nature'.[34] This involves, therefore, a denial of the claim that there is any such thing as a basic human need which can be isolated and used for any normative purposes. Rather:

> According to the historicist approach ... it is not possible to distinguish what is natural and what is social in this way. There are not two distinct and externally related components, a universal need on the one hand and a series of socially developed preferences on the other. There is only one thing: a socially modified need. Moreover, our needs are always modified by our social lives. They exist only in this socially developed form, and are mere abstractions apart from it. The natural and social aspects of our being always exist in concrete unity.[35]

On this model there is no sense in which human needs, desires and behaviours can be analysed to uncover something more fundamental or important underneath. There exists only successively socially modified needs, rather than some fundamental substratum of needs. This does not, however, mean that there is 'no such thing' as human nature, or that human nature is infinitely changeable. Sayers sees both of these claims as merely accepting the logic of the stratigraphic model I described above: 'If we are social beings "all the way down", then we are, at the same time and equally, natural and biological beings "all the way up"'.[36]

However, this does not mean that capitalism cannot be condemned whatsoever. Rather, history can be seen as developing through successive and progressive stages of human development, each of which contribute towards the development of human powers. As implied by the *Grundrisse* quotation I discuss in chapter 1, capitalism can be seen as both rapidly expanding and universalising human capacities, yet at the same time doing so in a way that denies possibilities for their realisation. Thus, capitalism can be condemned according to its failure to live up to these standards, as deficient from the point of view of the later historical form that it makes possible. This is part 'immanent critique', in the sense that capitalism produces needs and desires it cannot possibly meet,

---

34   Sayers 1998, p. 67.
35   Sayers 1998, p. 153.
36   Sayers 1998, p. 154.

but also involves "a humanist ideal which goes far beyond the minimal naturalistic idea of a condition in which basic needs are satisfied ... an ideal of the fullest possible development of human powers and potentialities, the vision of the human being 'rich in needs'."[37] In this sense, then, it is appropriate to talk about capitalism as thwarting human nature only in the sense that it thwarts this unfolding process of development. This is 'against human nature', but not in the sense that it conflicts with either some core essence or some ideal standard (some "predetermined yardstick" as Marx puts it). It is, rather, about the denial of development and the thwarting of potentialities.

I have already defended the enduring value of such 'visionary' accounts that do not rely on a fixed standard (either historical or ideal) for the criticism of capitalism. Nonetheless, this account (as Sayers acknowledges) leaves several questions open.[38] It allows for the normative condemnation of capitalism for failing to meet needs and desires that it creates. Yet it does not offer much criteria for identifying which needs and powers are worth developing. While capitalism might still be condemned for creating needs it cannot fill, there may also be certain needs that we wish to discourage, or that conflict with other needs in ways that must ultimately be resolved.[39] While this is not to say that certain desires and capacities are more real or more human in some transhistorical sense, it is to say that there must be (historically specific) reflection on which ones we want to encourage and discourage.[40] While the vision of broad and varied human development is not an empty one, it will be necessary to begin to 'fill in the gaps' to some degree, and at some point, in the course of development.

---

37   Sayers, 1998, p. 157.
38   See e.g. Sayers, 1998, p. 135: 'This is not to deny the distinction between 'true' and 'false' needs altogether. It is to insist that this distinction is a historical and relative one, and thus to abandon the attempt to use the fixed core of 'natural' needs as a standard by which all development beyond it may be judged.' (with similar remarks on p. 66. and p. 128.)
39   This might take the form of representing certain potentialities as themselves pathological, or representing certain pathologies as the result of certain thwarted potentialities, but in either case it seems a more substantive account of human (or good) potentialities is required.
40   See Eagleton 1999, p. 156: 'Which of the potentials which capitalism is currently obstructing should be fostered and which should not, bearing in mind that bourgeois legality currently restricts such "productive" human potentials as strangling one's guiltless neighbour with one's bare hands?'

3   Revolutionary Aristotelianism and Its Limits

The desire to fill in these gaps with more substantive values is often what drives a turn to more essentialist accounts of human nature. Generally speaking, these follow an Aristotelian approach, in which the good life is about exercising our distinctive human powers. In this sense, to ask what is good for people is to *ask the same kind of question* as what is good for a dolphin or a chrysanthemum. To know what is good for a thing is to be able to identify its *ergon* – its purpose, or the kind of activity that is characteristic of it.[41] Good and bad are defined in terms of shortfall or success in this kind of functioning. Of course, human beings have additional powers that plants and non-human animals do not have. Thus, as well as basic questions of survival, nutrition, growth etc., human beings are rational and capable of linguistic activity, capacities which must also be exercised if we are to be said to truly flourish. The human animal is more complex, but this complexity does not change the fact that we can talk about what is good for it in the same kind of objective terms as what is good for any other kind of animal.

This means that we have objective reasons to act in ways that are consistent with our *ergon*. The question 'what is it to be a good human' is the same kind of question as 'what is it to be a good pair of scissors', and has similarly objective answers. Goodness and badness are linked to the human life form, not separate matters of subjective or emotive judgements. Thus acting in accordance with our nature is *rational*. Moreover, at least under normal circumstances, we will want to act in accordance with nature. We will desire what is good, and act in accordance with it. In this sense, the development of human nature is an appropriate end in three senses: it is the natural purpose of human beings; it is the end point of a process of development; and it is what people naturally move towards, at least in 'normal' healthy conditions and when acting rationally.

There are certainly reasons to think that an idea like this lies behind Marx's remarks about human nature and his ideas about alienation. He appears to identify a particular activity which is characteristic of human beings, and which he (at least in his early writings) designates their essence. He identifies the failure to exercise that capacity consciously and freely as a reason to condemn society as it has historically existed, and as the cause of particular social, psychological and physical ills. He believes that the exercise of this capacity is something human beings will naturally find pleasurable and attractive – but

---

41   Foot 2001, MacIntyre 1999.

that where it is not properly or fully exercised (i.e. where labour is not consciously and freely undertaken) it will be repulsive.

However, he also historicises this capacity, and recognised that its failure to
be exercised is not merely a personal, individual failing, but a particular social
and historical product. Many interpreters suggest this is a fusion of Hegel and
Aristotle. For Hegel, the development of the human essence had to be understood historically as well as individually, and thus it was realised differently in
different stages of human development.[42] Thus, as well as analysing human
beings in terms of their function, we can analyse societies according to how
they help this function. According to this interpretation, social change and the
development of human nature are one and the same process. As Miekle puts
it:

> [T]he realised human society is a society of realised humans. The full real-
> isation of the potentiality inherent in human society as an essence, is at
> the same time the society in which the potentiality of the social essence
> of the human natural species is fully realised. A fully realised human
> essence, and the fully realised essence of human society, are products of
> one and the same process.[43]

Again, this seems to accord closely to what Marx says. However, this is precisely
the kind of essentialist account that critics of the idea of human nature are
worried about, since it seems to suggest that the entirety of human history and
development is somehow already contained in the human animal – and that
its trajectory can thus be understood before it has actually happened.

Moreover, historicising the Aristotelian account while still invoking a real
and identifiable human nature presents it with specific problems.[44] For one
thing, as Sayers stresses, once the essence is appropriately historicised, it is
questionable whether much of use remains: 'Once all specific local differences

---

42   See Fromm: 'For Marx, as for Hegel, the concept of alienation is based on the distinc-
      tion between existence and essence, on the fact that man's existence is alienated from
      his essence, that in reality he is not what he potentially is, or, to put it differently, that
      he is not what he ought to be and that he ought to be that which he could be' (Fromm 1961,
      p. 47).

43   Meikle 1985, p. 58.

44   Such accounts generally do see themselves as depending on a real and knowable nature,
      despite its different historical manifestations. See, e.g. Meikle, 1985, p. 43, Blackledge 2012,
      p. 33, Knight 2007, MacIntyre, 2009.

have been abstracted away, the resulting universal is so vague and general that it is no use either as a ground for social explanation or as a criterion of value.'[45] More significantly, though, according to the Aristotelian account, knowing the nature of a thing requires knowing it at all stages of its development. MacIntyre makes this clear:

> To understand any living being, an oak tree, say, or a dolphin, or a wolf, or a human being, or any group of living beings, a forest say, or a school of dolphins, or a pack of wolves, or a human society, we need to know three things: first, what its starting point was, how it originated, the biology of its coming to be; secondly, what by its nature it had and has in it to become, to flourish qua member of that particular species, so that it becomes a perfected member of that species; and thirdly, what in the course of its development from its starting point to its present condition either enabled it to move towards or to achieve that end-state or prevented it from so doing.[46]

Aristotle is capable of talking about the good for human beings because he has real exemplars of a good human being to look to. However, radical critics of capitalist society have no such luxury.

This is for the simple reason that to say that capitalist society systematically thwarts human self-realisation is to say that there exist no exemplars of people who have realised their human essence. Everyone is (to some degree) stunted. Adorno puts this starkly:

> Without exception, human beings have yet to become themselves. By the concept of the self we should properly mean their potential, and this potential stands in polemical opposition to the reality of the self.[47]

Indeed, as MacIntyre himself observes, our societies are organised in a way that makes even asking these questions difficult:

> It is clear that in our present culture learning how to ask Aristotelian questions at the level of practice, let alone formulating Aristotelian answers, is difficult precisely because of the institutional structures within which

---

45   Sayers, 1998, pp. 158–9.
46   MacIntyre 2011b, pp. 307–8.
47   Quoted in Freyenhagen 2013, p. 237n.

most contemporary practices are carried on ... So day after day our lives are compartmentalised into distinct areas to the norms of each of which we are expected to adapt, so that adaptability itself, social malleability, has become an important social characteristic. The problem, however, with this kind of compartmentalisation is that the point of such Aristotelian questions as 'What would it be for my life *as a whole* to be a flourishing life?' and 'What is my good *qua* human being and not just *qua* role-player in this or that type of situation?' disappears from view, so that such questions no longer get asked or become very difficult to ask.[48]

If there exist no exemplars, no 'healthy specimens' to examine, where are we to look to identify human nature? There are only two possible answers: Humans in the past, and humans in the present.

To take the first of these options, it is indeed true that we can take a great deal of insight from the societies of the past. Marx and Engels both did a great deal of research into these societies, and felt that such research was hugely important. However, they do not claim that any of this work can familiarise us with fully developed human beings. In the *Grundrisse* (see Chapter 1) Marx appears to suggest that pre-capitalist societies involved realisation, but only in a limited, one-sided fashion. Nonetheless, might so-called 'primitive communism' be taken as offering some sort of guide to a good life? There are a number of reasons to be sceptical of this approach. The first is the risk of a similar sort of error as naturalising the *status quo*, namely naturalising the past. The idea that the past was a more 'natural' way of living than the present is deeply rooted in much of our culture, but it is an idea we ought to be deeply suspicious of. There is no clear reason to think that to live like hunter-gatherers is more in line with our essence than anything else. Moreover, there is the sheer controversy of anthropological evidence. It *may* be possible to demonstrate that pre-class societies were more egalitarian, less violent, less divided according to gender, etc., but I would not like to hinge an entire project of human liberation on it![49]

---

48   MacIntyre 2011a, p. 12. Jaeggi, too, characterises the 'masking of practical questions' as an important component of alienation (Jaeggi 2015, p. 57).

49   There is an analogy to be drawn here with Phillips's criticism of attempts to 'prove' the equality of the sexes: 'In the very act of "disproving" the assumption, "proving" the equality of the sexes, our generous egalitarian would seem to acknowledge that if the results did not fit with his hypothesis, then regarding the sexes as unequal would be perfectly fair' (Phillips 2015, p. 45).

Finally, there is the problem of historical distance, of the extent to which we can even understand the societies of the past, let alone live like them. Indeed, we should recall in this context Marx's discussion of the ancients referred to in Chapter 3. It is precisely their distance, the fact that we could not live like them again, at least not in exactly the same way, that held their attraction for us. They are a *curiosity*, something we are entranced by because we cannot fully understand it.

Is it, then, possible to examine existing, unhealthy specimens? One version of this is simply to lapse into the stratigraphic approach discussed above, in which we attempt to isolate the true human behind the layers of cultural and historical modification. However, this is prone to all the same worries already identified. Alternatively, it might be suggested that a conception of a healthy specimen can be identified by merely negating or holding a mirror up to non-healthy specimens. This is an attractive thought, but I think it is inadequate. Certainly, being able to point to instances of ills and say 'avoid that, and avoid the things that cause that', is of great value. It gives a set of pointers and co-ordinates, just in the same way that 'here be dragons' tells us where to avoid. But it is a major step, and it seems to me an unwarranted one, to go from acknowledging that these sorts of observations are *useful*, perhaps even *necessary*, for identifying what a healthy specimen might look like, to claiming that they are *sufficient* to do so.[50]

This points in a new and different direction. Rather than seeing human essence as involving a particular set of capacities which can be discovered by investigation, it suggests an account of essence as something yet to be realised, not something, as it were, lying within human beings, but as an *achievement*. On this reading, it makes sense to talk of humans as alienated not from what they are, but what they could be. There are two ways of understanding this kind of 'anticipatory' approach. The first might be in terms of a formal account of what it means to live according to our essence. On this reading, human species-activity is simply freely self-determined activity, the kind of activity which is made possible under communism, as Ollman puts it, 'species-life activity is what people are moving towards rather than what people of all periods actually

---

50 It might be responded that knowledge of *all* potential ills might enable such knowledge of the good life, just as identifying *all* the regions of dragons might make our map complete. However, there doesn't seem any reason to think that we currently have full knowledge of these ills, nor ought we to have any desire to find it. Catastrophism has a certain pedigree in radical politics, but it is not a particularly healthy one. See also Freyenhagen 2013, Ch. 8.

engage in'.[51] This involves no substantive claims about what kinds of activity are good for people, so long as it is their own activity, and they are capable of recognising it as such.[52] On this account, alienation is not a separation from a pre-existing essence, but simply a failure of free action, a deficient relationship to the world (as Jaeggi puts it, a relation of relationlessness).[53] The second interpretation might be willing to concede that there *are* substantive questions of the human good which can, in principle, be answered, but insist that there are material barriers to answering those questions, and that asking those questions independent of confronting and overcoming those barriers is moot. This might be one way of understanding Erich Fromm's characterisation of Marxism as 'essentially prophetic Messianism in the language of the nineteenth century'[54] or even Trotsky's more wildly visionary speculations about the potentials for human transformation under democratic self-government.[55] These two interpretations are not identical, but they both point to the same conclusion: What it is to live according to our nature is something that is to be achieved and discovered in the future, not totally identifiable in the here and now.

4 The Human Bad

Where does this leave talk of alienation? Does rejecting the possibility of a knowable human essence mean rejecting the concept of alienation completely? I think it does not. The theory of alienation requires the claim that it is possible to develop a relationship to one's own activity which is in some sense pathological or deficient, to the extent that we fail to recognise that activity as our own, and that this can come about as a consequence of specific kinds of social relationships of production. In this sense, the theory of alienation only depends on a claim about what is *bad* for human beings.[56] This *is* a claim about

---

51 Ollman 1976, p. 116.
52 See e.g. Kouvelakis 2003, p. 306: 'As for the notion of species, it exists only as self-determination of the people, a moment in which the people actually attains its concept'.
53 Jaeggi 2014, pp. 28–30.
54 Fromm 1961, p. 3.
55 Trotsky 2005, pp. 207–9.
56 In describing alienation in these terms, I am not denying the claim that capitalist alienation has a progressive dimension in the sense that it also increases human capacities for self-realisation (see, e.g. Sayers, 1998, p. 140), but merely stressing that alienation is also, and necessarily, a failure of such self-realisation.

human nature, but it is of a very different form to the accounts discussed above. To have an alienated relationship to one's labour is the cause of physical, mental and social ills. I fail to see how it is possible to assert this without saying *something* about the human animal. Crucially, however, these are claims based on observable phenomena, and making speculative generalisations about why those phenomena arise. Even more crucially, the claims they make are *negative*, they describe the origins of certain ills, but make no immediate claim about the human good. They say, essentially, performing labour under conditions of domination is bad for the human animal. The authority of this claim rests on the fact that capitalist conditions of labour really can be linked to real experiences of suffering and distress.

Many will find even these kinds of claims controversial, but at the very least they ought to be controversial for a different reason than some of the other conceptions of human nature I described above. It might be useful to draw explicitly an analogy which has been present in the background, namely with medicine. This analogy is important, since very few would assert that the broad generalisations about the human organism employed in medicine are non-theoretical, idealist concepts (as Althusser thinks claims about the human essence are). Rather they are concepts which aim at an approximation to processes of material reality, and stand and fall (even if that fall can be rather slow) on their success in treatment. Yet effective medicine does not obviously depend on a fixed and fully specified model of the healthy human. Whatever a medical practitioner's wider picture of the good life, it is possible for them to treat specific illnesses without direct reference to it. The controversy which ought to arise concerns whether these generalisations are accurate ones, whether the diagnoses they make are helpful, and whether the methodology they are based on is sound.

Consider, by way of comparison, the work by Wilkinson and Pickett that I mentioned in Chapter 4. In an attempt to ground their findings in an account of human nature, they invoke a direct comparison between humans and non-human primates, specifically chimps and bonobos. Chimps are hierarchical and male-dominated, with the hierarchy being established and maintained largely through violent conflict. In contrast, bonobos, 'the caring, sharing ape', are significantly less hierarchical, and frequently use sexual activity to avoid conflict and smooth over the problems posed by scarce resources. Why bring this up, you might reasonably ask?

> Interestingly, a section of DNA, known to be important in the regulation of social, sexual and parenting behaviour, has been found to differ between chimps and bonobos. It is perhaps comforting to know that, at least in this

section of DNA humans have the bonobo rather than the chimp pattern, suggesting our common ancestor may have had a preference for making love rather than war.[57]

While some might feel relieved or comforted by this, just as many will see confirmation of their fears that any invocation of human nature risks a slide into biological essentialism, which reduces complex human relationships to social and sexual imperatives. Indeed, as I have suggested elsewhere, Wilkinson and Pickett themselves make some claims which appear to naturalise gender norms in a problematic way.[58] However, it would be wrong to think that either their wider arguments or the apparently causal links they identify stand and fall with this account. Just the opposite: the fact that they identify connections between social inequality and a variety of social ills holds irrespective of these claims, and offers vitally important insights. Even if they had not offered these slightly dubious claims (and one wishes they hadn't), there would still be strong reason to think that the connections they identify are real, and significant. They are still capable of making the substantive claim 'Inequality is bad for us'. This *is* a claim about the nature of human beings, but it stands independently of their particular claims about what is good for human beings (or our evolutionary heritage).

How do we assess the strength or weakness of a claim of this sort? It stands and falls on its *explanatory power*. Here it is useful to draw an analogy with the way in which Wood has attempted to defend Marx's views on human nature:

> Marx gives no real argument for identifying labour or production as the most basic or essential human function. But I think he may have been persuaded of this identification by considerations drawn from his materialist conception of history. According to this conception, the basic determinant of social life and historical development is the relentless tendency of human beings to develop and exercise their capacities to dominate nature and creatively shape it to satisfy human wants and express human aspirations ... Marx takes production to be the fundamental and encompassing human function because human beings, in practice, acknowledge it to be of fundamental importance to the character of their lives. And he believes the development and exercise of productive powers is man's most basic aspiration because it shows itself in history to be such. His justification

---

57   Wilkinson & Pickett 2009, p. 205.
58   See Swain 2013.

for this belief consists in whatever empirical evidence there is that the materialist conception of history is a correct conception.[59]

I don't wish to comment on Marx's theory of history here, but it seems to me that something analogous can be said about what is generally called the theory of alienation. The fact that the theory of alienation can offer us a real under-standing of a variety of phenomena in capitalist society necessarily counts in favour of the negative, causal claims about human nature on which it relies. This is not to say that such claims are indefeasible, or cannot be doubted, but they stand and fall alongside the explanatory claims to which they are intim-ately connected.

It is somewhat striking that, while Wood asserts that Marx's conception of human nature stands and falls with the theory of historical materialism, it is a cornerstone of Althusser's arguments that the two are incompatible. This sug-gests to me, if nothing else, how different the understandings of the notion of human nature which are at stake are. The kind of essentialist model of human nature which Althusser is understandably suspicious of is not really what we are left with. Rather, we are left with a set of claims about the human animal in specific situations, which are, to one extent or another, rooted in empirical evidence.

Against this, it might be responded that this depends on an overly subjective account of alienation, one that reduces alienation to mere subjective experi-ences rather than, as Marx stresses, objective social structures. I think this rests on a misunderstanding. The point is that certain subjective mental experiences have their roots in objective social structures. However, if it was never possible to link these two things together – if objective alienation was never the cause of subjective suffering and distress – I think we would lack (at least some) reas-ons to condemn these objective conditions. The subjective experiences thus matter, and are a crucial part of alienation itself. Continuing the medicine ana-logy, though they are the results of an underlying cause and do not exhaust the definition of flu, the symptoms of flu are *part of what it is to have flu*. Likewise, what it is to be alienated includes subjective suffering and distress. Of course, this puts a premium on being able to demonstrate links between more or less alienating conditions and better or worse symptoms, but there are some good reasons to think that this is possible.[60]

---

59   Wood 2004, p. 29.
60   See Crinson and Yuill 2008, for the beginnings of an attempt to link empirical data on healthcare inequalities to a theory of alienation.

This negativist conception of the human – or perhaps of the inhuman – can be combined with the 'anticipatory' conception of human nature as something yet to be achieved as the basis for a coherent theory of alienation. Labour under conditions of domination, in which we lack control over the subjective conditions of our labour, is bad for us. We *know* that it is bad for us because it is the cause of various physical and mental ills. However, we do not know positively and in any great detail what form activity might take which is good for us. We can know (at least one example of) what it is to live 'against our nature', but it does not follow that we can know in any substantive detail what it is to live 'in accordance with our nature', or even that there is one such way.[61] Rather, this remains something to be worked out in the course of and alongside establishing conditions of freedom. In this sense, such negative conceptions can be incorporated within the processes of emancipation, without short-circuiting or overdetermining them.

How does this get worked out? How might we begin to answer the questions that an anticipatory account leaves open? It does seem we might want answers to those questions, for two reasons. Firstly, we might want to go beyond the merely formal account of unalienated activity as self-determining activity. Even if we take a similar approach to Engels's remarks about sexuality (see Chapter 4) and argue that such questions are none of our business, we might hope they eventually becomes *someone's* business. Secondly, even limiting ourselves to a purely formal account, we might require at least some sense of the kind of values, capacities and norms (or perhaps virtues) which *make possible this self-determination*. If such questions are blocked by our contemporary forms of life, how do we unblock them?

Returning to the idiom of asking Aristotelian questions, MacIntyre makes some suggestive remarks about the role of resistance:

> [T]he resistance with which I am primarily concerned is the resistance of the established order, of the representatives of the established patterns of power, to any attempt to ask and answer Aristotelian questions at the level of practice. As you and I encounter the resistance elicited by any systematic attempt to achieve central human goods, we learn to define what we are politically.[62]

---

61   Remember that I above rejected the idea that the good could be the mere mirror image of the bads, even in scenarios where we have complete knowledge of the bad. See Freyenhagen 2013, Ch. 8, esp. Section II.

62   MacIntyre 2011a, p. 16.

It is, in other words, in the course of challenging the obstacles to our collective self-realisation that we create the spaces and contexts in which to work out
what such a realisation might look like. Yet in doing so we move unavoidably
into the field of politics. Peter Sedgwick, in his work on Marxist Psychiatry, also
stresses the importance of the political field for helping people clarify conceptions of the good life. His concern is that those labelled as (mentally) ill, and
who are genuinely suffering, are capable of articulating for themselves what
constitutes both their illness and what would constitute treatment. In response
to a 'technologising of illness' or 'medicalisation of moral values', he instead
asserts the importance of a 'politicisation of medical goals', in which it becomes
possible to clearly articulate demands on existing health services, and in so
doing clarify what might constitute better health.[63] These are questions which
take on an unavoidably political dimension, and, in as much as they exist as
demands, an unavoidably political structure.[64]

The idea that we might define questions of the human good in political contexts, in particular those in conflict with the existing order of things, returns us
to a familiar point from the previous chapters: the substantive content which
might guide and help fill in the detail of a vision of communism should emerge
politically, in the course of movements of resistance and reaction to specific ills,
rather than through pre-political standards, whether it be distributive ideals or
human essences. This, however, turns attention sharply to the question of politics, of its opportunities and limits, which will be considered in the next chapter.

---

63   Sedgwick 1982, p. 40.
64   Ironically, perhaps, this can be seen as agreeing with Laclau and Mouffe that there is no
      value to speaking of the human essence prior to its articulation in political terms, while
      disagreeing that this renders all talk of essence suspect.

Denouncing the Abyss

> The so-called revolutions of 1848 were but poor incidents – small fractures and fissures in the dry crust of European society. However, they denounced the abyss.
>
> MARX, Speech at the Anniversary of the People's Paper, 1856[1]

∴

1 Politics and the Political

The previous chapters have been concerned with practical questions largely from the point of view of the critical theorist. It is the question of what is wrong with capitalism, and the appropriate way of criticising it and developing alternatives from that criticism. In particular, I have suggested that these alternatives should emerge as part of political movements, rather than be seen as prior to them. As I have suggested already, these problems are ethical in the sense that they pose real practical problems for the relationships between theorists committed to emancipation and the social movements of which they are a part. However, these questions, of course, do not exhaust the issue of ethics within social movements. This chapter, then, focuses in particular on the question of politics and political action, precisely because it is in this area that questions of self-emancipation appear to be most complex and urgent. Marx insists that movements for emancipation must engage in and enter the sphere of politics, but it is also the sphere in which a commitment to self-emancipation is most tested.

By most modern understandings of politics Marx was a political thinker and activist. He was concerned with the analysis and criticism of social and political institutions and, however vaguely, advocated an alternative form of political organisation. However, this description is already fraught with difficulties, since the definition of politics remains vague and contested for both Marx and us. On the one hand, it has been a great achievement of success-

---

1 MECW 14, p. 655.

ive movements of liberation to force recognition that the personal is political. On the other hand, an increasingly narrow definition of politics abounds in both political philosophy and ordinary life, such that politics is identified with what politicians do, and questions of power beyond state authority, and that authority itself, disappear from view. It is possible for a London businessman to write an editorial for the *Evening Standard* insisting on 'taking the politics out of politics',[2] and for 'anti-political' electoral movements to win substantial representation in institutions of political power. No wonder, then, that when it comes to examining what Marx thought about politics, there is substantial room for disagreement, and discussion at cross purposes.

Disagreements about the proper scope of 'politics' focus on a number of different questions, with varying degrees of explicitness. One useful distinction is between processual and situated definitions of politics.[3] Processual definitions of politics emphasise politics as a kind of (human) activity that can take place in broadly any kind of society in which questions of power, co-operation and the proper use of resources arise. For example, Roberto Unger describes politics as 'struggle over the resources and arrangements that set the basic terms of our practical and passionate relations. Preeminent among these arrangements is the formative institutional and imaginative context of social life'.[4] For Young, 'politics in this sense concerns all aspects of institutional organization, public action, social practices and habits, and cultural meanings insofar as they are potentially subject to collective evaluation and decision-making'.[5] This approach is often aimed at making questions which have traditionally been placed in the private sphere explicitly political, most obviously questions of gender and sexuality.[6]

Situated definitions of politics, on the other hand, see politics as an activity taking place in a particular location or sphere. Usually, this sphere is the state, or at least questions of government and legitimate rule. These approaches, for a variety of different reasons, see the political realm as encompassing what states do, and how people operate within and in relation to the state's institutions and structures.[7] Thus, strictly speaking, the personal is not political, and only becomes political when it becomes, for example, a demand for state

---

2 Palumbo 2015.
3 See Leftwich 2004.
4 Unger 1987, p. 145.
5 Young 1990, p. 9.
6 Squires 2004.
7 See, e.g., and from wildly different intellectual starting points, Swift 2004, Schmitt 2007, Poulantzas 2000.

intervention into personal life (or, in the case of abortion rights, for example, to end it). However, it is also possible to have situated definitions that look outside the state. Murray Bookchin, for example, suggests that the state ought to be seen as 'a completely alien formation, a thorn in the side of human development, an exogenous entity that has incessantly encroached on the social and political realms' and 'has steadily invaded the political domain, which, for all its past shortcomings, had empowered communities, social groupings, and individuals'.[8] While Bookchin evidently shares many of the pre-occupations of processual accounts, he explicitly rules out the state as a site of politics. Instead, politics happens elsewhere, in democratic assemblies and municipalities.

A different point of disagreement about politics (overlapping with but distinct from the first) is the question of *force*. Some definitions see politics as fundamentally about force. For example, Nicholson argues that 'The use and control of force by some members of the society and the moves by others to influence their use of it, or to gain control of it for themselves, are the distinctively political human activities. On this view, there is politics in a society, and between societies, but nowhere else'.[9] An opposing view, however, sees politics as fundamentally about reaching agreement through discussion, and thus sees the use of force not as the central question of politics (nor as its continuation by other means), but as the moment that politics proper ends.[10] This conception of politics sees it as 'a unique form of rule, distinct from other forms of rule, such as autocracy or totalitarianism'.[11] Connected to this is a disagreement about the character of politics in general: Is it aimed at agreement and consensus, or fundamentally structured around antagonisms that are largely irresolvable? For example, Carl Schmitt suggests that 'The political entity cannot by its very nature be universal in the sense of embracing all of humanity and the entire world'.[12] Rather, politics is fundamentally structured by an irreducible friend/enemy relationship. To the extent such relationships are removed, and a political community expands to include everyone, it ceases to be political: 'What remains is neither politics nor state, but culture, civilisation, economics, morality, law, art, entertainment, etc'.[13]

---

8   Bookchin 2015. See also Critchley 2007, pp. 88–131.
9   Nicholson 2004, p. 50.
10   See Crick 2004, Arendt 1970.
11   Crick 2004, p. 67.
12   Schmitt 2007, p. 53.
13   Schmitt 2007, p. 53.

2   Politicising and Depoliticising

These contested definitions and notions of politics make talking about Marx and politics difficult. But so does Marx himself. In his early, pre-1845, works, the political sphere is presented as an alienated sphere of social relations. Thus, the state appears as an outgrowth of society that is unable to truly resolve its contradictions, and political emancipation is explicitly contrasted with social emancipation. In the 1843 critique of Hegel, Marx rejects the idea that any particular political estate can represent society as a whole, stressing instead the fundamental democratic power of the people (See Chapter 2). In *On the Jewish Question* he distinguishes sharply between human emancipation and political emancipation, which is limited to a set of rights within the state, while in *Notes on the King of Prussia and Social Reform* he rejects Ruge's condescension towards the struggles of the Silesian weavers, defending them against the charge that they are politically unsophisticated, and suggesting that their struggles are in fact far more radical. This is because the weavers revolted not just against political isolation, but against alienation in their own life: 'The community from which [their] own labour separates [them] is life itself, physical and spiritual life, human morality, human activity, human enjoyment, *human nature*'.[14] This sets up an apparent distinction between political and human revolution:

> Just as the disastrous isolation from this nature is disproportionately more far-reaching, unbearable, terrible and contradictory than the isolation from the political community, so too the transcending of this isolation and even a partial reaction, a *rebellion* against it, is so much greater, just as the *man* is greater than the citizen in human life than political life. Hence, however limited an industrial revolt may be, it contains within itself a universal soul: and however universal a political revolt may be, its colossal form conceals a narrow spirit.[15]

Marx goes on to explain that the political revolution takes as its point of view the state as 'an abstract totality which exists only through its separation from real life and which is *unthinkable* in the absence of an organised antithesis between the universal idea and the individual existence of man'.[16] A revolution

---

14   *Early Writings*, p. 418.
15   *Early Writings*, p. 419.
16   *Early Writings*, p. 419.

that possesses this 'limited and contradictory' soul only 'organises a dominant group within society at the cost of society'.[17]

These passages suggest an attitude towards politics that is largely negative, even 'anti-political'.[18] They express the idea that politics is situated, focused on the state and its institutions. Moreover, this sphere is a pale, shallow, reflection of truly human activity, and cannot itself provide revolutionary opportunities. Even in these passages, however, Marx stresses that 'All revolution – the *overthrow* of the existing ruling power and the *dissolution* of the old order – is a *political act*'. This is no different for the establishment of socialism, which 'stands in need of this political act just as it stands in need of *destruction and dissolution*. But as soon as its organising functions begin and its *goal*, its *soul* emerges, socialism throws its *political* mask aside'.[19] Thus even if what is desired is not a political *revolution*, a political *moment* within it remains essential. What distinguishes the socialist revolution from a merely political revolution is that, because its perspective originates outside of politics, it is capable of proceeding beyond this political moment, and ultimately undermining politics itself.

There are both affinities and differences between these passages and the 1843 manuscripts on Hegel, in which democracy is considered the basic genus of politics (the solution to the *riddle* of every constitution),[20] and thus any specific, narrow representation is necessarily a shallow form. In these writings, Marx stresses the importance of universal suffrage, and of the constituting power of the people themselves as political subject, independent of any estate. One way of interpreting this is as pitting a processual account of politics against a situated one – politics as a basic human capacity for self-government versus politics as the narrow sphere(s) of the state.[21] It is, on this reading, precisely when the people enters politics that this division becomes eroded. The importance of political emancipation remains emphasised in the 1844 manuscripts, where Marx argues that 'the emancipation of society from private property, etc., from servitude, is expressed in the *political* form of the *emancipation of workers*'.[22] In the *King of Prussia* Marx does not assert democracy against the state, but rather humanity against politics, but elements of the structure remain substantially the same. Firstly, it is only from the point of view of the

---

17   *Early Writings*, p. 419.
18   See Humphrys and Tietze 2013, and replies in Barker 2014 and Callinicos 2015.
19   *Early Writings*, p. 420.
20   *Early Writings*, p. 87.
21   See Kouvelakis 2003, Critchley 2007, pp. 114–19.
22   *Early Writings*, p. 333.

masses – now given specific form in the weavers – that it is possible to recognise and resolve social contradictions; and secondly, their arrival on the political scene cannot help transform politics itself, stretching its limits and expanding its reach.

This structure is carried through into the *Communist Manifesto*, which insists that 'the first step in the revolution by the working class is to raise the proletariat to the position of ruling class to win the battle of democracy',[23] and remains largely in place until the 1848 revolutions. It is arguably after the failure of those revolutions that Marx is at his most 'anti-political'. To give one example from 1852:

> The Communists can help accelerate the dissolution of bourgeois society and yet leave the dissolution of the Prussian state in the hands of bourgeois society. If a man whose immediate aim was the overthrow of the Prussian state were to preach the destruction of the social order as a means to this end he would be like that deranged engineer who wished to blow up the whole planet in order to remove a rubbish-heap. But if the final goal of the League is the overthrowing of the social order, the method by which this is to be achieved is necessarily that of political revolution and this entails the overthrow of the Prussian state, just as an earthquake entails the overthrow of a chicken-house.[24]

Here, the overthrow of the political state will appear as a trifling consequence of a much deeper, social revolution. This is the conception of 'politics' that dominates Marx's writings after this point, sharing the geological metaphor with the quotation at the beginning of this chapter. It is the basic theoretical approach that guides the writing of the *18th Brumaire* and is expressed succinctly in the *1859 Preface*. Broadly, it is a sense of the political as a sphere arising on the basis of a given form of production, and thus comprehensible only by reference to that form. Thus the state is an outgrowth of society, and the capitalist state an outgrowth of capitalist society. Conflicts in the political sphere are the reflection of contradictions in the economic and social sphere, and the sphere of politics itself cannot resolve the contradictions on which it arises.[25] Note that

---

23   *Communist Manifesto*, p. 104. See also *German Ideology*, pp. 52–3: 'every class which is aiming at domination, even when its domination, as is the case with the proletariat, leads to the abolition of the old form of society in its entirety and of domination in general, must first conquer political power'.
24   MECW 11, p. 404.
25   Callinicos 2004.

this sees the state not, like Bookchin, as exogenous, but as endogenous, in the sense that it arises from society itself. Not an infection, but the crust of a tectonic structure.

Yet throughout this, it remains important to stress that political activity by the working class is essential. This notion appears prominently in his writings about the Chartists and the Ten Hours Bill. It is clear that he still sees a political moment as being essential to working-class self-emancipation. For example, in 1871 he writes that:

> every movement in which the working class comes out as a *class* against the ruling classes and attempts to coerce them by *pressure from without* is a *political movement*. For instance, the attempt in a particular factory or even a particular trade, to force a shorter working day out of the individual capitalists by *strikes*, etc, is a purely economic movement. The movement to force through an eight-hour *law*, etc, however, is a *political* movement. And in this way, out of the separate economic movements of the workers there grows up everywhere a *political* movement, that is to say a movement of the *class*, with the object of achieving its interests in a general form, in a form possessing general, socially binding force.[26]

Here the binding together of the working class can only be achieved when its struggles are raised to the level of political demands, and this remains a necessary step, even if it is seen as something that happens more or less automatically, and as a reflection of far deeper processes at work. Similar ideas are repeatedly pressed by both Marx and Engels against Bakunin and his supporters in this period, who, they argue, fail to see that 'Every class movement *as a class movement*, is necessarily and was always a political movement.'[27]

The more processual account of politics makes a re-appearance again in the aftermath of the Paris Commune. For Marx, the commune was

> a thoroughly expansive political form, while all previous forms of government had been emphatically repressive. Its true secret was this. It was essentially a working-class government, the produce of the struggle of the producing against the appropriating class, the political form at last discovered under which to work out the economical emancipation of

---

26   MECW 44, p. 258.
27   MECW 43, p. 491. See Draper, 1990, Chapter 6, and Basso, 2015, pp. 163–70, for several further examples.

> Labour ... The political rule of the producer cannot coexist with the per-
> petuation of his social slavery. The Commune was therefore to serve as a
> lever for uprooting the economical foundations upon which rests the very
> existence of class rule. With labour emancipated, every man becomes a
> working man, and productive labour ceases to be a class attribute.[28]

It is hard to read this any other way than as reflecting a broader, processual account of politics that necessarily goes beyond the narrow, state-focused version. The commune is a political form, but it is necessarily broader and more expansive than any that has gone before. It can uproot the economic conditions of society, and resolve their contradictions. Again, it should be clear that this is a more expansive conception of politics than that expressed in some of the passages above. This is not the politics that arises out of contradictions but cannot remove them – it is the political form (at last discovered) which *can* remove them.[29]

It is in this period, only months after the commune, that Engels asserts that '[R]evolution is the supreme act of politics; whoever wants it must also want the means, political action, which prepares for it, which gives the education in revolution and without which the workers will be duped ... the day after the struggle'.[30]

Is it possible, from all of this, to say anything particularly general about Marx's approach to politics? There are, I think two key points: First, there is a narrow, situated sphere of politics that cannot ultimately resolve social questions but which working class struggles cannot avoid engaging in the course of their development; and second, that in the course of struggle the working class develops forms of self-organisation that institutionalise its capacity for self-rule, and that these will necessarily expand and transform the narrow bounds of 'politics-as-usual'.[31] This can be understood in terms of a dynamic of politicising and depoliticising. If 'politics' designates a narrow sphere that concentrates questions of power within it, this also acts to render those other spheres as 'unpolitical'. Thus the 'social' and, in particular, the 'economic' become perceived as non-political. This has a reifying effect, representing relationships

---

28   *First International and After*, p. 212.
29   See Kouvelakis 2007.
30   MECW 22, p. 417.
31   Basso, 2015, pp. 177–89, notes the repeated importance for Marx and Engels of the political
      articulation of workers acting or being 'in common', in particular in their discussions of
      the commune and the dictatorship of the proletariat, and links it to ideas of prefiguring
      communism itself.

in these spheres as natural, while political authority appears from outside, merely 'intervening'. This is, in capitalism, particularly acute. As I discussed in Chapter 1, capitalism has replaced a series of hierarchical distinctions of birth, religion, etc. with the cash nexus, and in doing so has translated a series of questions that were previously political into economic ones. Domination and exploitation are now (primarily) economic questions, while 'politics' is the reserve of a coercive state.[32] This is the sense in which politics is appropriately seen as reflecting and concentrating social contradictions, while also being unable to resolve them.

It is precisely this division that (good) revolutionary practice undermines. In the process of revolution, people see the political character of everyday life, recognise that what appear to be natural relations are human choices, and develop new ways of living. It is these contexts that allow for the articulation of shared conceptions of the good life and of appropriate social arrangements. This is *politicising*, to the extent that it helps make visible the political character of social and economic relationships. It is *depoliticising*, to the extent that it undermines the basis of any special sphere of the political, in particular one that concentrates political power. If politics is everywhere, it is nowhere. This approach stresses the importance of formations which recognise the political character of all economic questions, and thus fuse these questions together. For Marx, this was the Paris Commune, for later Marxists, the Mass Strike,[33] the Soviets, or 'the workers' councils in Hungary, the *shoras* in Iran, the *cordones* in Chile, the inter-factory strike committee in Poland'.[34]

Of course, questions of emphasis might matter here. The Marx of 1843 and of 1871 seems to emphasise the politicising side of this dynamic – the commune as expansive form, democracy as the solved riddle of all constitutions – while the Marx of 1844 and 1852 seems to emphasise the depoliticising side – either the truly human community sloughing off the atrophied political layer like a snake shedding its skin, or deep social earthquakes toppling the spires of politics like so many cowsheds. This difference of emphasis may matter for various reasons. For example, it may be more than a semantic question whether communism is seen as involving the abolition or the elevation of the political.[35] It

---

32   See Wood 1995, pp. 53–60.

33   'If the sophisticated theory proposes to make a clever logical dissection of the mass strike for the purpose of getting at the "purely political mass strike", it will by this dissection, as with any other, not perceive the phenomenon in its living essence, but will kill it altogether' (Luxemburg 2005).

34   Blackledge 2010, p. 123.

35   Berki 1983, pp. 166–8.

may also matter strategically, in terms of both where to focus activity and where to expect social transformation.

However, it is important to stress that whichever emphasise is preferred Marx does not suggest that either can avoid the narrow sphere of politics altogether. Both *still see political struggle as necessary for social transformation*. This is not a choice between a social strategy and a political strategy. Even at his least 'political', Marx still insists that the revolutionary process demands entering into the field of politics itself, that 'abortion of society'. In other words, whether the goal is expressed as politicisation or depoliticisation, *revolution itself is a substantively political act*.

Moreover, politics in this sense is always a matter of force and conflict, something Marx stresses again and again. Marx would have found the idea of politics ending when force begins ludicrous. Rather, 'the struggle between two political powers lies neither within the sphere of civil law, nor within the sphere of criminal law ... Only one power can supply the answer – history'[36] and 'Between equal right force decides'.[37] Elsewhere, Marx talks about political power being manifest in the form of the truncheon.[38] Indeed, much of his attitude to politics can be summarised in the following quotation from the *Poverty of Philosophy*:

> Do not say that social movement excludes political movement. There is never a political movement which is not at the same time social. It is only in an order of things in which there are no more classes and class antagonisms that social evolutions will cease to be political revolutions. Till then, on the eve of every general reshuffling of society, the last word of social science will always be:
> *Le combat ou la mort; la lutte sanguinaire ou le néant. C'est ainsi que la question est invinciblement posée*.[39]

3   Demanding, Smashing, Seizing

One reason that Marx stresses engagement with 'politics' in the narrower sense seems to concern the importance of *demands*. In the same letter of 1871 where he asserts the centrality of political struggle, he argues that:

---

36   MECW 8, p. 325.
37   *Capital Vol. 1*, p. 344.
38   MECW 14, p. 326.
39   MECW 6, p. 213.

Where the working class is not yet far enough advanced in its organisation to undertake a decisive campaign against the collective power, i.e., the political power of the ruling classes, it must at any rate be trained for this by continual agitation against, and a hostile attitude towards the policies of the ruling classes. Otherwise it will remain a plaything in their hands.[40]

This is part of the importance of maintaining class struggle in order to train and develop the capacities of the working class. Elsewhere, he emphasises the importance of mobilisation and struggle for the process of development, being profoundly scornful of strategies that would seek to avoid class struggle, since 'the continual conflicts between masters and men ... the indispensable means of holding up the spirit of the labouring class, and preventing them from becoming apathetic, thoughtless, more or less well-fed instruments of production'.[41] In a statement of 1879, Marx and Engels expressly link this to self-emancipation, suggesting that 'it is therefore impossible for us to co-operate with people who wish to expunge this class struggle from the movement'.[42]

The importance of this lies not so much in the success or failure of any particular conflict, as the opportunities it affords for developing working-class organisation. Engels writes about the Ten Hours Bill that:

The time and exertions spent in agitating so many years for the Ten Hours' Bill is not lost, although its immediate end be defeated. The working classes, in this agitation, found a mighty means to get acquainted with each other: to come to a knowledge of their social position and interests, to organise themselves and to know their strength. The working man, who has passed through such an agitation, is no longer the same he was before; and the whole working class, after passing through it, is a hundred times stronger, more enlightened, and better organised than it was at the out-set. It *was* an agglomeration of mere units, without any knowledge of each other, without any common tie; and now it is a powerful body, conscious of its strength, recognised as the 'Fourth Estate', and which will soon be the *first*.[43]

These demands, which are political at least to the extent they are directed at and can only be met by state authorities, play both an organisational and a

---

40   MECW 44, p. 258.
41   MECW 12, p. 169.
42   MECW 45, p. 408.
43   MECW 10, p. 275.

pedagogical role. Organisationally, it builds up campaign groups, trade unions and parties. It necessitates organisational cooperation, and builds ties of solidarity between workers. It also helps to bring more people into class struggle in general, and thus deepens the roots of these organisations, and widens their potential audience.

However, arguably more important is the pedagogical function, which has both a negative and a positive aspect. Negatively, as Engels observes, it helps the worker recognise their own location in society: to realise the limits of what can be achieved within the existing shape of things, and thus that deeper changes are required. This is the sense, expressed in the *Communist Manifesto*, in which certain measures, 'which appear economically insufficient and untenable ... in the course of the movement, necessitate further inroads upon the old social order'.[44] Positively, however, it also helps provide workers with the intellectual tools to develop alternative conceptions of social organisation.

Consider the following remarks from MacIntyre:

> To imagine a worthwhile revolution is to be able to envisage radically and systematically different types of social institutions and social relationships, institutions aimed at the achievement of the common good. Revolutions become possible only when enough members of some political society are not only able to imagine such alternatives, but are prepared to participate in realising them in order to achieve their common good ... For any group to satisfy these conditions requires a remarkable shift in social imagination and insight. How might such a shift be achieved?
>
> Only, I believe, by the experience of concurrently trying to make and remake the badly needed institutions of everyday life through grass-roots organisation, trade unions, cooperatives, small businesses that serve neighbourhood needs, schools, clinics, transport systems and the like, so that they may serve the common good, and, by doing so, learning that only by breaking with the political norms of the *status quo* can the relevant common goods be achieved. For those who engage in such making and remaking will encounter that resistance to any breach of those norms which is the characteristic response of the established order. It is that resistance that makes revolutionaries.[45]

44   *Communist Manifesto*, p. 104.
45   MacIntyre 2011a, pp. 319–20.

It is because of a similar dynamic between resistance and revolution that Marx emphasises the importance of maintaining class struggle, and of including within that class struggle political demands. This can be understood in the pedagogical terms I discussed in Chapter 2. Demands for specific measures have an expressive and proleptic function. They allow the workers to project themselves into a later stage of development, and in the process of attempting to enact that later stage come to a better awareness of their own desires and the barriers to achieving them. This process then reflects back, transforming the working class as a collective subject, and developing new capacities within them. De Smet argues that the archetypal form of this is the transitional demand, as articulated by Trotsky, which attempts to articulate demands that link the particular conditions of the proletariat to their general emancipation.

Another example might be the way David Harvey talks about the potential emancipatory content of the demand for the 'right to the city' as a 'political, class-based demand'.[46] For Harvey, diverse political campaigns around urban questions – rent, access to housing, water supply, electoral representation – might converge to form a far more radical call for control over the modern city:

> if these various oppositional movements did somehow come together – coalesce, for example, around the slogan of the right to the city – then what should they demand? The answer ... is simple enough: greater democratic control over the production and use of the surplus. Since the urban process is a major channel of use, then the right to the city is constituted by establishing democratic control over the deployment of the surpluses through urbanisation.[47]

Revolts over these sorts of issues pose political questions – in whose interests is the city run, how could we organise it differently? It is in beginning to politically organise in order to assert and achieve these demands that people take the steps required to re-organise social life. Harvey gives the example of the revolts over water privatisation in Bolivia between 2000 and 2005. He notes in particular the way in which the city of El Alto developed varying new forms of democratic organisation and politics, on the basis of the traditions developed in these opposition movements.[48]

---

46   Harvey 2012, p. 136.
47   Harvey 2012, pp. 22–3.
48   Harvey 2012, pp. 140–50 See also McNally 2013 for several similar examples.

This emphasis on demands speaks against a strategy of distancing or isolation from the state, sometimes described as an interstitial strategy. Such approaches emphasise the importance of operating in gaps at a distance from established politics, and thus eschew making direct demands on political authorities.[49] Against this position, Marx argues that conflict with and making demands of the state is a necessary part of political development. It is necessary to identify the state as an adversary and an antagonist, and enter into conflict with it. However, this alone might remain compatible with what Young calls a politics of insurgency, which challenges established powers without seeking to ultimately defeat or replace them. This sees politics as 'a dialectic between movements of insurgency that seek democratization, collective decision-making, and grass-roots empowerment, on the one hand, and established institutions and structures that seek to reabsorb such demands into a distributive framework, on the other'.[50] Within this dialectic, playing the role of the insurgent need not involve seeking political power in the form of the capture or replacement of existing institutions.

Marx, however, does not stop at this point. He does not merely assert the importance of demands that strengthen organisation and develop awareness – he insists that the conquest of political power is necessary. While this clearly has to take place in parallel to a process of development and learning, the development of new kinds of social relations, etc., it also seems to involve an important event or moment, in which political power is won.

In the aftermath of the Commune, Marx and Engels proposed the following motion to the International Working Men's Association:

> In presence of an unbridled reaction which violently crushes every effort at emancipation on the part of the working men, and pretends to maintain by brute force the distinction of classes and the political domination of the propertied classes;
>
> Considering that against this collective power of the propertied class the working class cannot act, as a class, except by constituting itself into a political party, distinct from, and opposed to, all old parties formed by the propertied classes;
>
> That this constitution of the working class into a political party is indispensable in order to ensure the triumph of the social revolution and its ultimate end – the abolition of classes;

---

49   See Critchley 2007, p. 112; Holloway 201; Wright 2006.
50   Young 1990, p. 91.

That the combination of forces which the working class has already effected by its economical struggles ought at the same time to serve as a lever for its struggles against the political power of landlords and capitalists –

The Conference recalls to the members of the international:

That in the militant state of the working class, its economical movement and political action are indissolubly united.[51]

This motion directly links the necessity of political action not just to the development of consciousness and organisational capacity, but to the need to address the repressive functions of the state. While what Marx meant by a 'party' in 1871 is not the same as what subsequent generations meant, it is clear here that organisation and engagement in politics is necessary in order to confront the organised power of the ruling class. However, it fails to spell out the precise connection between these two things. Thus we are told that the constitution of the working class into a political party that contests political power follows necessarily from the fact that state power is used directly on behalf of the ruling powers to thwart emancipation. It remains ambiguous, however, between two different possible reasons for this.

The first reason that might be given for this is simply that winning the political struggle is necessary to take control of the existing state apparatus. According to this reading, it is the fact that this apparatus is under the political control of the bourgeoisie that presents the problem. Thus, what is required is a successful political campaign that will put the working class in charge of the state, instead of the existing ruling classes. This appears consistent with the logic of the *Communist Manifesto*. Here, the working class must win the battle for democracy in order to gain control over the existing political apparatus, and then use their power to make 'despotic inroads' into existing society. The measures themselves revolutionise society. Of course, these measures will necessarily revolutionise the state itself, since they will begin to undermine the basis of the separate sphere of politics.[52] Nonetheless, a prerequisite to this is seizing hold of the existing state.

However, in Marx's discussions of the Commune we see a different logic at work. There he asserts that 'the working class cannot simply lay hold of the ready-made state machinery, and wield it for its own purposes'.[53] A huge

---

51   *First International and After*, p. 270.
52   Avineri 1968, pp. 205–8.
53   *First International and After*, p. 206.

amount of both rhetorical and intellectual work is being done by the word 'simply' here. In the case of the commune, the alternative to 'simply laying hold' is quite clear:

> Instead of continuing to be the agent of the Central Government, the police was at once stripped of its political attributes, and turned into the responsible, and at all times revocable, agent of the Commune. So were the officials of all other branches of the administration. From the members of the Commune downwards, the public service had to be done at *workman's wage*. The vested interests and the representation allowances of the high dignitaries of state disappeared along with the high dignitaries themselves. Public functions ceased to be the private property of the tools of the Central Government. Not only municipal administration, but the whole initiative hitherto exercised by the state was laid into the hands of the Commune ... While the merely repressive organs of the old governmental power were to be amputated, its legitimate functions were to be wrested from an authority usurping pre-eminence over society itself, and restored to the responsible agents of society.[54]

Here, rather than seizing hold of the existing state, the idea is that its various functions are aggregated to an alternative, more democratic institution, and at the same time revolutionised and transformed. This involves transforming those powers so that they cease to be a power set above society, and instead become an expression of society itself.[55]

However, this approach necessarily calls into question the legitimacy of the existing state in a way that the 'seizing' dynamic does not. As a result it places the movement in far more direct conflict with the repressive functions of the state, at least those that are unwilling to have their roles and privileges transformed. This, then, also requires that the remaining repressive functions be confronted, and ultimately smashed. As Tomba shows, this question is hinted at already in the *18th Brumaire*, where Marx suggests that "all political upheavals perfected this machine instead of smashing it",[56] and Marx confirms even more explicitly in a letter of 1872 that this implies "that the next attempt of the French revolution will be no longer, as before, to transfer the bureaucratic-military machine from one hand to another, but to smash it, and this is essential for every real people's revolution on the Continent."[57]

---

54   *First International and After*, p. 212.
55   See Basso, 2015, pp. 177–80.
56   Surveys from Exile, p. 238. Tomba, 2013, p. 56.
57   Tomba 2013, p. 56.

These two different dynamics – seizing and smashing – continue to co-exist in Marx. While the Commune clearly does have a major impact on Marx's thinking, it is somewhat hard to pin down what it is. Already, in 1872, he can be found suggesting that direct conflict with the repressive powers of the state might be avoided in countries like Britain and the Netherlands.[58] This is where the word 'simply' seems to carry a great deal of weight. The working class cannot 'simply' lay hold; any laying hold must also involve revolutionising and transformation. But precisely how this revolutionising is to be achieved, by which means, through which institutions, appears deeply context specific.

These two dynamics should not be confused with later distinctions between reform and revolution, though they may well have laid the basis for them. Both these strategies are conceived as revolutionary (by Marx at least), to the extent that they are political acts that at the same time radically reconfigure the scope of politics and precipitate social transformations.[59] Nor is this primarily about violent revolution vs peaceful transition. Both strategies are fundamentally conflictual, and involve the use of force to some degree or another. Nor should they be seen as two necessarily incompatible strategies, though they might pull in different directions at times. It ought to be possible to pursue strategies that attempt to win power in the existing state, while simultaneously developing alternative structures which can challenge it, though it clearly requires careful thought to balance the two – as numerous examples in the twentieth century attest. Indeed, this might be the very reason for Marx's somewhat coy and ambiguous formulations here – he wanted to be able to praise the Commune without identifying it as the sole means of political action. The purpose of identifying these different trends is not to identify one or the other as either better, or more truly Marxist. There is a century and a half worth of history after Marx to do that. My concern is their impact on a practical commitment to self-emancipation.

4   Politics and Self-Emancipation

These different modes of engaging in politics all pose different challenges when it comes to a commitment to self-emancipation. In some ways, the logic of demanding appears to be the least problematic. As noted, this can be done

---

58   *First International and After*, p. 324. Marx nonetheless acknowledges immediately afterwards that 'in most continental revolutions the lever will have to be force'.

59   Avineri 1968, p. 230.

without intending to take power or replace the existing state, and thus it does not raise some of the organisational challenges involved in doing so. However, important practical questions still remain even here. One of these is avoiding the pathologies that De Smet identifies, which I mentioned in Chapter 2. These involve proleptic demands and proposals that fall outside of what he (following Vygotsky) calls the zone of proximal development. These demands can be voluntaristic – i.e., they lie far beyond the zone of proximal development, or they can be pessimistic – falling short of it. Voluntaristic demands have a demobilising, rather than empowering effect. They collapse, as Lenin puts it, 'in phrasemongering and clowning'.[60] Instead of helping a process of development, they stall it. Pessimistic suggestions, on the other hand, hold movements back. Of course, this zone is not fixed – it can expand and contract depending on real developments: 'There is no general formula of "always be one step ahead of the masses"; sometimes it is necessary to be two, three or four steps ahead'.[61]

A related, but different, worry is about demands which serve only to strengthen the hand of the state, or reinforce narrowly defined, existing structures of power. This is the kind of concern that leads some to be worried of demands in general, precisely because they appear to legitimise the existing state of affairs. Returning to Harvey's discussion of the 'right to the city' might help flesh this out. Harvey's hope is that such a demand forms the basis of more radical transformative struggles: that it might be part of asserting democratic control over the way we make our social life. However, there is no guarantee that it will do so. Indeed, as Harvey is aware, the language of 'rights' is not necessarily emancipatory if it is restricted to narrowly individual rights to the actually existing city. On the one hand, the right to the city has to be different from the abstract, individualistic form in which rights are usually understood in capitalist society. On the other, it has to be stressed that we do not merely want a right just to *these* cities, in *these* forms:

> It is for this reason that the right to the city has to be construed not as a right to that which already exists, but as a right to rebuild and re-create the city as a socialist body politic in a completely different image – one that eradicates poverty and social inequality, and one that heals the wounds of disastrous environmental degradation.[62]

---

60   Lenin 1970, p. 9.
61   De Smet 2015, p. 117.
62   Harvey 2012, p. 138.

To ensure that the right to the city does not become construed as a narrow, reformist demand, but remains linked to fundamental questions of democratic control and self-organisation, requires a particular sort of approach by those involved in demanding it. It requires raising these issues as fundamental to any campaign, and resisting attempts to displace them from the agenda. It requires always attempting to connect what might appear to be disparate questions to the overall goal of social transformation.

This reflects a general problem of a dynamic between seeking to move and mobilise people into action on the one hand, and educating and empowering them on the other. If demands are intended both to draw more people into campaigns of resistance, *and* to form part of a process of both organisational strengthening and pedagogical development, these functions do not always go together so smoothly. Stanley Moore offers an example of the dilemmas this can pose:

> Those who stress the task of organising the working class are likely to concentrate on activating the maximum number. This may incline them to put forward attainable demands and to emphasise immediate advantages. The danger of this policy is that such tactics may result in blunting rather than sharpening the revolutionary consciousness of the workers. On the other hand, those who stress the task of educating the working class are likely to concentrate on turning the maximum number into revolutionaries. This may incline them to put forward unattainable demands and to ignore immediate advantages. The danger of this policy is that such tactics may result in isolating the revolutionary socialists from less class conscious workers. These two ways of falling off the tightrope – sacrificing revolutionary fervour to numbers and sacrificing numbers to revolutionary fervour – are forms of what came to be known, in the era after Marx, as right and left deviations.[63]

Picking a path between these various extremes is not easy. Firstly, it requires close engagement with movements themselves. Knowing the 'zone of proximal development' of a movement is not a matter of calculation or applying an external schema, it requires engaged practice and commitment. Secondly, however, it requires political *judgement*. It is not about finding a simple midpoint between two extremes, but about identifying the appropriate course of action.

---

63   Moore 1963, p. 60.

When it comes to smashing or seizing the state, however, different problems arise. One particular cluster of these concerns force or violence: When, if ever, is it acceptable to use force and violence in the service of revolutionary action? To this, it seems, there is no easy answer. Marx is evidently not among those thinkers who believes that politics ends when violence is engaged and he would make little sense of the modern distinction between 'civil disobedience' and the use of force. Moreover, any revolutionary violence must be weighed against the violence of the state and the systematic violence of capitalist exploitation. This is a point he drives home most notably in discussions of the commune.[64] On the other hand, there is no reason to take Marx as thinking that violence is a fundamental part of revolutionary activity. There is very little evidence in Marx for a position that is sometimes ascribed to him, such that revolutionary violence is considered to be a virtue because it is the dialectical opposite of the future society. Marx does endorse the Hegelian idea that history proceeds by its bad side,[65] and the references to *la lutte sanguinaire* in the quotation above might suggest a more bloodthirsty approach. However, he can also be found hoping that violence be kept to a minimum, and blaming those who provoke it,[66] and the central motor for him is *struggle*, rather than violence *per se*. Thus, Brenkert is over-stating the case when he says that:

> It is far, then, from Marx's view that the use of revolution and the violent acts which may attend it might contaminate the people who would build a new society. The views of Gandhi, Martin Luther King, and the like are quite remote from Marx's views. One ought not engage in passive disobedience, a la Thoreau, so as to prepare oneself for a society in which there will be no violence, in which coercion is ended. Rather, the use of violence is fully compatible with the end Marx demands and indeed helps to foster it, rather than infect it, as others have claimed.[67]

It is true that Marx would have rejected the views of these sorts of thinkers as 'distinctly non-dialectical'.[68] This is because they make the mistake of the more

---

64   See, e.g., *First International and After*, p. 228.
65   'It is the bad side that produces the movement that makes history, by providing a struggle' (MECW 6, p. 174).
66   Avineri 1968, p. 215. In this context it is worth also recalling the distinction employed in the *Communist Manifesto* between abolishing the bourgeoisie as a class and eliminating specific members of it. *Communist Manifesto*, p. 99.
67   Brenkert 1983, p. 181.
68   Brenkert 1983, p. 182.

naïve accounts of prefigurative politics I discussed in Chapter 2 of assuming a strict identity between means and ends – that we can live the society of the future in the present without recognising the immense gap that exists between. It does not follow from this, however, that the means need to be in some sense the *opposite* of the ends.

The other crucial area where this matters is organisation. Winning state power, whatever the means, requires a degree of organisation that goes well beyond simple associations or campaign groups. It requires a certain amount of division of labour, of structure and organisation, and of bureaucracy. All of this brings with it challenges which Marx only partially recognised.[69] One commonly cited example is Robert Michels' 'iron law of oligarchy', which suggests that such institutions inevitably develop bureaucratic structures which subvert their goals. The maintenance of these structures, and the interests of the groups at the top of them, inevitably becomes more important than the particular goals of a democratic society. In this way, organisation and democracy end up fundamentally in tension: 'Organisation is, in fact, the source from which the conservative currents flow over the plain of democracy, occasioning there disastrous floods and rendering the plain unrecognisable'.[70] Michels' picture is a deeply pessimistic one, and it is also far too general. It is far from clear that it is any sort of iron law. As Colin Barker has argued, Michels fails adequately to distinguish different kinds of organisation and their different goals – giving the particular sins of social democratic organisations a more universal application.[71] Nonetheless, the risks he identifies – putting organisational needs ahead of political ones, and narrowing decision-making to a small group – are real, and borne out by experience in a host of organisations, whether explicitly social democratic or not.

Similarly, any organisation aimed towards contesting the political sphere must be hierarchically structured to at least some extent. Elections require candidates, who will inevitably be identified to some degree as 'leaders'. Decisions over strategy and tactics cannot always be made by the fullest democratic decision-making procedures – sometimes individuals or smaller groups will have to make decisions for which they later have to be held accountable. Even where decisions can be subject to democratic debate and discussion, someone makes the proposal(s), and chooses the form of words used and the scope of the choice, and someone draws up the agenda, determining the order of debate, the structure of motions, and the range of legitimate and viable options.

---

69   Przeworski 1985, pp. 239–41.
70   Michels 1959, p. 22.
71   Barker 2001.

Someone, too, needs to book the meeting hall, and have an awareness of how long the meeting can reasonably continue before a decision must be made. And someone has to look after the children.

The crucial question here, then, is how can an organisation remain committed to self-emancipation despite these challenges – what kinds of norms, practices and standards must it institute to avoid these risks? This applies both in the structures and relationships *within* specific organisations and the relationships *between* them and the particular movements they seek to be involved in, influence and shape. It is not enough to avoid hierarchy within your own organisation if it is combined with a pathologically (in the sense discussed in Chapter 2) voluntarist, vanguardist or elitist approach to movements outside of it. But the reverse is also true. Of course, these questions are irrelevant in the absence of such a movement. If there is simply no movement to engage with, the highest standards in the world will not prevent such an organisation collapsing into irrelevance. But here the reverse is *not* true – appropriate organisational norms, both within an organisation and in its relationship to the movement, are crucial. They do not flow automatically from being part of a growing and developing movement. Getting these norms right remains vital, and in the final chapter I will consider some examples of how they might be spelled out.

Self-Emancipation and Revolutionary Practice

> The way to tell the difference is to keep the notion of autonomous demo-
> cracy in mind: militancy is sound when it remains loyal to the idea that
> people should rule themselves.
>
> STEPHEN D'ARCY, *Languages of the Unheard*[1]

∴

1 Introduction

I ended the previous chapter by suggesting that engagement in the sphere
of politics present real problems for those committed to self-emancipation.
Questions of organisation, conflict and violence present challenges which must
be addressed. These political challenges generate ethical problems which are
complex and specific, but flow directly from the recognition of political struggle as a necessary stage in self-emancipation. In this final chapter, I turn my
attention directly to these problems, and to attempting to find solutions to
them.

It is worth noting that these challenges in part flow from the fact that the
locus of action of Marx and Marxists is not, despite all of the talk of class
struggle, the ruling classes, but the ruled classes. This point is exemplified in
the picket line. The picket line's practical value exists not in a direct confrontation with the capitalist class, but in an attempt to win solidarity amongst other
workers, and to prevent them undermining the strike. Thus, while direct conflicts between the working class and the ruling class are certainly relevant, what
is more important is political activity within and between different currents in
the working class itself.

Marx himself does not have a great deal to say about these questions. In part,
this is because he is suspicious of the moralism and hypocrisy of those who
would condemn the revolt of the oppressed and exploited while committing
far greater systemic violence themselves. Thus he often adopts a kind of amoralist stance, in which those who question revolutionary tactics are dismissed,

---

1 D'Arcy 2013, p. 73.

and their criticisms seen as irrelevant. This silence leads many to think he has nothing to say about it, or at best endorses a form of long-term consequentialism, such that the distant goal of a good society is the only thing that justifies (or fails to justify) action in the present.[2] This, of course, becomes weaker the further off the goal appears to be.

However, the focus on self-emancipation as both means and goal of revolutionary action suggests something quite different, in which means and ends are pulled closer together, rather than pushed further apart. Can this commitment help give justifications and criteria for appropriate revolutionary action? In this chapter, I will consider four different theoretical approaches that suggest it can. Two of these are concerned explicitly with the justification of certain practices of struggle, while the other two are more general practical principles; two are from the revolutionary Third International tradition, while the other two are organisers, activists and commentators from contemporary social struggles. In presenting these I don't suggest that any one should be seen as the best way of thinking about these questions, but collectively I think they show a commitment to self-emancipation can be a real, practical guide to action in the here and now.

2   Leon Trotsky and the Interdependence of Means and Ends

One particularly famous attempt to engage with the question of ethics in the context of revolutionary politics comes in Leon Trotsky's pamphlet *Their Morals and Ours*. Trotsky's starting point is a defence of revolutionary violence, and in particular his own conduct, against both liberal and neo-Kantian critics. In particular, he is concerned with defending himself against the charge that he adopts the 'Jesuit' principle that the ends justify the means. A great deal of his argument involves rhetorically skewering the hypocrisy of his liberal critics and arguing against any notion of trans-historical duties in a society divided by class, but his positive alternative hinges on the following passage:

> A means can be justified only by its end. But the end in its turn needs to be justified. From the Marxist point of view, which expresses the historical interests of the proletariat, the end is justified if it leads to increasing the power of humanity over nature and to the abolition of the power of one person over another.[3]

---

2   Lukes 1987, p. 142.
3   Trotsky 1973, p. 54.

Thus certain acts are justified if they further the cause of human emancipation, understood as ending the oppression of some by others and expanding
the possibility of humans to realise themselves in nature. It is important for
Trotsky that these means *genuinely do* advance the cause of emancipation. Not
all means are justified:

> Permissible and obligatory are those and only those means, we answer,
> which unite the revolutionary proletariat, fill their hearts with irrecon-
> cilable hostility to oppression, teach them contempt for official moral-
> ity and its democratic echoers, imbue them with consciousness of their
> own historic mission, raise their courage and spirit of self-sacrifice in the
> struggle.[4]

Here Trotsky is at pains to argue that this is different from the 'Jesuit principle' –
he is rather suggesting an intimate interdependence of means and ends. What,
however, is the difference? After all, no-one argues that an *un*justified end can
justify any means. In a rare intersection between the revolutionary left and academic philosophy, John Dewey wrote a brief response to Trotsky. Dewey shares
with Trotsky the view that the only thing which can justify actions is the ends
which result from them. Furthermore, he offers a plausible interpretation of
Trotsky's claims based on the distinction between what he calls the 'end-in-
view' and the actual result. Dewey notes that often when people talk about the
ends justifying the means they are referring to appalling crimes being done in
the name of some vague greater good in the far future:

> What has given the maxim ... that the end justifies the means a bad name
> is that the end-in-view, the end professed and entertained ... justifies the
> use of certain means, and so justifies the latter that it is not necessary to
> examine what the actual consequences of the chosen means will be.[5]

Trotsky's argument can thus be seen as rejecting this kind of argument, arguing
for the permissibility only of actions which *demonstrably do* advance the cause
of human liberation.

However, Dewey believes that Trotsky is not consistent with this line of
thought. In particular he latches on to Trotsky's invocation of Marxist laws
of historical development. The logical conclusion of Trotsky's argument is,

---

4 Trotsky 1973, p. 54.
5 Dewey 1973, p. 76.

according to Dewey, 'that with the idea of the liberation of mankind as the end-in-view, there would be an examination of *all* means that are likely to attain this end without any fixed preconceptions as to what they *must* be'.[6] However, this is not what Trotsky does: 'On the contrary means are deduced from an independent source, an alleged law of history which is the law of all laws of social development'.[7] Dewey argues that Trotsky ends up subordinating the 'inductive' question, of whether revolutionary methods do sincerely lead to the liberation of humanity, with a 'deductive' judgement, which assumes that they must be based on a law of history. Trotsky has, in the final analysis, committed an idealist error: 'Orthodox Marxism shares with orthodox religion-ism and with traditional idealism the belief that human ends are interwoven into the very texture and structure of existence – a conception inherited pre-sumably from its Hegelian origin'.[8] Dewey takes Trotsky as ending up with the same model that he seems to be attacking, of thinking that the end-in-view of a communist future justifies a host of means that appear unconnec-ted.

Yet a careful reading of Trotsky's remarks suggests a more nuanced interpret-ation. It is important to stress that Trotsky does not simply argue that anything goes, but that the standards for what is permissible in the service of a revolu-tion are set by the nature of the revolution itself. Actions which disempower the proletariat, and thwart the possibility of their self-emancipation, are imper-missible. For example, he argues the following:

> The liberation of the workers can come only through the workers them-
> selves. There is, therefore, no greater crime than deceiving the masses,
> palming off defeats as victories, friends as enemies, bribing workers' lead-
> ers, fabricating legends, staging false trials, in a word, doing what the
> Stalinists do.[9]

Here we have a fairly clear statement of something that can never be legitimate, which makes explicit reference to the principle of self-emancipation.[10] On the same grounds, Trotsky criticises terrorism as a distraction from mass political

---

6   Dewey 1973, p. 76.

7   Dewey 1973, p. 77.

8   Dewey 1973, p. 79.

9   Trotsky 1973, p. 56.

10   See also Geras, 2017, Chapter 9, which offers an interpretation of *Their Morals and Ours*
      in terms of the significance of working class development and self-education, and also
      highlights the example of lying as of particular significance.

activity: 'To the terrorist we say: It is impossible to replace the masses; only in the mass movement can you find expression for your heroism'.[11]

These kinds of concerns are consonant with another of Trotsky's contributions to Marxist thought, namely his critique of substitutionism (See Chapter 2). In 1903 Trotsky writes:

> [H]istory, having placed a definite task on the agenda, is observing us sharply. For good or ill (more for ill), we are leading the masses to revolution, awakening in them the most elementary political instincts. But in so far as we have to deal with a more complex task – transforming these 'instincts' into conscious aspirations of a working class which is determining itself politically – we tend to resort to the short-cuts and over-simplifications of 'thinking-for-others' and 'substitutionism'.
>
> In the internal politics of the Party these methods lead ... to the Party organisation 'substituting' itself for the Party, the Central Committee substituting itself for the Party organisation, and finally the dictator substituting himself for the Central Committee; on the other hand, this leads the committees to supply an 'orientation' – and to change it – while 'the people keep silent' ... All in all, these 'methods' lead to the complete disappearance of questions of political tactics in Social Democracy.[12]

These remarks are often seen as prophetic of the direction of the Russian Revolution. In that context it should be stressed that Trotsky is not saying that party organisation, or indeed revolutionary activity, inevitably leads to such substitution, merely that it is an attendant risk, and consciousness of it must guide action. It is striking, in particular, that he is wary of the complete disappearance of tactical questions from the field of revolution. A serious engagement with revolution as self-emancipation means thinking through the difficult questions of what it requires, what *really* advances the cause? Where these sorts of questions disappear from view, self-emancipation becomes a phrase and not a reality.

This suggests that the notion of interdependence of means and ends needn't necessarily be seen as a purely 'end-in-view' approach, in which specific details are eroded and any actions are justified in service of an abstract revolution. Indeed, it suggests precisely the opposite – we should care deeply about wheth-

---

11   Trotsky 1973, p. 56.
12   Trotsky 1904.

er the means employed really do strengthen the capacity for self-emancipation. As Bensaïd puts it:

> If the ultimate criterion of concrete morality was, as Trotsky affirmed, not even the interest of the proletariat, but the universal development of consciousness and of culture (of which the proletariat was only the particular mediation), in other words what frees a humanity that is really human from its religious and social alienation, then all means are not permitted, even to a revolutionary infidel.[13]

In particular, Trotsky's emphasis on revolutionary honesty – in contrast to the Stalinist approach, chimes with Marx's own emphasis on self-criticism and patience in the *18th Brumaire*:

> Proletarian revolutions ... constantly engage in self-criticism, and in repeated interruptions of their own course. They return to what has apparently been accomplished, in order to begin the task again; with merciless thoroughness they mock the inadequate, weak and wretched aspects of their first attempts; they seem to throw their opponent to the ground only to see him draw new strength from the earth and rise before them more colossal than ever; they shrink back again and again before the indeterminate immensity of their own goals, until the situation is created in which any retreat is impossible, and the conditions themselves cry out: '*Hic Rhodus, hic salta!*'[14]

This reading of Trotsky suggests a way of embedding the principle of working class self-emancipation into practical judgements about ethical choices. If self-emancipation is both the means and the ends of revolutionary action, this does make it possible to identify certain practices as impermissible, and lying and substitutionism are paradigm examples. Nonetheless, in phrasing this in terms of means and ends, Trotsky still leaves many questions open. In particular, while lying to the working class may always be wrong, many other things are far more context dependent (Trotsky's own example of hostage-taking being a case in point). In such situations, it may be demanding too much to undertake the kind of 'inductive' analysis demanded by Dewey in order to decide whether a given practice really strengthens the revolution. In cases like this,

---

13   Bensaïd 2009, pp. 178–80.
14   *Surveys from Exile*, p. 150.

there appears a real risk of slipping into the kind of 'end-in-view' arguments Dewey warns of. The question, then, is whether the core insight suggested by Trotsky – that a commitment to the goal of revolution as self-emancipation can give substance to an ethics of revolution in the present – might be developed into a more systematic standard for action.

3   Stephen D'Arcy and the Democratic Standard for Militancy

A sense of how these insights might be developed can be found in the work of Stephen D'Arcy, who proposes a more rigorous standard for considering various practices of resistance and social transformation. Following Martin Luther King's characterisation of rioting as 'the language of the unheard', D'Arcy offers what he calls the democratic standard for assessing militant politics. This democratic standard is linked directly to a conception of democracy as public autonomy:

> Public autonomy requires that people dictate the terms of social co-operation based on a broadly shared understanding of the common good and the requirements of justice, after a thorough process of inclusive, wide ranging discussion. Public autonomy, in this more demanding sense, means genuine self-rule.[15]

A vital component of this self-rule is giving *voice* to people. One of the roles of militant protest is thus to 'usher the unheard directly onto centre stage, offering them a language, a vehicle to make themselves heard'.[16]

Militancy, for D'Arcy encompasses a wider range of tactics and practices, united by four key features. Firstly, militancy arises from *grievance*: Thus rioting against police violence can count as militancy, rioting because your hockey team lost cannot. Secondly, militancy is adversarial, identifying an opponent that is in some way intransigent or unreceptive to reason-based argument. They have no choice but to treat 'the target of their resistance as an adversary, to be defeated in struggle, or at least to be forced into retreat or pressured into making concessions'.[17] However, as well as being adversarial, militancy is also confrontational:

---

15   D'Arcy 2013, pp. 23–4.
16   D'Arcy 2013, p. 22.
17   D'Arcy 2013, pp. 26–7.

A group of workers, motivated by unfair pay and conditions and convinced that their employer could never be persuaded to treat them with
fairness, could decide to quit their jobs *en masse* and launch a workers'
co-operative. This might be radical, in one way, but it stops short of militancy. Militancy seeks out direct conflict. Adversarial acts of protest are
not militant unless they are also confrontational.[18]

Finally, militancy is a kind of collective action, not an individual lashing out,
but a more or less planned and co-ordinated activity in concert with others.

Whatever one thinks about this definition of militancy (and I think it's a
good one), it has the virtue of bringing into focus precisely the kinds of actions,
strategies and practices that are most controversial. It is precisely the identification of enemies to be defeated and confrontational attempts to defeat them
that cause consternation and concern, and seem most in need of both justification, and a standard to discriminate between appropriate and inappropriate
uses. Indeed, D'Arcy's development of such a standard proceeds as a sort of
inversion of the standard liberal critique of such practices. For many liberal critics, such protest risks becoming profoundly anti-democratic. This is because it
seeks to use means other than reasoned debate to achieve its ends. These means
include disruption, sabotage and maybe even armed struggle. In standard liberal accounts such means often appear as a kind of 'blackmail' or coercion,
moving outside the bounds of reasonable democratic debate.

D'Arcy's response is that, in the face of intransigent elites and unresponsive
structures of power, good militant protest in fact redeems and defends democracy. When people are denied a voice, denied the capacity to influence and
shape democratic life, the appropriately democratic thing to do is to switch to
confrontation: '[F]ar from undermining democracy by switching from dialogue
to confrontation, militancy defends and upholds the democratic ideal by making this shift ... by weakening the capacity of elites and institutions to thwart
reason-guided public discussion from dictating the terms of social cooperation'.[19] Thus militancy appears as a civic virtue, an essential part of a democratic
society, 'not a foe, but the best friend of reason-guided public discussion'.[20]

However, militancy is only a virtue if it meets what D'Arcy calls the democratic standard. This has four features, which function as criteria for judging
sound militancy. The first principle is the opportunity principle: 'This principle

---

18   D'Arcy 2013, p. 27.
19   D'Arcy 2013, p. 71.
20   D'Arcy 2013, p. 71.

highlights three features of sound militancy: it addresses substantive and pressing grievances; it effectively creates opportunities to hasten or facilitate the resolution of those grievances; and it proceeds only when nonmilitant tactics have proven fruitless, due to obstruction by intransigent elites or unresponsive systems of power'.[21] To unpick this: grievances must be genuine. The demands of men's rights activists, racists, or tax dodgers may be keenly felt, but society is substantially organised in their interest. Militant activity should open up new opportunities for resolving grievances, rather than shut them down. It is worth stressing that this is not to say that people must necessarily actively exhaust every opportunity every time. There is ample evidence that certain powerholders will be intransigent, and there is no need to perform a charade of checking first.[22] There are plenty of occasions where it is reasonable and plausible to assume intransigence from the beginning. For D'Arcy, militancy ought to be seen as a remedial virtue, aimed precisely at dealing with the real fact of the intransigence of elites.

The second and third principles concern more directly the democratic empowerment of the participants and those who suffer the grievance concerned. These are the agency principle and the autonomy principle. The agency principle concerns encouraging those most affected by a grievance to take the lead in securing their own solution to that grievance. This recognises how 'one of the ways that militancy can be unsound is that it can reproduce the very silencing and marginalisation that it purports to oppose'.[23] This principle explicitly discourages people from acting on behalf of others without their active participation. The autonomy principle extends and expands upon this, suggesting more broadly that 'militancy should enhance the power of people to govern themselves through inclusive, reason-guided public discussion'.[24] One way of applying this principle is negatively: thus, measures which tend to have the result of extending and empowering the state or the dominant classes violate this principle. For example, taking the state on at its strongest – the fields of law on the one hand and military struggle on the other – should be tackled with extreme care and sensitivity, since this risks empowering it still further.

The fourth principle stresses the importance of public justification. This D'Arcy calls the accountability principle, which asserts that 'Militancy should limit itself to acts that can be defended publicly, plausibly, and in good faith as

---

21   D'Arcy 2013, p. 66.
22   D'Arcy 2013, p. 67.
23   D'Arcy 2013, p. 68.
24   D'Arcy 2013, p. 69.

duly sensitive to the democratic values of common decency and the common good'. This is intended to be sensitive to the moral and practical fact that people within resistance movements have to be able to justify to themselves and others the actions they take, something that D'Arcy thinks amoralist and consequentialist theories (including, wrongly in my opinion, Trotsky's) fail to recognise. This is not, it is worth stressing, about needing to justify their actions to the powerful or to the same intransigent elites one is challenging. Rather, it is about justifying actions within and between groups struggling for emancipation and recognition. This, like the others, flows directly from D'Arcy's commitment to public autonomy: 'to act in ways that one cannot, or would not, be willing or able to defend in these terms is to exempt oneself improperly from one of the constitutive demands of democratic politics, the demand to give an account of oneself to one's peers. Acting in this way shows scorn for the value of public autonomy'.[25]

Having spelled out these principles, D'Arcy demonstrates their relevance for judging real life strategies of resistance, from civil disobedience to armed struggle. Indeed, foregrounding the democratic standard brings out strikingly different results than other standards that are sometimes employed. So, for example, while non-violent civil disobedience is held up as the most virtuous form of militancy by many liberal theorists, its willingness to accept legal consequences can actually fall foul of the autonomy principle by empowering and recognising the authority of the state and legal system. On the other hand, rioting and armed struggle may, under certain conditions be perfectly legitimate forms of resistance – since the standard is not violence or non-violence, but democratic empowerment.

The significance of D'Arcy's account is that it gives a standard for assessing the validity of various resistance (and revolutionary) strategies that is linked to the desire for democratic self-management. Its application can be far broader than to revolutionary struggle aimed at radical transformation – indeed many of the notions of protest and civic virtue could still be of value within a liberal democratic society, without any intention of building an alternative. However, a conception of self-emancipation as central to revolution clearly lies at the heart of D'Arcy's account.[26] The standard that D'Arcy offers falls short of categorical-imperative-style universal duties. They are severely context dependent and themselves open to debate, but they do provide some sort of standards to judge and guide action.

---

25   D'Arcy 2013, p. 70.
26   D'Arcy 2013, pp. 183–6.

One argument against this account might run like this: Virtues are only meaningful and relevant as part of certain social practices. Thus it may be true that militancy can be a remedial virtue within a democratic society – but we do not live in one. So it is irrelevant to point to the virtues appropriate for that kind of society as a standard to judge the activity aimed at getting there. This brings into view an ambiguity in D'Arcy's account: is the virtuous democratic citizen a militant, or is the virtuous militant a democrat? If the former, then it seems this presents a problem, for in a radically undemocratic society the virtues of a democratic citizen might well be irrelevant. However, it is worth noting that, for all that D'Arcy speaks of ideals, his discussions are firmly rooted in real life protests and struggles. His model of militancy comes from the land defence of the Kanehsata':ke Mohawk community in 1990, and he is clear that at high points, like the Arab Spring or the Battle of Seattle, this ideal is a real possibility. Thus we have real virtuous archetypes with which to compare our activity – real practices from within our bad society. Perhaps, then, the democratic principle is not so much a measure of democratic virtue, but of militant virtue – a standard not to measure ourselves as democratic citizens, but as radical democrats in an undemocratic context. In any case, the significance of D'Arcy's account is that it demonstrates the possibility of using a clear commitment to democratic self-empowerment as both the means and end of political struggle to generate real standards for assessing practices within these struggles: 'The autonomy of the people is not only the goal of anticapitalism; it must also be its method'.[27]

4   Georg Lukács and the Actuality of Revolution

Georg Lukács offers an ambitious interpretation of Marxism that sees the core of the revolutionary project as a process of dereifying social relationships. Following Marx's treatment of commodity fetishism (and influenced by Weber and Neo-Kantian criticisms of modernity), Lukács treats capitalism as a system in which reification – perceiving social relationships as relationships between things – dominated social life. However, at the core of Lukács's model is the claim that the proletariat is uniquely capable of overcoming and seeing through that reification, and thus of becoming aware of the contingency and historical specificity of capitalism, and realising the capacity to live differently. Lukács is a controversial figure for a variety of reasons, and any interpretation of him is likely to be contested. Indeed, many will think it bizarre that his ideas are

---

27   D'Arcy 2013, p. 184.

mentioned in the context of a project dealing with self-emancipation. However, in this section I want to stress the significance of Lukács as someone who 1) emphasises an irreducible role for the consciousness of the proletariat and 2) offers an important and essential role for those who would seek to help develop that consciousness. In particular, I suggest that Lukács' notion of 'the actuality of revolution' can offer something like a guide to practice for revolutionary action.

Lukács believed that under capitalism workers were uniquely located to become aware of capitalism's reified nature. This was because of their dual character as both bearers of labour power and as producers themselves. They were thus both fetishised commodities, bearers of abstract labour, and living breathing people. When they become aware of this fact it

> brings about an objective structural change in the object of knowledge ... Beneath the cloak of the thing lay a relation between men ... beneath the quantifying crust there was a qualitative, living core. Now that this core is revealed it becomes possible to recognise the fetish character of every commodity.[28]

As Andrew Feenberg puts it,

> The patterns of behaviour that flow from and reproduce reification are altered by social self-consciousness. Instead of facing apparently solid social facts individually, workers recognize their own collective implication in these so-called facts and in so doing dereify them: the social world no longer appears as a collection of things but as a complex of processes in which the workers are always already engaged.[29]

Moreover, because of the fundamental role played by the economy in shaping social relations under capitalism, the economic struggles of the proletariat could have a broader dereifying effect, loosening the sense of capitalism as a natural social order:

> In normal times, the isolated individual agents confront the corporation as an overwhelming power, a 'reality' to which they must adjust. But during a strike, social form and content are juxtaposed and clash. The

---

28   Lukács 1971, p. 169.
29   Feenberg 2014, p. 238.

corporation is revealed to be a complex of human relations that can be challenged, exposing it to transformation at every level: economic, social, political. The revolution is such a dereifying practice writ large, encompassing the entire society.[30]

A fundamental part of this class consciousness, then, is the recognition that capitalism is not a natural state of affairs governed by universal rules of human behaviour, but a specific historical product that can be organised differently. In this sense, class consciousness reveals practically what Marxism also seeks to demonstrate intellectually – capitalism's historical specificity and the possibility of its transcendence.

However, for Lukács, this class consciousness is an ideal type (understood in largely Weberian terms), that should not necessarily be identified with the actual consciousness of the proletariat at any particular time.[31] It was conceived as a consciousness that the working class was capable of, and which was in their interests, but not necessarily one they possessed. This gap between the ideal type and the reality is the source of much controversy in interpretations of Lukács, because it is here where he introduces a specific role for organisation. Because of this gap, there is a necessary role for organisation, a party, in drawing out and developing class consciousness, in attempting to bridge the gap.

Inevitably, given both the actual trajectory of both the revolution and Lukács's intellectual career, people have seen in this account the roots of an idea that grants intellectual authority to the party.[32] However, this is not Lukács's intention. He does not intend to develop a theory of an elite who make a revolution, but rather to produce a way of thinking about the role of active socialists – and their organisations – in encouraging and bringing forward class consciousness.[33] Lukács talks about the role of organisations as follows:

> So this mysterious 'third place', this 'historical demon', the Communist Party ... possesses a curious characteristic: it is a *content* that is necessarily tied to becoming conscious ... Forms of organisation are there in order to bring this process into being, to accelerate it, in order *to make* such contents conscious in the working class (in a part of the working class), which

---

30   Feenberg 2014, p. 238.
31   See Feenberg 2014, pp. 223–43, Lukács 2000, pp. 63–70.
32   See, e.g., Kolakowski 1981, Honneth 2008.
33   See Dean 2012, LeBlanc 2013, Feenberg 2014.

once made conscious turn the workers into class conscious workers, precisely those contents that correspond as adequately as possible to their
objective class situation.[34]

Dean elaborates this process through analogy with psychoanalysis: 'As it learns
from the struggling masses, the party provides a vehicle through which they
can understand their actions and express their collective will, much as the psy-
choanalyst provides a means for the analysand to become conscious of her
desire'.[35] The role of the party is to *bring out* certain kinds of consciousness,
ones it does not automatically possess on its own: 'If ... historical materialism
alone is in a position to offer objective and correct knowledge of capitalist society, it does not deliver this knowledge independently of the class standpoint of
the proletariat, but rather *precisely from this standpoint*'.[36]

The inevitable response to this is to suggest that this cannot help but give a
privileged role to the party, since it is ultimately the party that appears as the
bearer of the ideal type of consciousness, which it then needs only to teach to
the masses. Indeed, Lukács is not entirely innocent here. His reference to the
ideal type of class consciousness as 'imputed' lends itself to this interpretation
(though he makes clear he is not particularly attached to it).[37] This can lend
itself to a reading by which the 'thoughts and feelings that men would have in a
particular position if they were able to assess both it and the interests arising in
it in their impact on immediate action and on the whole structure of society'[38]
are somehow better available to the party's intellectuals than to workers themselves. If this were the case, if true class consciousness could be divined from
the correct application of theory, then this really would be a problem, since
there is no reason to think that developing this theory needs the proletariat
at all except as passive recipients.[39] In this schema the development of class
consciousness would not really be any sort of development – it would be the
bending of existing consciousness towards a pre-ordained schema. However,
whatever errors Lukács makes in presentation, it is clear enough his intention
points in another direction. For example, he suggests that knowledge that can
liberate 'cannot be of the abstract kind that remains in one's head – many

---

34   Lukács 2000, p. 84.
35   Dean 2012, p. 243.
36   Lukács 2000, pp. 80–1.
37   Lukács 2000, p. 63.
38   Lukács 1971, p. 51. See also Lukács 2000, pp. 71–3.
39   Indeed, there is a case for saying that this reflects a somewhat narrow conception of the
      nature of knowledge on Lukács's part: see Renton 2013.

'socialists' have possessed that sort of knowledge. It must be knowledge that has become flesh and blood; to use Marx's phrase, it must be 'practical critical activity'.[40]

Thus we have a model in which the real consciousness of the working class comes first, but there is also a role for organisation in helping it develop, in representing it to itself in order to better understand it. How does this work? We see some clues in Lukács's short book on Lenin, in which he introduces the concept of 'the actuality of the revolution'. This can be seen as operating on three levels. Firstly, the revolution is actual in the sense that it is a real historical possibility:

> For historical materialism as the conceptual expression of the proletariat's struggle for liberation could only be conceived and formulated theoretically when revolution was already on the historical agenda as a practical reality; when, in the misery of the proletariat, in Marx's words, was to be seen not only the misery itself, but also the revolutionary element 'which will bring down the old order'.[41]

This was a real historic possibility in the sense that capitalism had simultaneously developed the forces of production to a sufficient degree, and created a class capable of overthrowing the old regime and building a new one. This level of 'actuality' is a broad one, as true today as it was in Lukács's time, but not necessarily particularly valuable as a guide to action.

The second level of actuality is the specific set of conjunctural conditions that make a revolution possible. This is not just about the existence of a class, but its degree of confidence and organisation, its level of consciousness, etc. Moreover, it is also about the strength of the other side – the extent to which the state and economy are suffering from crises and splits, and whether it is possible to take advantage of it. In Lukács's pamphlet, not helped by its status as a eulogy on the occasion of Lenin's death, recognising these factors appear as a particular feature of Lenin's genius.

For my purposes, however, it is a third sense in which Lukács seems to use the actuality of revolution that is relevant. Loosely, this is as the kind of practice capable of linking the two other levels – of linking the broad fact that a revolution is historically possible to the specific moment of its success. This begins to emerge when Lukács draws the contrast with what is likely his real target: the social-democratic parties of the Second International, who had relegated the

---

40   Lukács 1971, p. 262.
41   Lukács 1977, p. 11.

socialist revolution to a far-off end goal. This had turned revolution into a mere phrase, and led to an absence of concern for the immediate questions of trans-forming social organisation, and for the questions of what *really* empowered the proletariat in this task, what *actually* prepared the ground for social trans-formation:

> For the *realpolitik* of the Social Democrats, who consistently treated all questions of the day only as such, unrelated to the whole historical pro-cess and without reference to the ultimate problems of the class struggle, thus never pointing realistically and concretely beyond the horizon of bourgeois society, gave socialism once again a utopian character in the eyes of the workers. The separation of the final aim from the movement not only distorts the assessment of everyday questions – those of the movement – but also makes the aim utopian.[42]

Another risk of this is, as Rosa Luxemburg warns, the eventual abandonment of revolution as any sort of goal whatsoever.[43]

On this reading, the actuality of revolution is not about *knowing* that revolu-tion is on the agenda, but of acting to *keep* it on the agenda: 'This means that the actuality of the proletarian revolution is no longer only a world historical horizon arching above the self-liberating working class, *but that revolution is already on its agenda*'.[44] It is about the capacity to see in the struggles of the present the possibilities of the future, and the ability to link the present to the future:

> The actuality of the revolution therefore implies study of each individual daily problem in concrete association with the socio-historic whole, as moments in the liberation of the proletariat ... It merely means that every question of the day – precisely as a question of the day – at the same time became a fundamental problem of the revolution.[45]

This is a matter not just of theory – of analysing the situation to see revolu-tionary possibilities – but of method and skill. It involves a keen sense for the relationship between political action in the present and the future seizure of power by the proletariat.

---

42   Lukács 1977, p. 72.
43   See Luxemburg 2005.
44   Lukács 1977, p. 13.
45   Lukács 1977, p. 13.

This can be explicitly contrasted with Lukes's interpretation of Marxist ethics as 'a form of consequentialism that is long range and perfectionist'. Leaving aside whether it is best to consider this ethics as a form of consequentialism, it is not one that is long range. Lukes's concern is that Marxism is unable to offer any meaningful practical guide to action, as everything becomes indexed to the far-off goal of a communist society. Whilst actions are judged according to the extent to which they contribute to this society, the society itself is so distant as to entirely obscure any detailed consideration of how they might contribute towards it. However, the notion of 'the actuality of revolution', as well as the interpretation of Trotsky above, suggest a response to Lukes's position. To talk about the actuality of the revolution is precisely to avoid seeing the future society as merely a far-off end goal, to which anyone and anything can be sacrificed; it means to see the possibility of revolution as being on the agenda, and to keep it there.

This is not, it should be stressed, to say that it allows us to transparently read off and disclose a particular course of action in its entirety. Indeed, it is partly in reaction to such a position that the concept is developed. As Dean notes,

> That revolution is actual means that decisions, actions, and judgement cannot be perpetually deferred. When we take them, we are exposed to our lack of coverage in history, to the chaos of the revolutionary moment. We have to be confident that the revolutionary process will bring about new constellations, arrangements, skills and convictions, that through it we will make something else, something we haven't yet imagined.[46]

The kind of proposals which issue from this approach will always be open-ended, not fixed. They will always require, as Lukács's appropriation of Lenin puts it, 'a concrete analysis of a concrete situation'.[47] However, that does not mean there is nothing to be said about them, or that they become utterly obscured by fidelity to a vague future. Rather, they are motivated by a concern for self-emancipation, which gives them shape and content.

Whether or not you agree with the whole package of Lukács's philosophical system, the strength of this model is that it sees the practical struggles of the working class as primary while still recognising a role for activists and organisations within this process. Indeed, you may not even accept Lukács's idea that a *party* (as a specific form of organisation) is central to this process – or

---

46   Dean 2012, pp. 240–1.
47   Lukács 1977, p. 35. See also Lenin 1965, where Lenin describes the concrete analysis of the concrete situation as 'the very gist, the living soul, of Marxism'.

even ascribe a special role to the proletariat as a labouring class – and yet still recognise this model's significance as a partial answer to the question 'what should we do if we are committed to self-emancipation?' Taking seriously the actuality of the revolution involves posing at every stage the question of what empowers people, what prepares them for changing the world. This is more than just a process of deepening organisation; it means helping to transform consciousness by helping people recognise their own capacities to transform the world. The final approach I discuss can be seen as a practical example of this.

5   Jane McAlevey and Whole Worker Organising

Jane McAlevey's notion of 'whole worker organising' develops out of an intellectual and practical critique of the dominant mode of organising in US Trade Unionism, and an attempt to develop effective alternatives. While primarily understood as a method for worker organisation, it is rooted in a desire to empower the workers and for them to come to recognise their own power through collective activity. However, it also asserts that this approach is the most practically effective, as well as principled, approach to worker organising: it gets results better than anything else. Given McAlevey's role and record as an organiser, she has a plausible claim to this.

The broad emancipatory concern of whole worker organising is clear in McAlevey's own description of it:

> Whole-worker organizing seeks to engage 'whole workers' in the betterment of their lives. To keep them consistently acting in their self-interest, while constantly expanding their vision of who that self-interest includes, from their immediate peers in their unit, to their shift, their workplace, their street, their kids' school, their community, their watershed, their nation and their world.[48]

This notion of self-interested action that consistently expands its focus has clear affinities with the notions of revolutionary practice discussed in Chapter 2, of the broadening and expanding of social needs. It is a method designed to aid and enhance this process, to help people work through the process of their own emancipation.

---

48   McAlevey 2012 Kindle Loc. 284–321.

The first step in this is recognising the worker as a single, unitary being, not someone compartmentalised into different categories or lives:

> Whole-worker organizing begins with the recognition that real people do not live two separate lives, one beginning when they arrive at work and punch the clock and another when they punch out at the end of their shift. The pressing concerns that bear down on them every day are not divided into two neat piles, only one of which is of concern to unions. At the end of each shift workers go home, through streets that are sometimes violent, past their kids' crumbling schools, to their often substandard housing, where the tap water is likely unsafe.[49]

Thus, this is explicitly contrasted with strategies that tend to compartmentalise people and reinforce this notion of compartmentalisation. At its worst, this is a strategy that sees workers as merely 'one actor in relationship to a dozen others'; as merely a piece of the 'available leverage points used to get the employer to agree to union demands'. It is a flaw that is also contained in the notion of building alliances between workers and community:

> The term itself reinforces the idea that shop floor issues of wages and working conditions are the proper domain of unions and that when unions move beyond this narrowly defined terrain they are in the foreign land of 'community', where they must exercise a sort of diplomacy.[50]

This has simple, practical problems – there are only so many meetings a human being can take – but it also misses the fact that we are ultimately talking about one set of people – workers (or potential workers) who live in a community. According to McAlevey: 'It is not an overstatement to assert that when unions buy into this labour/community dichotomy it is the end of organized labour as a progressive force'.[51]

There are three particularly important features of whole-worker organising to emphasise. Firstly, McAlevey stresses the importance of building majorities. As well as being practically necessary for recognition and industrial power, building a majority is essential to the notion of a union being an organisation for collective struggle.[52] A focus not concerned with putting the work-

---

49   McAlevey 2012 Kindle Loc. 284–321.
50   McAlevey 2012 Kindle Loc. 284–321.
51   McAlevey 2012 Kindle Loc. 284–321.
52   See McAlevey 2015.

ers themselves at the heart of the campaign can rely on a few spokespeople taken from the workforce – whole worker organising as a strategy requires sustained work to build convinced majorities within certain locations and workplaces.

Part of building a majority requires identifying what McAlevey describes as organic worker-leaders. These are not necessarily the most militant, and certainly not necessarily the loudest or quickest to speak up. They are the workers that other workers are most likely to listen to, take seriously and go to with their problems. It is the task of organisers to identify who these people are and convince them of the importance of building the union:

> You might ask which person on a shift the others would go to if they wanted to learn how do things better. Or whom they would talk to if they had a problem with their supervisor or a coworker. You proceed systematically, really listening to what people say.[53]

Identifying these people helps recognise the key people who have to be convinced in order to convince a wider work force. Getting these people onside is essential. However, this idea of leadership is also important in recognising that the leaders and the *organisers are not the same thing*. Moreover, the leaders are not the same as the people who shout the loudest, or necessarily have the most radical ideas, or the best theory. They are the people who others trust and listen to.

Finally, there is the power structure analysis. This attempts to develop a clear picture of the power holders relevant to a given campaign or workplace:

> The power structure analysis gives workers a map of the resources available to them and of the weak points in the power structure where their resources could be most effectively applied. This technique became the basis for a cycle of expanding returns: new skills and understandings spread broadly among our members, leading to meaningful victories that deepened the ties among our members and between them and others in their communities – which fed back into yet more skills and understanding, eventually enabling the workers to challenge the political and economic power structure that dominated their lives.[54]

---

53   McAlevey 2012 Kindle Loc: 692–706.
54   McAlevey 2012 Kindle Loc: 284–321.

Thus while this required a heavy degree of analysis and expertise, it was necessarily also a collective process, developed in concert with and among the workers themselves. The power analysis in fact functioned as 'a power-building process in itself, as workers began to realize they had resources they never even knew about – personal relationships, social networks, and knowledge of their community – which could be mobilized on their behalf'.[55] The power analysis thus acts as both a guide to strategy and a tool for workers to recognise their own power and better understand the social relations in which they exist: 'The workers themselves are a key source of knowledge in this regard, but they are often unaware of the strategic nature of the knowledge they have. Showing them how to put it all together takes a lot of time, invested by skilled organizers'.[56]

It is also worth stressing that whole worker organising shows that a focus on self-emancipation as a process and long-term goal needn't be contrasted with effective wins in the here and now. It is precisely the capacity of this kind of organising to deliver results that enables it to be of continuing relevance to the workers it seeks to empower. This should, partially, answer the concern that a commitment to self-emancipation is likely to pull away from the achievement of immediate gains and achievements in the here and now. McAlevey shows that, in this field at least, it is actually the self-emancipation approach that gets results. This is not to say that this is always the case – there can be real tensions between mobilising and empowering (for example in the precise formulation of demands), but it is at least to say that they needn't always pull apart.

Would it be hyperbole to say whole worker organising is the actuality of revolution in practice? Perhaps, after all, it is first and foremost a strategy for trade union organisers; but there are clear analogies: it stresses the centrality of the struggling classes themselves, placing them in the centre of their own liberation. It seeks to make everyday questions – both in and outside the workplace – simultaneously questions of democratic empowerment and self-organisation, which broaden the horizons of struggle (it would certainly, for example, meet D'Arcy's democratic standard). It is attuned to real strategic challenges, without collapsing into realpolitik and petty bargaining. Finally, it seeks to help workers recognise their own power and how they can exercise it, with this coming from a collective and dialogical process.

On the other hand, it might be objected that McAlevey's model depends on a skilled organiser coming in from outside with a plan (Just like Lukács per-

---

55   McAlevey 2015 Kindle Loc: 682.
56   McAlevey 2012 Kindle Loc: 1055–9.

haps depends too heavily on the super-Leninist activist). It is certainly the case that McAlevey stresses the important role of these skilled organisers – they are seen as fundamental to the model of organising she describes. To an extent, this is a result of the fact that she focuses on trade union organising, with resources, full-time staff and so on. However, it might thus be suggested that this reproduces precisely the problematic division it is intended to erode – the organiser remains primary, the more fundamental directing agency. This division needn't be cast so starkly – firstly, the organiser evidently does not have all the answers – every stage of developing a strategy has to happen in concert with workers themselves. Secondly, there is no theoretical reason, even if there might be practical reasons, why the organiser should come from 'outside', or be separate from the workers themselves. Finally, being a good organiser *is* a matter of skill, just like being a good educator is. This is not to say that only a small elite can do it, but to stress that there are skills and capacities for judgement that need to be honed through practice and experience.

6   Conclusion (Once More on Theory and Practice)

In this book I have offered a multitude of metaphors and examples for understanding the role of those committed to self-emancipation: Cliff's companions in struggle, Rancière and De Smet's different critical pedagogues, Bensaid's strategists in an infinite game, Levitas's archaeologists and architects of utopia, and to these we can now add D'Arcy's virtuous militants and McAlevey's whole worker organisers. These different examples all offer resources for thinking about the relationships necessary within and between organisations and social movements committed to emancipation. While some might be thought of as more important than others, all have their place, and all attempt to describe a role which aids struggles without taking them over and displacing the struggling people at the heart of them.

Do these examples add up to an over-demanding vision of the role of activists and theorists in these movements? It is certainly demanding; but no one said it was going to be easy. A politics of self-emancipation is difficult in the same way that politics as usual is easy. But it would be wrong to say it is over-demanding to the point of impossibility. It is in the nature of capitalist society that while we do not have exemplars of self-realised and realising human beings, we *do* have exemplars of militants who have resisted capitalism and helped empower themselves and others in forms that point towards democratic alternatives. Some I have mentioned already, if only in passing: The Egyptian revolutionaries on whom De Smet bases his analysis, the Kanehsata':ke Mohawk community that inspires D'Arcy, the men and women of the Paris Commune, and, for a time at least, Lenin and the Bolsheviks. But these are only a few examples, to which might be added many more in the past and future. It is possible to look to these real exemplars for inspiration and guidance, as well as to learn concrete and practical lessons.

Moreover, these roles only make sense as part of collective endeavours. These are not about heroic individuals, but practices and commitments that must be embedded in an organisational context if they are to thrive and function effectively. The bigger these organisations are, the more able they will be to play these roles – to encourage, strengthen and learn from struggles, to develop strategies based on collective historical experience, and to begin to articulate a vision of an alternative. The smaller they are, the more modest they must be about their capacities. But this does not mean they can do nothing, or that the practical challenges and demands revealed by a commitment to self-emancipation can be postponed until we have the organisations (or organisation) we want. How we get to that point is a question as urgent as it is difficult, and one largely beyond this book, but it seems unlikely that it will be possible unless self-emancipation is a guiding principle, as it was for Marx and Engels, from the very beginning.

One final question may remain: where does this leave Marxism as a specific doctrine? MacIntyre expresses this concern clearly:

> The problem is that even Lenin's party, however admirable its aspirations, did not and could not have satisfied two conditions that enable genuinely centralised authority to coexist with the self-management and self-governance of those over whom that authority is exercised. The first is that information must flow from the centre to the periphery, from periphery to centre, and from different points on the periphery to each other, so that everybody understands what is happening in more or less the same terms. The second is that those at the periphery must be able to put not only the actions of those of the centre in question, but even from time to time the theoretical and other beliefs presupposed by those actions. Marxist leaderships have never been able to satisfy these conditions, just because of their view that any just and deep-rooted expression of the convictions of the working-class will or will soon come to coincide with the party's conception of 'the road to socialism' and of itself as representing a collective subject with a universal interest.[57]

---

57   MacIntyre 2011b, p. 321.

The worry for MacIntyre is, in essence, that to meet the kinds of conditions that would allow the real working-class to have ownership of the revolutionary process and its organisations would be to risk compromising the Marxist character of the organisation.

This worry might be put in two ways. Firstly: How does one square the relationship between a maximal commitment to democratic self-emancipation and the goal of communism itself? What if, to put it crudely, the self-emancipation of the working-class leads to something else?[58] Here, I think we should reflect on what this question might mean. It assumes a model which conceives of socialism as one of many paths away from capitalism, as merely one option among several. On this model, it is reasonable to ask the question: how do we ensure the working class take the 'right path'?

It seems important to move away from this model, towards one which sees socialism not as one possible consequence of the self-emancipation of the working-class, but as *being* the self-emancipation of the working class. It is not one of many routes away from capitalism that the working class might choose; rather, it is the name for escaping capitalism and the unfreedom it necessarily involves. This suggests a way of thinking about social revolution that is far more about an escape route out of the present than about a particular path towards the future.[59] This has some affinities with Benjamin's notion of a revolution as pulling the brake rather than pushing the accelerator.[60] This is, it is worth stressing, not to say that there are no constraints on what can constitute self-emancipation. The very fact that it is self-*emancipation* imposes some quite important constraints – one cannot emancipate oneself into slavery, for example.

But this still leaves a deeper worry, that the experience of the working class might be essentially non-Marxist, that it might lead to a wholesale revision of Marxism itself.

One response to this is to suggest simply that Marxism should not be understood as any particular set of theoretical claims, but as a way of conceiving the *relationship between theory and practice*. In this sense we might well end up revising a series of particular claims of Marx, maybe even all of them, whilst

---

58   This question is put explicitly in David Marjoribanks' review of Blackledge's book. See Marjoribanks 2012.

59   Rejecting the 'one true path' model of revolution is also important for the discussion of revolutionary organisation I gave above. Most notably, it means that the role of the organisation is not to guide the working class along the correct path!

60   'Marx said that revolutions are the locomotive of world history. But perhaps things are very different. It may be that revolutions are the act by which the human race travelling in the train applies the emergency brake' (Benjamin 1977, p. 1232).

still maintaining a commitment to a certain way of relating social theory to social emancipation. If this is genuinely the result of the experience of mass struggles, that would hardly be a tragedy.

However, the theoretical core of Marxism holds relevance as long as it can genuinely help contribute to an understanding of the world around us, and to grasp how it could be made different. If it can continue to do this, then Marxism – appropriately renewed and refreshed – can retain its significance. Blackledge, adapting arguments from Lucien Goldmann, describes the attitude of Marxists in the late twentieth century in terms of a wager on the revolutionary potential of the working class.[61] In the absence of the visible mass struggles which characterised the early part of the century, Marxists were left in the semi-tragic position of betting that the working class remained potentially revolutionary. Yet for all that this is a wager, it is not a blind one. It is not a kind of article of faith or a shot in the dark; rather it is a decision based on a balance of probabilities, informed by theoretical judgements. To wager on the revolutionary potential of the proletariat is to *test* one of Marx's central claims, and thus be open to the possibility that it might be proven false.

It seems to me that these points constitute a partial answer to MacIntyre's concern. It is through an organisation (or organisations) of the type that he describes that the theoretical core of Marxism becomes tested. It is in the ability or otherwise of Marxism to adequately provide answers to the practical problems of the working class and others that capitalism dominates and oppresses that it will be judged. If Marxism is to offer this kind of guidance – and I hope I have made some contribution in this work towards showing that it can – it must be capable of correction and revision. It must be possible for people to say 'I think you badly miscalculated the odds – that was the wrong wager'. If the theoretical core consistently provides bad explanations for phenomena, and bad recommendations for action, then it is obvious that it ought to be revised, and perhaps abandoned completely. But it doesn't seem to me that Marxism has reached that point quite yet.

---

61   Blackledge 2012, Chapter 4.

Bibliography

Adorno, Theodor W. 1973. *Negative Dialectics*. New York: Continuum.

Aeschylus, 1897. *Prometheus Bound and the Seven Against Thebes*. Philadelphia: McKay.

Albert, Michael 2003. *Parecon: Life After Capitalism*. London: Verso.

Althusser, Louis 2005. *For Marx*. London: Verso.

Arendt, Hannah 1951. *The Origins of Totalitarianism*. New York: Harcourt, Brace and Co.

Arendt, Hannah 1970. *On Violence*. London: Allen Lane.

Arendt, Hannah 1998. *The Human Condition*. Chicago: University of Chicago Press.

Arneson, R.J. 1981. 'What's Wrong with Exploitation?'. *Ethics*, Volume 91, pp. 202–27.

Arthur, Christopher J. 1986. *Dialectics of Labour: Marx and his Relation to Hegel*. Oxford: Basil Blackwell.

Ash, William 1964. *Marxism and Moral Concepts*. New York: Monthly Review Press.

Asimov, Isaac 1952. *Foundation and Empire*. New York: Gnome Press.

Auerbach, Eric 1984. *Scenes from the Drama of European Literature*. Minneapolis: University of Minnesota Press.

Avineri, Shlomo 1968. *The Social and Political Thought of Karl Marx*. Cambridge: CUP.

Barker, Colin 2001. 'Robert Michels and "The Cruel Game"'. In *Leadership in Social Movements*. Edited by C. Barker, M. Lavalette and A. Johnson. Manchester: Manchester University Press, pp. 24–43.

Barker, Colin 2014. 'The Elephant is Political'. *rs21*, 30 October.

Basso, Luca 2015. *Marx and the Common*. Leiden: Brill.

Benjamin, Walter 1968. 'Theses on the Philosophy of History'. In: *Illuminations*. New York: Schocken, pp. 253–64.

Benjamin, Walter 1977. *Gesammelte Schriften*. Frankfurt/Main: Suhrkamp Verlag.

Bensaïd, Daniel 2002. *Marx for Our Times*. London: Verso.

Bensaïd, Daniel 2009. *Strategies of Resistance*. London: Resistance Books.

Berki, R. 1983. *Insight and Vision: The Problem of Communism in Marx's Thought*. London: Everyman.

Bhattacharya, Tithi. 2017. 'How Not to Skip Class: Social Reproduction of Labour and the Global Working Class'. In *Social Reproduction Theory*. Edited by Tithi Bhattacharya. London: Pluto. Blackledge, Paul 2010. 'Marxism, Nihilism and the Problem of Ethical Politics Today'. *Socialism and Democracy*, Volume 24, pp. 101–23.

Blackledge, Paul 2012. *Marxism and Ethics: Freedom, Desire, and Revolution*. New York: SUNY.

Blunden, Andy 2010. *An Interdisciplinary Theory of Activity*. Leiden: Brill.

Bohmer, Carol 2000. *The Wages of Seeking Help: Sexual Exploitation by Professionals*. West Port: Praeger.

Bookchin, Murray 2015. *The Next Revolution*. London: Verso.

Braverman, Harry 1998. *Labour and Monopoly Capital*. New York: Monthly Review Press.

Breines, Wini 1982. *The Great Refusal: Community Organisation in the New Left: 1962–1968*. New York: Praeger.

Brenkert, George G., 1983. *Marx's Ethics of Freedom*. London: Routledge and Kegan Paul.

Callinicos, Alex 1995. *Theories and Narratives*. Durham, NC: Duke University Press.

Callinicos, Alex 2004. 'Marxism and Politics'. In *What is Politics?*. Edited by A. Leftwich. Cambridge: Polity, pp. 53–66.

Callinicos, Alex 2006. *Resources of Critique*. London: Polity.

Callinicos, Alex 2009. *Making History*. Leiden: Brill.

Callinicos, Alex 2015. 'Anti-politics and the social illusion: A reply to Tietze and Humphrys'. *International Socialism*, 2 (145).

Carver, Terrell 1988. 'Communism for Critical Critics? The German Ideology and the Problem of Technology'. *History of Political Thought*, 9 (1), pp. 129–36.

Christman, John 2009. *The Politics of Persons: Individual Autonomy and Socio-historical Selves*. Cambridge: CUP.

Cliff, Tony 1960. 'Trotsky on Substitutionism'. *International Socialism*, 1(2), pp. 14–17 & 21–6.

Cohen, G.A., 1988. 'The Dialectic of Labour in Marx'. In *History, Labour and Freedom*. Oxford: Clarendon Press, pp. 132–54.

Cohen, G.A. 1990. 'Self-Ownership, Communism and Equality'. *Proceedings of the Aristotelian Society*, Volume Supplementary Volume 1990, pp. 25–44.

Cohen, G.A. 2001. *If You're An Egalitarian How Come You're So Rich?*. Cambridge, MA: Harvard University Press.

Cohen, G.A. 2008. *Rescuing Justice and Equality*. Cambridge MA: Harvard University Press.

Cornu, Auguste 1957. *The Origins of Marxian Thought*. Springfield: Charles C. Thomas.

Crick, Bernard 2004. 'Politics as a form of Rule: Politics, Citizenship and Democracy'. In *What is Politics?* Edited by A. Leftwich. Cambridge: Polity, pp. 67–85.

Crinson, I. and Yuill, C. 2008. 'What alienation theory can contribute to the study of health inequalities'. *International Journal of Health Service*, 38 (3).

Critchley, Simon 2007. *Infinitely Demanding*. London: Verso.

D'Arcy, Stephen 2013. *Languages of the Unheard*. London: Zed Books.

De Smet, Bret 2015. *A Dialectical Pedagogy of Revolt: Gramsci, Vygotsky and the Egyptian Revolution*. Leiden: Brill.

Dean, Jodi 2012. *The Communist Horizon*. London: Verso.

Dewey, John 1973. 'Means and Ends'. In *Their Morals and Ours*. London: Pathfinder, pp. 73–80.

Draper, Hal 1971. 'Marx's Principle of Self-Emancipation'. *Socialist Register 8*, pp. 81–109.

Draper, Hal 1977. *Karl Marx's Theory of Revolution, Volume 1: State and Bureaucracy*. New York: Monthly Review Press.

Draper, Hal. 1990. *Karl Marx's Theory of Revolution, Vol. IV: Critique of Other Socialisms*. New York: Monthly Review Press.

Dworkin, Gerald 1988. *The Theory and Practice of Autonomy*. Cambridge: CUP.

Eagleton, Terry 1999. 'Self-Realization, Ethics, and Socialism'. *New Left Review*, 1(237), pp. 150–61.

Eagleton, Terry. 2011. *Why Marx Was Right*. London: Yale University Press.

Elster, Jon 1985. *Making Sense of Marx*. Cambridge: CUP.

Farber, Samuel 2014. 'Reflections on Pre-Figurative Politics'. *International Socialist Review*, Volume 92.

Feenberg, Andrew 2014. *The Philosophy of Praxis: Marx, Lukacs and the Frankfurt School*. London: Verso.

Finlayson, Lorna 2015. *The Political is Political*. London: Rowman and Littlefield.

Foot, Philippa 2001. *Natural Goodness*. Oxford: Oxford University Press.

Franks, Benjamin. 2006. *Rebel Alliances: The Means and Ends of Contemporary British Anarchisms*. Oakland, CA: AK Press.

Freyenhagen, Fabian 2013. *Adorno's Practical Philosophy*. Cambridge: CUP.

Fromm, Erich 1961. *Marx's Concept of Man*. New York: Frederick Ungar Publishing.

Geertz, Clifford 1993. *The Interpretation of Cultures*. London: Fontana.

Geoghegan, Vincent 2008. *Utopianism and Marxism*. Oxford: Peter Laing.

Geras, Norman 1983. *Marx and Human Nature: Refutation of a Legend*. London: Verso.

Geras, Norman 1985. 'The Controversy About Marx and Justice'. *New Left Review*, Volume 1/150, pp. 47–85.

Geras, Norman. 2017. *Literature of Revolution*. London: Verso.

Geuss, Raymond 2005. *Outside Ethics*. Princeton: Princeton University Press.

Geuss, Raymond 2008. *Philosophy and Real Politics*. Princeton: Princeton University Press.

Goodwin, Barbara and Keith Taylor 2009. *The Politics of Utopia*. Oxford: Peter Lang.

Gordon, Uri. 2018. 'Prefigurative Politics between Ethical Practice and Absent Promise'. *Political Studies*, 66(2), pp. 521–537. Gould, Carol C. 1978. *Marx's Social Ontology*. Boston: MIT.

Gray, John 2007. *Black Mass: Apocalyptic Religion and the Death of Utopia*. London: Allen Lane.

Habermas, Jürgen 1972. *Knowledge and Human Interests*. London: Heidemann.

Harvey, David 2012. *Rebel Cities*. London: Verso.

Hendrix, B.A., 2012. 'Where should we expect social change in non-ideal theory?' *Political Theory*, Volume 41, pp. 116–43.

Holloway, John 2010. *Crack Capitalism*. London: Pluto Press.

Holmstrom, Nancy 1977. 'Exploitation'. *Canadian Journal of Philosophy*, Volume 7, pp. 353–69.

Honneth, Axel 2008. *Reification: A New Look at an Old Idea*. Oxford: Oxford University Press.

Honneth, Axel 2014, 'Foreword'. In *Alienation*, by Rahel Jaeggi. New York: Columbia University Press, pp. vii–x.

Hudis, Peter 2012. *Marx's Concept of the Alternative to Capitalism*. Leiden: Brill.

Humphrys, Elizabeth and Tad Tietze 2013. 'Anti-Politics: Elephant in the Room'. *Left Flank*, 31 October.

Hurka, Thomas 1993. *Perfectionism*. Oxford: Oxford University Press.

Jacoby, Russell 2005. *Picture Imperfect*. New York: Columbia University Press.

Jaeggi, Rahel 2014. *Alienation*. New York: Columbia University Press.

Kain, Philip J. 1988. *Marx and Ethics*. Oxford: Clarendon Press.

Kamenka, Eugene 1962. *The Ethical Foundations of Marxism*. London: Routledge and Kegan Paul.

Kautsky, Karl 1918. *Ethics and the Materialist Conception of History*. Chicago: Charles H. Kerr.

Knight, Kelvin 2007. *Aristotelian Philosophy: Ethics and Politics from Aristotle to MacIntyre*. Cambridge: Polity.

Kolakowski, Leszek 1981. *Main Currents of Marxism Vol. III*. Oxford: Oxford University Press.

Kouvelakis, Stathis 2003. *Philosophy and Revolution: From Kant to Marx*. London: Verso.

Kouvelakis, Stathis 2007. 'Marx's Critique of the Political'. *Situations*, 2(2), pp. 81–93.

Kuroń, Jacek and Karol Modzelewski 1982. 'Open Letter to the Party'. In *Solidarność: The Missing Link*. Edited by Colin Barker. London: Bookmarks.

Laclau, Ernesto and Chantel Mouffe 2014. *Hegemony and Socialist Strategy*. London: Verso.

Laycock, Henry 1999. 'Exploitation via Labour Power in Marx'. *The Journal of Ethics*, Volume 3, pp. 121–31.

LeBlanc, Paul 2013. 'Spider and Fly: The Leninist Philosophy of Georg Lukács'. *Historical Materialism*, 21 (2), pp. 47–75.

Lebowitz, Michael 2003. *Beyond Capital*. 2nd ed. London: Palgrave McMillan.

Leftwich, Adrian 2004. 'The Political Approach to Human Behaviour: People, Resources and Power'. In *What is Politics?*. Edited by Adrian Leftwich. Cambridge: Polity, pp. 100–18.

Lenin, V.I., 1965. 'Kommunismus'. In *Collected Works*. Moscow: Progress Publishers, pp. 165–7.

Lenin, V.I., 1970. *Left Wing Communism: An Infantile Disorder*. Moscow: Progress.

Leopold, David 2007. *The Young Karl Marx: German Philosophy, Modern Politics and Human Flourishing*. Cambridge: CUP.

Levitas, Ruth 2013. *Utopia as Method: The Imaginary Reconstruction of Society*. London: Palgrave MacMillan.

Liebich, Andre 1979. *Between Ideology and Utopia: The Politics and Philosophy of August Cieszkowski*. London: D. Riedel Publishing.

Löwy, Michael 2005. *The Theory of Revolution in the Young Marx*. Chicago: Haymarket.

Lukács, György 1971. *History and Class Consciousness*. Cambridge MA: MIT.

Lukács, György 1977. *Lenin: A Study in the Unity of His Thought*. London: New Left Books.

Lukács, György 1995. 'Bolshevism as an Ethical Problem'. In *The Lukács Reader*. Edited by A. Kadarkay. Oxford: Blackwell, pp. 216–21.

Lukács, György 2000. *A Defence of History and Class Consciousness*. London: Verso.

Lukes, Steven 1987. *Marxism and Morality*. Oxford: OUP.

Luxemburg, Rosa 2005. *The Mass Strike*. London: Bookmarks.

MacIntyre, Alasdair 1999. *Dependent Rational Animals*. London: Open Court.

MacIntyre, Alasdair 2009. 'Notes from the Moral Wilderness'. In *MacIntyre's Engagement with Marxism*. Edited by Paul Blackledge and Neil Davidson. Chicago: Haymarket, pp. 45–68.

MacIntyre, Alasdair 2011a. 'How Can Aristotelianism Become Revolutionary?' In *Virtue and Politics*. Edited by Paul Blackledge and Kelvin Knight. Notre Dame: Notre Dame Press.

MacIntyre, Alasdair 2011b. 'Where We Were, Where We Are, Where We Need to Be'. In *Virtue and Politics*. Edited by Paul Blackledge and Kelvin Knight. Notre Dame: Notre Dame Press.

Maeckelbergh, Marianne 2011. 'Doing is Believing: Prefiguration as Strategic Practice in the Alterglobalisation Movement'. *Social Movement Studies*, Volume 10, pp. 1–20.

Mannheim, Karl 1936. *Ideology and Utopia*. London: Kegan Paul.

Marjoribanks, David 2012. 'Review of Paul Blackledge Marxism and Ethics'. *Marx and Philosophy Review of Books*.

McAlevey, Jane 2012. *Raising Expectations and Raising Hell*. London: Verso.

McAlevey, Jane 2015. 'The Crisis of New Labor and Alinsky's Legacy: Revisiting the Role of the Organic Grassroots Leaders in Building Powerful Organisations and Movements'. *Politics and Society*, 43 (3), pp. 415–41.

McNally, David 2013. '"Unity of the Diverse": Working-Class Formations and Popular Uprisings from Cochabamba to Cairo'. In *Marxism and Social Movements*. Edited by Colin Barker. Leiden: Brill, pp. 401–24.

Meikle, Scott 1985. *Essentialism in the Thought of Karl Marx*. London: Duckworth.

Merleau-Ponty, Maurice 1969. *Humanism and Terror*. Boston: Beacon Press.

Merleau-Ponty, Maurice 2002. *Phenomenology of Perception*. London: Routledge.

Mészáros, Istvan 1970. *Marx's Theory of Alienation*. London: Merlin.

Michels, Robert 1959. *Political Parties*. London: Simon and Schuster.

Mills, C. Wright 2005. 'Ideal Theory as Ideology'. *Hypatia*, 20 (3), pp. 165–84.

Miłosz, Czesław 1980. *The Captive Mind*. London: Penguin.

Moore, Stanley 1963. *Three Tactics: the Background in Marx*. New York: Monthly Review Press.

Morris, William 2003. *News From Nowhere*. Oxford: Oxford University Press.

Nicholson, P.P., 2004. 'Politics and the Exercise of Force'. In *What is Politics?* Edited by Adrian Leftwich. Cambridge: Polity, pp. 41–52.

Nielsen, Kai 1989. *Marxism and the Moral Point of View*. Boulder: Westview Press.

Nilsen, Alf Gunvald and Laurence Cox 2013. 'What Would a Marxist Theory of Social Movements Look Like?' In *Marxism and Social Movements*. Edited by Colin Barker. Leiden: Brill, pp. 63–82.

Nozick, Robert 1974. *Anarchy, State and Utopia*. London: Blackwell.

Ollman, Bertell 1976. *Alienation: Marx's Conception of Man in Capitalist Society*. Cambridge: Cambridge University Press.

Ollman, Bertell 1977. 'Marx's Vision of Communism: A Reconstruction'. *Critique*, Volume 8, pp. 4–41.

Ollman, Bertell 2005. 'The Utopian Vision of the Future (Then and Now): A Marxist Critique'. *Monthly Review*, 53 (3).

O'Rourke, James J. 1974. *The Problem of Freedom in Marxist Thought*. Boston: D. Riedel Publishing.

Paden, Roger 2002. 'Marx's Critique of the Utopian Socialists'. *Utopian Studies*, 13 (2), pp. 67–91.

Palumbo, James 2015. 'We will only see new change by taking the politics out of politics'. *London Evening Standard*, 10 March.

Pettit, Philip 2001. *A Theory of Freedom: From the Psychology to the Politics of Agency*. Oxford: OUP.

Phillips, Anne 2015. *The Politics of the Human*. Cambridge: Cambridge University Press.

Plekhanov, Georgi 1967. *The Role of the Individual in History*. New York: International Publishers.

Popper, Karl 1966. *The Open Society and Its Enemies Vol. 2*. Princeton: Princeton University Press.

Poulantzas, Nicos 2000. *State, Power, Socialism*. London: Verso.

Prawer, S.S. 1976. *Karl Marx and World Literature*. Oxford: Clarendon Press.

Przeworski, Adam 1985. *Capitalism and Social Democracy*. Cambridge: Cambridge University Press.

Rancière, Jacques 1991. *The Ignorant Schoolmaster*. Stanford: Stanford University Press.

Rancière, Jacques 2009. *The Emancipated Spectator*. London: Verso.

Rancière, Jacques 2011. *Althusser's Lesson*. London: Continuum.

Rawls, John 1999. *A Theory of Justice: Revised Second Edition*. Oxford: OUP.

Reiman, Jeffrey 1987. 'Exploitation, Force, and the Moral Assessment of Capitalism: Thoughts on Roemer and Cohen'. *Philosophy & Public Affairs*, Volume 16, pp. 3–41.

Reiman, Jeffrey, 2012. *As Free and as Just as Possible*. London: Wiley Blackwell.

Renton, David 2013. *Socialism From Below: Writings From an Unfinished Tradition*. London: Unkant Publishers.

Ricoeur, Paul 1986. *Lectures on Ideology and Utopia*. New York: Columbia University Press.

Rockmore, Tom 1980. *Fichte, Marx and the German Philosophical Tradition*. Carbondale: Southern Illinois University Press.

Roemer, Jon 1985. 'Should Marxists Be Interested in Exploitation?' *Philosophy & Public Affairs*, Volume 14, pp. 30–65.

Roemer, Jon 1988. *Free to Lose*. Cambridge: Cambridge University Press.

Sargent, L.T. 2010. *Utopianism: A Very Short Introduction*. Oxford: Oxford University Press.

Sayers, Sean 1998. *Marxism and Human Nature*. London: Taylor & Francis.

Sayers, Sean 2011. *Marx and Alienation*. London: Palgrave McMillan.

Schmidt, Alfred 2014. *The Concept of Nature in Marx*. London: Verso.

Schmitt, Carl 2007 [1932]. *The Concept of the Political*. Chicago: University of Chicago Press.

Schwartz, Justin 1995. 'What's Wrong with Exploitation?'. *Nous*, Volume 29, pp. 158–88.

Sedgwick, Peter 1982. *Psycho Politics*. London: Pluto Press.

Sen, Amartya 2009. *The Idea of Justice*. Cambridge: Harvard University Press.

Simmons, A. John 2010. 'Ideal and Non-Ideal Theory'. *Philosophy & Public Affairs*, Volume 38, pp. 5–36.

Singer, Daniel 1993. 'In Defence of Utopia'. *Socialist Register*, Volume 29, pp. 249–56.

Singer, Peter 1972. 'Famine, Affluence, and Morality'. *Philosophy and Public Affairs*, Volume 1, pp. 229–43.

Squires, Judith 2004. 'Politics Beyond Boundaries: A Feminist Perspective'. In *What is Politics?* Edited by Adrian Leftwich. Cambridge: Polity, pp. 119–34.

Steiner, Hillel 1984. 'A Liberal Theory of Exploitation'. *Ethics*, Volume 94, pp. 225–41.

Stemplowska, Zofia 2008. 'What's Ideal About Ideal Theory'. *Social Theory and Practice*, 34 (3).

Swain, Dan 2012a. *Alienation: An Introduction to Marx's Theory*. London: Bookmarks.

Swain, Dan 2012b. 'Review of Hudis, Peter, Marx's Concept of an Alternative to Capitalism'. *Marx and Philosophy Review of Books*, 1 December.

Swain, Dan 2013. 'Alienation and The Spirit Level'. *Oxford Left Review*, Volume 11, pp. 38–44.

Swain, Dan 2015. 'Review of Blackledge, Paul, "Marxism and Ethics"'. *Reason Papers*, 37 (1), pp. 170–5.

Swift, Adam 2004. 'Political Philosophy and Politics'. In *What is Politics?*. Adrian Leftwich. Cambridge: Polity, pp. 135–46.

Tabak, Mehmet 2012. *Dialectics of Human Nature in Marx's Philosophy*. New York: Palgrave MacMillan.

Talmon, J.F. 1970. *The Origins of Totalitarian Democracy*. London: Sphere Books.

Tolstoy, Leo 1869. *War and Peace*. London: Simon and Schuster.

Tomba, Massimiliano. 2013. *Marx's Temporalities*. Leiden: Brill.

Trotsky, Leon 1904. *Our Political Tasks*. s.l.: Trotsky Internet Archive.

Trotsky, Leon 1973. *Their Morals and Ours*. London: Pathfinder.

Trotsky, Leon 2005. *Literature and Revolution*. Chicago: Haymarket.

Tucker, Robert 1961. *Philosophy and Myth in Karl Marx*. Cambridge: Cambridge University Press.

Unger, Roberto 1987. *Social Theory: Its Situation and Its Task*. Cambridge: Cambridge University Press.

Valentini, Laura 2009. 'On the Apparent Paradox of Ideal Theory'. *The Journal of Political Philosophy*, Volume 17, pp. 332–55.

Van Parijs, Philip 1993. *Marxism Recycled*. Cambridge: Cambride University Press.

Vogel, Lise 2013. *Marxism and the Oppression of Women*. Leiden: Brill.

Vrousalis, Nicholas 2013. 'Exploitation, Vulnerability and Social Domination'. *Philosophy & Public Affairs*, Volume 41, pp. 131–57.

Wall, Steven 2012. 'Perfectionism in Moral and Political Philosophy'. In *The Stanford Encyclopedia of Philosophy*. s.l.: s.n., pp. URL = http://plato.stanford.edu/archives/win2012/entries/perfectionism-moral/. Edited by E.N. Zalta.

Warren, Paul 1994. 'Self-Ownership, Reciprocity and Exploitation, or Why Marxists Shouldn't Be Afraid of Robert Nozick'. *Canadian Journal of Philosophy*, Volume 24, pp. 33–56.

Webb, Darren 2000. *Marx, Marxism and Utopia*. London: Ashgate.

Wertheimer, Alan 1996. *Exploitation*. Princeton: Princeton University Press.

Wilkinson, Richard and Kate Pickett 2009. *The Spirit Level*. London: Penguin.

Williams, Bernard 2005. *In the Beginning Was the Deed*. Princeton: Princeton University Press.

Wood, Alan 1972. 'The Marxian Critique of Justice'. *Philosophy and Public Affairs*, 1(3), pp. 244–82.

Wood, Alan 2004. *Karl Marx*. London: Routledge.

Wood, Ellen Meiksins, 1995. *Democracy Against Capitalism*. Cambridge: CUP.

Woolf, Virginia 1938. *Three Guineas*. London: Shakespeare's Head Press.

Wright, Erik Olin 2006. 'Compass Points'. *New Left Review*, Volume 41, pp. 93–124.

Wright, Erik Olin 2010. *Envisioning Real Utopias*. London: Verso.

Yates, Luke 2015. 'Rethinking Prefiguration: Alternatives, Micropolitics and Goals in Social Movements'. *Social Movement Studies*, 14 (1), pp. 1–21.

Young, Iris Marion 1990. *Justice and the Politics of Difference*. Princeton: Princeton University Press.

Index

CPSIA information can be obtained
at www.ICGtesting.com
Printed in the USA
JSHW012303170820
7294JS00005BA/8